1989 Children's Writer's & Illustrator's Market

1 9 8 9
Children's
Writer's &
Illustrator's
Market®

Edited by
Connie Wright Eidenier

Assisted by
Katherine Jobst

Writer's
Digest
Books

Cincinnati, Ohio

Distributed in Canada by Prentice-Hall of Canada Ltd., 1870 Birchmount Road, Scarborough, Ontario M1P 2J7.

Managing Editor, Market Books Department:
Constance J. Achabal

International Standard Serial Number 0897-9790
International Standard Book Number 0-89879-342-4

Children's Writer's & Illustrator's Market *reserves the right to exclude any listing which does not meet its requirements.*

Contents

1   From the Editor
3   How to Use Children's Writer's & Illustrator's Market
6   The Business of Children's Writing & Illustrating

6   *Marketing Your Work*
7   *Format for Submitting Work*
9   *Packing and Mailing*
10 *Pricing*
11 *Business Records*
12 *Recording Submissions*

12 *Rights*
15 *Taxes*
15 *Building Skills*
16 *Books of Interest*
16 *Publications of Interest*

The Markets

17   Book Publishers
80   Magazine Publishers
116 Young Writer's/Illustrator's Markets
127 Contests and Awards

Resources

138 Agents
148 Organizations
153 Workshops
157 Glossary
161 Newbery Medal Winners
165 Caldecott Medal Winers
169 Age-Level Index
175 General Index
180 Record of Submissions

Eye Spy

Look carefully at the big picture to spy with your little eye each of the things below.

Chickadee, a publication designed to interest 4-9 year olds in the world and environment around them, used this two-page, (left side shown here) 4-color piece by illustrator Vesna Krstanovich. ''Vesna has a gentle humor in her art, which is just right for the younger market,'' begins Catherine Ripley, senior issue editor of Chickadee. The artwork was designed to be an observation puzzle for children, Ripley explains. ''It's fun to look at and kids understand what to do without having to read the copy.'' Krstanovich, Toronto, Ontario, was paid $650 for the piece.

Other examples of artwork purchased by editors or art directors can be found throughout the Book Publishers, Magazine Publishers, and Young Writer's/Illustrator's Markets sections. Information describing why each was salable is also provided. If you have sold any artwork to a listing included in this edition of Children's Writer's & Illustrator's Market, we invite you to submit the piece to us for possible publication. Please include information about who purchased it, how it was used, and why you feel it was marketable.

Children's books and magazines have become a viable force in today's publishing industry thanks to growing interest from parents, teachers and librarians eager to see today's youth develop an interest in reading. According to a December, 1988, issue of _Newsweek_, more than 4,600 children's books were published in 1987: This is a 50 percent growth over 1978 statistics. In this same article, it was reported that publishers sold $334 million in hardcover books in 1987 (compared to $136 million in 1977), and $150 million in paperbacks (compared to $26 million a decade ago). Other positive signs of the profitability of children's books can be seen in the increasing number of children's bookstores which today number between 300 and 400. They were almost nonexistent 10 years ago.

The growth in this very specialized segment of the publishing industry is particularly evident in the enthusiasm with which editors are seeking ideas for picture books and stories, young and middle readers, and young adult material. Here at Writer's Digest Books, we've been closely monitoring this growth and decided the time had come to compile a market directory listing the needs of the children's book and magazine industry. How appropriate that our first edition of _Children's Writer's & Illustrator's Market_ comes out in 1989—The Year of the Young Reader as designated by the Library of Congress.

Book publishers

In compiling this first edition, more than one hundred book publishers responded to our questionnaires and phone calls with a variety of manuscript and illustration needs for new books they are interested in pursuing. Each book publisher's listing specifies not only manuscript and illustration needs, but the approximate manuscript length preferred, styles and mediums of art they wish to review, and a list of recently published books you may wish to research for a feel of each publisher's style. Many publishers also share information about royalty or other pay arrangements for writers and artists, and others provide a time frame (in weeks or months) on which they report back on queries, manuscript or art submissions.

Children's publishing is a market receptive to new writers and artists, but quality is also the buzz word for submissions because editors and art directors deal with very discriminating buyers. The retail bookstore owner, who is a chief vehicle for generating the profits publishers enjoy, responded to a _Publishers Weekly_ survey questioning what components of a book they reviewed prior to purchase as inventory. The responses—based on 410 retail bookstores polled— listed 98 percent as considering book content foremost, followed by 95 percent looking at illustration quality, 94 percent weighing the author's reputation, and 93 percent evaluating both cover design and retail price. This information will help you to appreciate what the publisher has to consider when evaluating what new book ideas to market.

Magazines

The children's and teen's magazine market incorporates a variety of educational, entertainment and inspirational material from religious and commercial publishers. Each magazine listing will give you information about the type of subject matter reviewed for fiction and nonfiction material, and what types of illustrations are preferred. Pay ranges also are given as well as rights typically purchased by the editor or art director.

Many of the publications listed in the magazine section are also included in a special section of markets for the work of young writers and illustrators. While pay may be in copies of the publication rather than in actual cash, the satisfaction of seeing their article or drawing published is reward enough for many children and teenagers.

Contests

Be sure to read through the contest section, too. There are numerous writing and art organizations that sponsor annual competitions. Awards may range from plaques and medals to sizable cash prizes. Many times contests provide you with a measuring stick to compare your work against other peers. And, the winners have a handy PR tool to incorporate into future self-promotional efforts.

Other helpful sections

We have also included, for your benefit, sections on Organizations and Workshops. It is important to stay on top of developments in your profession, especially with increasing competition from new writers and illustrators. These listings will provide you with background material about what each organization and workshop can offer for your professional education and growth.

If you've thought about signing up with an agent, be sure to read through the section introduction for Agents. Advice on what to consider when interviewing for an agent should provide you with some solid questions to ask prior to acquiring representation. Only agents open to representing new clients are included in this section.

Be sure to read through the Business of Children's Writing & Illustrating at the front of this book. In it you will find helpful information about keeping business records, marketing your work, properly mailing writing and art submissions so they arrive in a presentable condition, preparing for tax season, and an in-depth presentation of copyrights and rights sold in the marketplace. Being a brilliant writer or artist isn't quite enough to guarantee your financial success . . . competency at running your business will ensure you can continue to enjoy your creative endeavors—and your house and car!

I hope you enjoy and profit from this premiere edition of *Children's Writer's & Illustrator's Market*. Let me know of your successes . . .

Connie Eidenier

How to Use
Children's Writer's &
Illustrator's Market

Before you study the listings in this book, take time to read through the explanations for the sample listing. It will help you to properly use the information so you can more effectively market your writing and illustrations to editors, publishers and agents.

It's important to remember that anytime you see a "SASE" it is referring to a self-addressed, stamped envelope. If a listing specifies that you include a SASE with your query or manuscript/illustration submission, be sure to do this to ensure its return. For unsolicited submissions, you should always include a SASE whether or not one is requested in the listing. Also, a "ms" or "mss" appearing within a listing refers to "manuscript" or "manuscripts" respectively.

For your reference when reading each listing, be aware that "picture books" are written/illustrated for preschool-8 year olds, "young readers" for 5-8 year olds, "middle readers" for 9-11 year olds, and "young adults" for those 12 years and older.

The numbers in the sample listing below correspond to the numbered explanations that run after the listing.

(1) McELDERRY BOOKS, imprint of Macmillan Publishing Co., **(2)** 866 Third Ave., New York NY 10022. (212)702-7855. **(3)** Book publisher. **(4)** Publisher: Margaret K. McElderry. **(5)** Publishes 10-12 picture books/year; 2-4 young reader titles/year; 8-10 middle reader titles/year; 3-5 young adult titles/year. 33% of books by first-time authors; 33% of books from agented writers. **(6)** (Some listings will provide information on the % of books subsidy published.)

Fiction: (7) Picture books: animal, contemporary. Young readers: animal, contemporary, easy-to-read. Middle readers: animal, contemporary, fantasy, science fiction, spy/mystery/adventure. Young adults: contemporary, fantasy, science fiction. **(8)** Average word length: picture books—500; young readers—2,000; middle readers—5,000-6,000; young adults—45,000-50,000. **(9)** Recently published *A Family Project*, by Sara Ellis (ages 10-14, contemporary story involving crib death); *Memory*, by Margaret Mahy (ages 14 and up, contemporary story involving Alzheimer's Disease); *Another Shore*, by Nancy Bond (ages 12 and up, time travel story).

Nonfiction: (10) Picture books: animal, history, nature/environment. Young readers: animal, history, nature/environment, science, sports. Middle readers: animal, biography, history, music/dance, nature/environment, science, sports. Young adults: biography, music/dance, nature/environment. **(11)** Average word length: picture books—500-1,000; young readers—1,500-3,000; middle readers—5,000-7,500; young adults—30,000-45,000. **(12)** Recently published *There was a Place*, by Myra Cohn Livingston (ages 8-12, poetry); *Story of a Main Street*, by John S. Goodall (all ages, pictorial social history).

How to Contact/Writers: (13) Fiction & Nonfiction: Submit complete ms or query. **(14)** SASE (IRC) for return of ms. **(15)** Reports on queries in 2-3 weeks; on mss in 8 weeks. **(16)** Publishes a book 18 months after acceptance. **(17)** Will consider simultaneous (only if indicated as such), and computer printout submissions.

Illustration: (18) Number of illustrations used for fiction: picture books — "every page"; young readers — 15-20; middle readers — 15-20. Number of illustrations used for nonfiction: picture books — "every page"; young readers — 20-30; middle readers — 15-25. **(19)** Editorial will review ms/illustration packages submitted by authors/artists; ms/illustration packages submitted by authors with illustrations done by separate artists, and an illustrator's work for possible use in author's texts. **(20)** (Some listings will include information about the medium/style/size of artwork the editor or art director will prefer to review.)

How to Contact/Illustrators: (21) Ms/illustration packages: Send ms (complete) and 2 or 3 pieces of finished art. Illustrations only: Send resume and slides or sketches. **(22)** Reports on art samples in 6-8 weeks. **(23)** Original artwork returned at job's completion.

Terms/Writers & Illustrators: (24) Pays authors in royalties based on retail price. (Some listings will also specify whether or not they buy material outright or use other methods of payment.) **(25)** (Some listings will give an average figure for advances paid to authors/illustrators.) **(26)** Pay for separate authors and illustrators: "50-50 as a rule for picture books." Pay for illustrators: By the project. (Some listings will also include additional payment for ms/illustration packages and/or factors that determine final payment for artwork such as number of illustrations used and/or b&w vs. color work.) **(27)** Sends galleys to authors; dummies to illustrators, "they make the dummies for picture books." **(28)(29)** Book catalog, manuscript/artist's guidelines free on request.

Tips: (30) Writers: "Read widely in the field and write constantly." Illustrators: "Look at books already published and go to exhibitions of all sorts, sketch constantly." **(31)** (Some listings provide Tips about what type of manuscript or illustration the firm most needs.) **(32)** There is an "emphasis on books for babies and young children, on nonfiction, on poetry."

(1)(2) The full name, mailing address, and phone number of the book or magazine publishing company, agency, organization, workshop, or contest. A phone number in a listing does not mean the market accepts phone queries. Make a phone query only when your story's timeliness would be lost by following the usual procedures. As a rule, don't call unless you have been invited to do so.

(3) The type of business.

(4) Title and name of contact person. Address your query or submission to a specific name when possible. If no contact name is given consult a sample copy of the publication or catalog. As a last resort, you can address your query to "Editor" or "Art Director" or whatever is appropriate.

(5) The next series of information is a breakdown of the type and number of books published annually: picture books, young readers, middle readers, young adults. If you submit a book for young readers to a company that only publishes two young reader titles a year, it decreases your chances of getting published. Use this breakdown to help you choose a company most receptive to your type of book. The percentage of books by first-time authors will give you an indication of how open a market is to new authors. Also given is the percentage of submissions accepted through agents.

(6) Information to let you know which companies subsidy publish.

(7) The specific fictional material desired (and material not desired) is listed. Follow the guidelines. Do not submit a picture book about sports if it isn't what a market wants.

(8) Editors know the length of most material they buy; follow their word or page range. If your manuscript is longer or shorter by a large margin, submit to a more appropriate market.

(9) A list of recently published fiction is provided. Use this list to see what types of fiction a market publishes.

(10) Specific nonfiction material desired.

(11) The appropriate page or word length for nonfiction material is given.

(12) A list of recently published nonfiction.

(13) It is important to contact a market in the manner it states. If you send material (e.g., a complete manuscript) a market doesn't ask for, it shows a lack of adequate market research on your part.

(14) This states whether or not you should include a SASE for return of your manuscript. Submissions to foreign countries should include a self-addressed envelope (SAE) and International Reply Coupons (IRC) available at most major post offices.

(15) Reporting times indicate how soon a market will respond to your query or manuscript, but times listed are approximate. Wait four weeks beyond the stated reporting time before you send a polite inquiry.

(16) If your material is accepted this information gives you the approximate time it will take for your manuscript to be published.

(17) Submission requirements can include the actual form of the submission (such as original typewritten copy preferred over a photocopied version) or whether a computer printout is acceptable or the possibility of sending a manuscript via floppy disk or modem. Send manuscripts or queries to one market at a time unless it indicates simultaneous submissions are OK. If you do send your manuscript to more than one market at a time, always mention in your cover letter that it is a simultaneous submission.

(18) The average number of illustrations required per type of book gives the illustrator an idea of how much work a project might entail.

(19) The information in this area tells the illustrator if the company is interested in seeing manuscripts with illustrations by the same person and/or manuscripts by an author with illustrations done by a separate artist. It will also tell if the market is open to the use of freelance illustrators for the company's own book projects.

(20)(21) Submit illustrations only in the manner an art director/editor asks. Many times this section will give the name of the art director to whom illustrators wishing to work on a freelance basis with the company should submit their resumes, samples, etc.

(22) The approximate amount of time taken to report back on illustrations is provided. If an art director/editor doesn't respond within the stated time, wait four weeks before sending a polite inquiry.

(23) If it doesn't state that original artwork is returned, then it is not returned to the artist.

(24) Terms for payment of authors.

(25) If an advance is given, the average amount will be provided here.

(26) Payment information for ms/illustration packages and freelance illustration projects is provided here.

(27) If galleys are sent to authors and/or dummies to illustrators for review prior to publication, you will read the notification here.

(28)(29) If catalogs and/or guidelines are available, it's important to send for them.

(30)(31)(32) Helpful suggestions for writers and illustrators are listed under the subhead "Tips."

The Business of Children's Writing & Illustrating

Writing and illustrating material for children and teenagers require a special insight into how young people think and feel, and also how they react to various situations in life. Along with this aptitude, however, there is another skill important to becoming a professional in the children's publishing industry — knowledge of running your own business. It takes business acumen to keep accurate financial records and prepare tax forms, to effectively — and cost-efficiently — promote your work through writing snappy query or cover letters, submitting manuscripts in the correct format, plus packing and mailing manuscripts and illustrations properly to present an initially professional appearance to the editor or art director receiving them. Being a professional also involves understanding what a copyright can do to protect you as the creator, and a familiarity with what rights are typically sold in the marketplace.

Before setting up your own business you may wish to talk to other established writers and illustrators to determine what type of bookkeeping methods they've adopted, what business equipment they've invested in and what kind of self-promotion campaigns they incorporate to increase their business. Also, read through the organizations listed in this book to determine if you would like to join any. In addition to building your writing and illustration skills, many of these groups can advise you on business and legal considerations you need to address.

Marketing your work

There is really no mystery to submitting your work successfully in the marketplace; the basic elements are good research and persistence. First, you need to familiarize yourself with the publications that interest you. Read through the listings of those markets in this book to determine what type of material is wanted; who the contact is; how the editor or art director wishes to be contacted initially; and what types of rights they acquire to your work as well as how much they pay. (If a listing accepts unsolicited manuscripts, be sure you enclose a self-addressed, stamped envelope [SASE] for its return.)

Get copies of all these publications — or copies of their books — and study their writing and illustration styles and formats. Does the type of material they publish match the type of work you produce? Next you will want to request writer's or illustrator's guidelines to more carefully match work you will be submitting to their needs. If a particular market has changed its direction since *Children's Writer's & Illustrator's Market* has gone to press, these guidelines will reflect current needs. Also, many times throughout the year publishers will have special seasonal or holiday needs that will be explained in the guidelines.

Format review for submitting work

Throughout these listings you will read editors' requests for a query letter, cover letter, book proposal, complete manuscript or resume as all or part of the initial contact procedure.

Query letters. A query letter should be no more than a one-page, well written, concise piece to arouse an editor's interest in your manuscript. Queries are usually required from writers submitting nonfiction material to a publisher. Such a letter should be single-spaced and include the editor's name, if available, though you will want to avoid using a first name during an initial contact until more familiarity is established. In the query letter you want to convince the editor that your idea is perfect for his readership and that you're the writer qualified to do the job. Include any previous writing experience in your letter plus published samples to prove your credentials, especially any samples that relate to the subject matter you're querying on.

Many query letters start with a lead similar to the lead that would be used in the actual manuscript. Next, you want to briefly outline the work and include facts, anecdotes, interviews or any other pertinent information that give the editor a feel for the manuscript's premise. Your goal is to entice him to want to know more. End your letter with a straight-forward request to write the work, and include information on its approximate length, date it could be completed, and the availability of accompanying photos or artwork.

Queries are rarely used for fiction manuscripts, but occasionally there are exceptions. For a fiction query you want to explain the story's plot, main characters, conflict and resolution. Just as in nonfiction queries, you want to make the editor eager to see more. For more information on writing good queries, consult *How to Write Irresistible Query Letters*, by Lisa Collier Cool (Writer's Digest Books).

Cover letters. Many editors prefer to review a complete manuscript, especially for fiction. In such a case, the cover letter will serve to introduce you and establish your credentials as a writer plus give the editor an overview of the manuscript. Unlike the query letter, a cover letter sent with a manuscript doesn't need to take a hard-sell orientation; the manuscript, at this point, will be the selling mechanism. Be sure to let the editor know whether the unsolicited manuscript is a simultaneous submission. However, if you're just sending a photocopy of your manuscript, and not a simultaneous submission, you might want to reassure him that he is the only one considering your work at this time. Some editors might assume a photocopied manuscript is being considered elsewhere. If you're sending the manuscript after a "go-ahead" from the editor, the cover letter should serve as a reminder of this commitment.

For an illustrator, the cover letter also will serve as your introduction to the art director and establish your credentials as a professional artist. Type the cover letter on your letterhead, and in addition to introducing yourself and your abilities, be sure to explain what services you can provide as well as what type of follow-up contact you plan to make, if any. If you are sending samples of your work, indicate whether they should be returned or filed. If you wish them returned include a self-addressed, stamped envelope (SASE) with your submission packet. Cover letters, like the query, should be no longer than one page.

Resumes. Many times illustrators are asked to submit a resume with their cover letter and samples. A resume provides you with a vehicle to showcase your experience, education, and awards. Resumes can be created in a variety of formats ranging from a single page listing information to color brochures featuring your art. Keep the resume brief, and focus on your artistic achievements, not your whole life. On your resume you want to include your name and address, your clients, and the work you did for them. Also include your educational background and any awards you've won.

Book proposals. Throughout the listings in the Book Publishers section you will find references to submission of a synopsis, outline and sample chapters. Depending on an editor's preference, some or all of these components, as well as inclusion of a cover letter, comprise a book proposal.

A synopsis summarizes the book. Such a summary includes the basic plot of the book (including the ending), is easy to read, and flows well.

An outline can also be used to set up fiction, but is more effective as a tool for nonfiction. The outline covers your book chapter by chapter and provides highlights of each. If you are developing an outline for fiction you will want to include major characters, plots and subplots, and length of the book. An outline can run 3 to 30 pages depending on the complexity of your manuscript.

Sample chapters give a more comprehensive idea of your writing skill. Some editors may request the first two or three chapters to see how your material is set up; others may request a beginning, middle and ending chapter to get a better feel for the entire plot. Be sure to determine what the editor needs to see before investing time in writing sample chapters.

Many picture book editors require an outline or synopsis, sample chapters and a variation of roughs or finished illustrations from the author/illustrator. Listings specifying an interest in picture books will detail what type of artwork should accompany manuscripts. You will also want to query the editor or art director prior to submitting material for more detailed information to tailor your illustrations to their needs. If you want to know more about putting together a book proposal, read *How to Write a Book Proposal*, by Richard Balkin (Writer's Digest Books).

Manuscript formats. If an editor specifies that you submit a complete manuscript for review, here is some format information to guide you. In the upper left corner type your legal name (not pseudonym), address, phone number and Social Security number (publishers must have this to file payment records with the government). In the upper right corner you should type the approximate word length, what rights are being offered for sale (this is not necessary for book manuscripts; rights will be covered in your contract) and your copyright notice, which should appear as © Joe Writer 1989. (A handwritten copyright notice is acceptable.) All material in the upper corners should be typed single-spaced, not double.

There is no need for a cover page or title page on a manuscript: The first page should include the title (centered) one-third of the way down. Two spaces under that type "by" and your name or pseudonym. To begin the body of your manuscript, drop down two double spaces and indent five spaces for each new paragraph. There should be 1¼ inch margins around all sides of a full typewritten page. Be sure to set your typewriter on "double-space" for the manuscript body. From page 2 to the end of your manuscript just include your last name followed by a dash and the page number in the upper left corner. You can include the title of your piece under your name if you wish. Drop down two double spaces to begin the body of the page and follow this format throughout the manuscript. If you're submitting a novel, type the chapter title one-third of the way down the page. On subsequent pages you again will want to include your name, dash symbol, page number and title of the manuscript.

On the last page of your manuscript skip down three double spaces after your last sentence and type "The End." Some nonfiction writers use the journalistic symbols "###" or "-30-." For more information on manuscript formats read *The Writer's Digest Guide to Manuscript Formats*, by Dian Dincin Buchman and Seli Groves (Writer's Digest Books).

To get an approximate word count for your manuscript, first count the number of characters and spaces in an average line, next count the number of lines on a representative page and multiply these two factors to get your average number of characters per page. Finally, count the number of pages in your manuscript, multiply by the characters per page, then divide by 6 (the average number of characters in a word). You will have your approximate word count.

Packing and mailing submissions

Your primary concern in packaging material is to ensure that it arrives undamaged, although proper packaging also presents the image of an organized professional who takes pride in his work.

If your manuscript is fewer than six pages it is safe to simply fold it in thirds and send it out in a #10 (business-size) envelope. For a self-addressed, stamped envelope (SASE) you could then fold another #10 envelope in thirds or insert a #9 (reply) envelope which fits in a #10 neatly without any folding at all. Some editors appreciate receiving a manuscript folded in half into a 6x9 envelope. For larger manuscripts you will want to use a 9x12 envelope both for mailing the submission out and as a SASE for its return. The SASE envelope can be folded in half. Book manuscripts will require a sturdy box such as a typing paper or envelope box for mailing. Just include a self-addressed mailing label and return postage so it can also double as your SASE.

Artwork requires a bit more packaging care to guarantee that it arrives in presentable form. Sandwich illustrations between heavy cardboard that is slightly larger than the work and tape it closed. You will want to write your name and address on each piece in case the inside material becomes separated from the outer envelope upon receipt. For the outer wrapping you can use either a manila envelope, foam-padded envelope, a mailer with plastic air bubbles as a liner, or brown wrapping paper. Bind nonjoined edges with reinforced mailing tape and clearly write your address.

Most often you will be mailing material first class. Mail sent within this classification usually is processed and delivered quickly. Also, first-class mail is forwarded for one year if the addressee has moved (which does happen with some magazine and book publishers), and can be returned if undeliverable. If you are mailing a package that weighs between one and 70 pounds it can go fourth class unless you specifically request first-class mail treatment. Fourth-class mail tends to be handled a bit more roughly so pack your material so it is protected. If you have enclosed a letter write "first-class letter enclosed" on the package and add the correct amount of postage. Also write "return postage guaranteed" on your package so it can be returned to you if undeliverable.

If you are concerned about your material safely reaching its destination you may wish to send it certified mail. Material sent this way must be signed when it reaches its destination, and if you wish, a return receipt will be sent to you. There is an 85¢ charge for this service in addition to the postage which is determined by the weight, size and destination of your package. Material sent certified mail also is automatically insured for $100.

Your packages can also be sent UPS, though they aren't legally allowed to carry first-class mail so your letter will have to be mailed separately. UPS also has wrapping restrictions: packages must be in heavy, corrugated cardboard; no string or paper can be on the outside; and packages must be sealed with reinforced tape.

If material needs to reach your editor or art director quickly, you can elect to use overnight deliveries such as U.S. Priority Mail and Express Mail Next Day Services, UPS's Two-Day Blue Label Air Service, and dozens of privately owned overnight services such as Federal Express, Emery Worldwide or Purolater Courier. Fees and delivery destinations vary.

Occasionally throughout this book you will see the term International Reply Coupon (IRC). IRCs are used in lieu of U.S. postage when mailing packages abroad. The U.S. Post Office can help you determine, based on your package's weight, the correct number of IRCs to include to ensure its return. The current cost of an IRC is 95¢ per ounce traveling surface mail; two IRCs are recommended for packages being shipped via air.

If you're sending a photocopy of a manuscript or copies of artwork samples, you may wish to specify to the editor that the material doesn't need to be returned if not used. It may be cheaper in the long run on your postage bill. In the latter case you can track the status of your submissions by enclosing a postage-paid reply postcard listing "yes, I am interested" or "no, the material is not appropriate for my needs at this time" options. Some writers or illustrators simply set a deadline date after which the manuscript or artwork is withdrawn from consideration if nothing is heard from the editor or art director.

Pricing, negotiating, and contracts

For many writers there is a predetermined range at which to negotiate for sale of a manuscript to a book publishing company or sale of an article or story to a magazine. For artists, however, payment for illustrations is set by such factors as: Are they rendered in 4-color or black-and-white? How many illustrations are purchased? What is the track record of the artist (this actually figures into payment for writers, also)? For a beginning illustrator, market research will be necessary to determine an hourly rate. Such a rate can be arrived at by using the annual salary of a staff artist doing similar work (try to find an artist willing to share this information), then dividing that salary by 52 (the number of weeks in a year) and again by 40 (the number of hours in a work week) to get the answer. You will want to add your overhead expenses such as rent, utilities, art supplies, etc. to this answer by multiplying your hourly rate by 2.5. Research, again, may have to come into play to be sure your rate is competitive within the marketplace.

Even though you may feel comfortable with the hourly rate you have set for your services, many art directors still will want to negotiate to be sure they are paying a good price for services rendered. Negotiation is a two-way process, and hopefully at the end both parties feel comfortable with what they are getting. The most important aspect of negotiating lies in your ability to listen to the other party; don't be so concerned with your needs that you miss what the other person is really saying he wants. On the other hand, take time to voice any questions or concerns you may have about the fee or other stipulations being offered; this is the only way you will be able to establish your needs to the art buyer. Negotiating is a process that can only be "perfected" by doing it often ... if one meeting doesn't go well, use that experience to build your negotiating skills for the next "client."

Once you make a sale you will probably sign a contract. A contract is an agreement between two or more parties that specifies the fee to be paid, services to be rendered, deadlines, rights purchased and, for artists, return (or not) of original artwork. Be sure to get a contract in writing rather than agreeing to oral stipulations; written contracts protect both parties from misunderstandings and faulty memories. Also, look out for clauses that may not be in your best interest, such as "work-for-hire." If there are clauses that appear vague or confusing, get some legal advice. The time and money invested in counseling upfront could protect you from more serious problems down the road. If you have an agent, he will review any contract.

Business records

The only way to determine if you are making a profit as a writer or illustrator is to keep accurate business records. You will definitely want to keep a separate bank account and ledger apart from your personal finances. Also, if writing or illustrating is secondary to another freelance career, maintain separate business records from that career.

There are many ledgers available in office-supply stores. Look through some samples to decide what works best for your needs. Most ledgers use a single-entry system in which you list any business-related expenses as well as income. If you're just starting your career, you will most likely be accumulating some business expenses prior to showing any profit. To substantiate your income and expenses to the IRS be sure to keep all invoices, cash receipts, sales slips, bank statements, cancelled checks plus receipts related to entertaining clients such as for dinner and parking. For entertainment expenditures you also will want to record the date, place and purpose of the business meeting as well as gas mileage. Be sure to file all receipts in chronological order; if you maintain a separate file for each month of the year it will provide for easier retrieval of records at year's end. Keeping receipts is especially important for purchases of $25 or more.

When setting up a single-entry bookkeeping system you will want to record income and expenses separately. It may prove easier to use some of the sub-heads that appear on Schedule C of the 1040 tax form, this way you can transfer information more easily onto the tax form when filing your return. In your ledger you will want to include a description of each transaction—date, source of income (or debts from business purchases), description of what was purchased or sold; whether pay was by cash, check or credit card, and the amount of the transaction.

You don't have to wait until January 1 to start keeping records, either. The moment you first make a business-related purchase or sell an article, book manuscript or illustrations you will need to begin tracking your profits and losses. If you keep records from January 1 to December 31 you are using a calendar-year accounting method. Any other accounting period is known as a fiscal year. You also can choose between two types of accounting methods—the cash method and the accrual method. The cash method is used more often: You record income when it is received and expenses when they are disbursed. Under the accrual method you report income at the time you earn it rather than when it is actually received. Similarly, expenses are recorded at the time they are incurred rather than when you actually pay them. If you choose this method you will need to keep separate records for "accounts receivable" and "accounts payable."

Recording submissions

An offshoot of recording income and expenses is keeping track of submissions under consideration in the marketplace. Many times writers and illustrators devote their attention to submitting material to editors or art directors, then fail to follow-up on overdue responses because they feel the situation is out of their hands. By tracking what submissions are still under consideration and then following up, you may be able to refresh a buyer's memory who temporarily forgot about your submission, or revise a troublesome point to make your work more enticing to him. At the very least you will receive a definite "no" thereby freeing you to send your material to another market.

When recording your submissions be sure to include the date they were sent; the business and contact name; and any enclosures that were inserted such as samples of writing, artwork or photography. Keep copies of the article or manuscript as well as related correspondence for easier follow-up. When you sell rights to a manuscript or artwork you can "close" your file by noting the date the material was accepted, what rights were purchased, the publication date and payment. (See sample forms after the General Index.)

Rights for the writer and illustrator

Without a copyright you would have no control over the work you create. Copyright protection ensures that you, the writer or illustrator, have the power to decide how the work is used and that you receive payment for each use. Not only does a copyright protect you, it essentially encourages you to create new works by guaranteeing you the power to sell rights to their use in the marketplace. As the copyright holder you can print, reprint or copy your work; sell or distribute copies of your work; or prepare derivative works such as plays, collages or recordings. The Copyright Law of 1976, which became effective January 1, 1978, is designed to protect a writer's or illustrator's work for his lifetime plus 50 years. If you collaborate with someone else on a written or artistic project, the copyright will last for the lifetime of the last survivor plus 50 years. In addition, works created anonymously or under a pseudonym are protected for 100 years, or 75 years after publication, whichever is shorter. Incidentally, this latter rule is also true of work-for-hire agreements. Under work-for-hire you relinquish your copyright to your "employer." Try to avoid agreeing to such terms.

Your work is copyrighted the moment you create it: Be sure, however, to include the universally accepted notice: © (your name) (year of work's creation), for example: © Joe Illustrator 1989. For further protection you can register your work with the Copyright Office in Washington D.C. Though this isn't absolutely necessary there are advantages to registering your work. You can bring a copyright infringement suit to court and sue for actual damages, statutory damages and recovery of attorney's fees. It's possible to register for a copyright after an infringement against you but you are limited to suing for actual damages only. Also, registering before an infringement will give you a stronger case in court. If you suspect that someone might infringe upon your work, register it. Infringements are relatively rare, however.

For more information about the proper procedure to register works, contact the Register of Copyrights, Library of Congress, Washington D.C. 20559. The registration fee is $10 per form, although you can register a group of articles or illustrations if:
- the group is assembled in order, such as in a notebook;
- the works bear a single title, such as "Works by (your name)";
- they are the work of one writer or artist;
- the material is the subject of a single claim to copyright.

The copyright law specifies that writers generally sell one-time rights to their work unless they and the buyer agree otherwise in writing. Be forewarned that many editors aren't aware of this. Many publications will want more exclusive rights from you than just one-time usage of your work, some will even require you to sell all rights to your work. Be sure that you are monetarily compensated for the additional rights you give up to your material. It is always to your benefit to retain as much control as possible over your work. Writers who give up limited rights to their work can then sell reprint rights to other publications, foreign rights to international publications, or even movie rights should the opportunity arise. Likewise, artists can sell their illustrations to other book and magazine markets as well as to paper-product companies who may use an image on a calendar or greeting card. You can see that exercising more control over ownership of your work gives you a greater marketing edge for resale. If you do have to give up all rights to a work, think about the price you are being offered to determine whether it will compensate you for the loss of other sales.

Rights acquired through sale of a book manuscript are explained in each publisher's contract. Take the time to read through relevant clauses to be sure you understand what each contract is specifying prior to signing. The rights you will most often be selling to periodicals in the marketplace are:
- One-time rights—The buyer has no guarantee that he is the first to use a piece. One-time permission to run a written or illustrated work is acquired, then the rights revert back to the creator.
- First serial rights—The creator offers rights to use the work for the first time in any periodical. All other rights remain with the creator. When material is excerpted from a soon-to-be-published book for use in a newspaper or periodical, first serial rights also are purchased.
- First North American serial rights—This is similar to first serial rights, except

that publishers who distribute both in the U.S. and Canada will stipulate these rights to ensure that a publication in the other country won't come out with simultaneous usage of the same work.

● Second serial (reprint) rights—In this case newspapers and magazines are granted the right to reproduce a work that already has appeared in another publication. These rights also are purchased by a newspaper or magazine editor who wants to publish part of a book after the book has been published. The proceeds from reprint rights are often split 50/50 between the author and his publishing company.

● Simultaneous rights—Use of such rights occurs among magazines with circulations that don't overlap, such as many religious publications. Many "moral guidance" stories or illustrations are appropriate for a variety of denominational publications. Be sure you submit to a publication that allows simultaneous submissions, and be sure to state in your cover letter to the editor that the submission is being considered elsewhere.

● All rights—Rights such as this are purchased by publishers who pay premium usage fees, have an exclusive format, or have other book or magazine interests from which the purchased work can generate more "mileage" for their interests. When the writer or illustrator sells all rights to a market he no longer has any say in who acquires rights to use his piece. Synonymous with purchase of all rights is the term "work-for-hire." Under such an agreement the creator of a work gives away all rights—and his copyright—to the company buying his work. Try to avoid such agreements; they're not in your best interest. If a market is insistent upon acquiring all rights to your work, see if you can negotiate for the rights to revert back to you after a reasonable period of time. It can't hurt to ask. If they're agreeable to such a proposal, be sure you get it in writing.

● Foreign serial rights—Be sure before you market to foreign publications that you have only sold North American—not worldwide—serial rights to previous markets. If not, you are free to market to publications you think may be interested in using material that has appeared in a U.S. or North American-based periodical.

● Syndication rights—This is a division of serial rights. For example, if a syndicate prints portions of a book in installments in its newspapers, they would be syndicating second serial rights. The syndicate would receive a commission and leave the remainder to be split between the author and publisher.

● Subsidiary rights—These are rights, other than book rights, and should be specified in a book contract. Subsidiary rights include serial rights, dramatic rights or translation rights. The contract should specify what percentage of these rights go to the author and publisher.

● Dramatic, television and motion picture rights—Purchase of such rights usually begin with a one-year option (usually 10 percent of the total price). During this time the interested party tries to sell the story to a producer or director. Many times options are renewed because the selling process can be lengthy. Currently there is a good market for nonfiction as well as fiction; biographies of famous people are an example of nonfiction that has become salable for this market.

Taxes

To successfully (and legally) compete in the business of writing or illustrating you must have knowledge of what income you should report and deductions you can claim. Before you can do this however, you must prove to the IRS that you are in business to make a profit, that your writing or illustrations are not merely a hobby. Under the Tax Reform Act of 1986 it was determined that you should show a profit for three years out of a five-year period to attain professional status. What does the IRS look for as proof of your professionalism? Keeping accurate financial records (see Business records), maintaining a business bank account separate from your personal account, the time you devote to your profession and whether it is your main or secondary source of income, and your history of profits and losses. The amount of training you have invested in your field also is a contributing factor to your professional status, as well as your expertise in the field.

If your business is unincorporated, you will fill out tax information on Schedule C of Form 1040. If you're unsure of what deductions you can take, request Publication 553 from the IRS. Under the tax reform act only 80 percent (formerly it was 100 percent) of business meals, entertainment and related tips and parking charges are deductible. If you're working out of a home office, a portion of your mortgage (or rent), related utilities, property taxes, repair costs and depreciation can be deducted as business expenses. To qualify though, your office must be used only for business activities, it can't double as a family room during nonbusiness hours. To determine what portion of business deductions can be taken, simply divide the square footage of your business area into the total square footage of your house. You will want to keep a log of what business activities, and sales and business transactions occur each day; the IRS may want to see records to substantiate your home office deductions.

Depending on your net income you may be liable for a self-employment tax. This is a Social Security tax designed for those who don't have Social Security withheld from their paychecks. You're liable if your net income is $400 or more per year. Net income is the difference between your income and allowable business deductions. Request Schedule SE, Computation of Social Security Self-Employment Tax if you qualify.

If completing your income tax return proves to be a complex affair call the IRS for assistance. In addition to walk-in centers, the IRS has 90 publications to instruct you in various facets of preparing a tax return. Some of the publications available include: 334 – Tax Guide for Small Business; 463 – Travel, Entertainment and Gift Expense; 505 – Tax Withholding and Estimated Tax; 525 – Taxable and Nontaxable Income; 533 – Self-Employment Tax; 535 – Business Expenses; 538 – Accounting Periods and Methods; 587 – Business Use of Your Home; 910 – Guide to Free Tax Services; 917 – Business Use of Car.

Building business – and creative – skills

Now that you have an idea of what it takes to set up your freelance writing or illustrating practice, you may want to consult further publications to read about business, writing or illustrating specialties you don't feel quite as comfortable with. Many of the publications recommended here incorporate business-oriented material with information about how to write or illustrate more creatively and skillfully.

Books of interest

The Artist's Friendly Legal Guide. Conner, Floyd; Karlen, Peter; Perwin, Jean; Spatt, David M. North Light Books, 1988.
Children's Media Marketplace. Jones, Delores B., ed. Neal-Schuman, 1988.
The Children's Picture Book: How to Write It, How to Sell It. Roberts, Ellen E.M. Writer's Digest Books, 1984.
The Children's Writer's Marketplace. Tomajczyk, S.F. Running Press, 1987.
How to Write and Illustrate Children's Books. Bicknell, Treld Pelkey; Trotman, Felicity, eds. North Light Books, 1988.
Illustrating Children's Books. Hands, Nancy S. Prentice Hall Press, 1986.
Market Guide for Young Writers. Henderson, Kathy. Shoe Tree Press, 1988.
Nonfiction for Children: How to Write It, How to Sell It. Roberts, Ellen E.M. Writer's Digest Books, 1986.
Writing Books for Children. Yolen, Jane. The Writer, Inc., 1983.
Writing for Children & Teenagers. Wyndham, Lee. Writer's Digest Books, 1987.
Writing Short Stories for Young People. Stanley, George Edward. Writer's Digest Books, 1987.
Writing Young Adult Novels. Irwin, Hadley and Eyerly, Jeannette. Writer's Digest Books, 1988.

Publications of interest

The Basics of Writing for Children. Writer's Digest Books, 1507 Dana Ave., Cincinnati OH 45207.
Children's Magazine Guide. Sinclair, Patti, ed. 7 North Pinckney St., Madison WI 53703.
The Horn Book. Silvey, Anita, ed. The Horn Book, Inc., Park Square Building, 31 St. James Ave., Boston MA 02116.
Society of Children's Book Writers Bulletin. Mooser, Stephen; Oliver, Lin, eds. Society of Children's Book Writers, Box 296, Mar Vista Station, Los Angeles CA 90066.

Important listing information

When using listings in the book and magazine sections, be aware that age categories can be found under the "Fiction" and "Nonfiction" headings for solicited material. They are given to aid you in targeting material for those age groups for which you write/illustrate. "Picture books" are geared toward the preschool-8-year-old group; "Young readers" to 5-8-year-olds; "Middle readers" to 9-11 year-olds; and "Young adults" to those 12 and up. These age breakdowns may vary slightly from publisher to publisher.

The Markets

Book Publishers

The baby boomers' babies who are coming-of-reading-age account for today's growth in children's publishing—and the expanded market for writers and illustrators in this field. Add to this, large numbers of teachers and parents concerned with the lack of reading ability and the low level of comprehension exhibited by current school-age students, and it is clear that the publishing of quality juvenile material will be a strong commitment for some time to come.

Many of the larger publishers listed in this section specify a wide range of fiction and nonfiction needs for the pre-school picture-book set to the young-adult readers. Nonfiction titles are on the increase, and are being solicited by trade book publishers eager to form a niche in the market. Such titles range from how books are made to titles describing different types of bugs or the developmental stages of a fetus. For fiction, editors look for tightly plotted stories that also show insight into the reader's feelings through use of believable characters.

Sharing the importance of a well-paced story is the need for talented illustrators who can bring the story to life through dynamic artwork. A *Publishers Weekly* survey of children's booksellers showed that 95% felt illustrations were the most important criterion in selling a book. Also in demand for all age levels are brightly illustrated nonfiction books. This trend has been encouraged by librarians eager to see more educational material in book format but who also realize that today's TV-oriented students need visuals to learn effectively. The expanded use of illustrations will likely affect textbook publishers also.

Young adult novels are undergoing a reorientation in today's market. The problem novels popular a decade ago are being replaced by a wide range of fiction titles. Identifying the young adult market is difficult partly because many of these readers tend to go from middle-reader books to mainstream adult novels. Still, notable fiction is being written for young adults—and is being purchased. You will want to work closely with an editor to determine the type of material deemed salable to teens.

Researching the market

Despite the healthy market for children's books it is still important for aspiring authors and illustrators to research what is selling, and what type(s) of books each publisher publishes. Be sure to read each listing in this section carefully. You are provided with general subject needs, the age group the publisher specializes in, and tips regarding the specific styles or needs of each publisher. The best way to ensure that you send the appropriate manuscript and/or illustrations to each publisher is to request their writer's and illustrator's guidelines, if available, and a recent book catalog to determine the particular genre of publications. After this initial step, go to your local library to read some selections from each publisher you are interested in sending a query and/or a manuscript to. This will enable you to become acquainted more thoroughly with the writing and illustration styles of each.

The business of submitting work

Pay attention to the method of submission each publishing house requests. Some only want a query, others sample chapters with a synopsis, and others will want to review an entire manuscript. Also, if the publisher prefers to have material sent through an agent, be sure that is the method you use, otherwise your unsolicited manuscript will be thrown into a slush pile and never be read.

For manuscript/illustration packages (i.e., picture books or some young reader titles) you will want to refer to the Illustration and How to Contact/Illustrators portions of the listing to determine the appropriate procedure for querying the editor or art director. Publishers reviewing such packages usually wish to see the entire manuscript plus a variety of finished and rough pieces of artwork to get a feel for how the book will work. If you're interested only in illustrating juvenile books you will want to check those same portions of each listing to determine whether to contact the editor or art director as well as determine what you need to submit regarding finished vs. rough art samples, or resumes or tearsheets to be kept on file. Many publishers express the desire to consider manuscripts and illustrations separately so the artist whose style most closely matches the flavor of a specific manuscript can be assigned by the editor or art director.

In your query letter, or cover letter if you're sending a complete manuscript, be sure to include any publishing credits. Give the editor a sense of your work by including the intended age group for your book, reasons why it is different than anything else on the market, and any competition. This effort at research will be appreciated by an editor. When sending out queries or cover letters/manuscripts, be sure to check in the listing whether a publisher will review simultaneous submissions. Children's book editors seem to be more open to simultaneous submissions than other trade book editors. If you are sending simultaneous submissions, let the editor know the material is being considered elsewhere, and send a personalized cover letter—not a form letter.

Most book publishing companies pay writers 3-20% of the wholesale or retail price (you, of course, will want to negotiate for retail price as your base). Illustrators' fees come in a variety of arrangements such as a flat fee for artwork based on the number of drawings and color vs. black-and-white work, to a royalty arrangement similar to the writers' percentages already mentioned.

Sometimes writers and illustrators split the royalties 50-50 on collaborative projects. It is important for you as a writer or illustrator to develop sound negotiating skills, and to be generally aware of pay ranges in the publishing industry so you can negotiate effectively.

Few writers (or illustrators) are ever published the first time they submit material to an editor. Some of the best, award-winning children's books have entailed years of rewriting by the author. Contrary to popular opinion (or misconception), children's writing is not easier than writing for adults. Many authors of juvenile material describe how difficult it can be to create a solid story line, using vocabulary appropriate to their intended audience. It also takes a special person to relive his own youth and remember how he reacted to situations that in adult years seem less traumatic or memorable. (These same qualities are also very important for illustrators to communicate effectively with youth, otherwise the picture's message can be lost.) Very few authors can create stories that relate to children's special needs and feelings without talking down to them. Editors are always thrilled to find the exceptions after wading through hundreds, or even thousands, of inappropriate manuscripts. But children's book editors remain open to new writers and unsolicited submissions — and probably rely less on agents than any other area of publishing.

Book packagers

Occasionally at the beginning of each listing you will notice markets that describe themselves as "book packagers" rather than "publishers." While the majority of packaged books for children have been nonfiction, there is currently an increase in the production of picture books. Book packagers, or "book producers" or "developers," work for publishers and offer services that range from hiring writers, photographers and/or illustrators to editing and producing the final book. What they don't do is market the book; you won't see a catalog of books a packager has produced since such publications will appear in the client/publisher's catalog instead. Book packagers can offer experienced manpower to a small publisher in which, for instance, the inhouse staff may not be skilled in a certain subject area or where experience in dealing with illustrations may be lacking.

What is the difference, besides marketing, between a book publisher and book packager? The book publisher reviews (and hopefully accepts) queries and/or manuscripts (mss) sent to them by writers. The book packager already has the book idea, they then go out to hire a writer and/or illustrator whose skills match their needs. It is often felt that this is a good outlet for the fledgling writer who wants to get started in book publishing. This isn't necessarily true ... book packagers will ask to see a writer's credentials to ensure they are getting the best person for the job. Also, writing and/or illustrating for a book packager won't always give you credit for the work you have done. Many times you will labor under a work-for-hire arrangement, or will be offered a large advance with low royalty percentage.

Subsidy publishing

You will notice that some of the listings in this section give percentages of subsidy-published material. Subsidy publishers ask writers to pay all or part of the costs of producing a book. There are different reasons people use subsidy publishers: they have had their material rejected by other publishers and believe they can't improve the work with further rewrites, or writing is more of a hobby and they want a book they can share with family and friends. Aspiring writers will want to strongly consider working only with publishers who pay. Paying publishers will more actively market your work because this is where they make their profit; subsidy publishers make their money from each writer who pays them to publish a book. If you are comfortable with the idea of working with a subsidy publisher, be sure you understand all points of a contract. If you're willing to underwrite the cost of producing a book, you should be willing to have an attorney look over your contract to clarify any unclear terms.

Being a professional

Having a great book idea is the first step ... but you will increase your chances of selling that book idea by handling yourself and your work as professionally as possible. If you haven't already done so, take a few minutes to read through the Business of Children's Writing & Illustrating at the beginning of this book. In it you will find information on the correct form for preparing a manuscript and writing a cover or query letter, marketing yourself more effectively, keeping accurate submission and business records, and a list of rights purchased in the marketplace.

ABINGDON PRESS, div. of United Methodist Publishing House, 201 Eighth Ave. S., Nashville TN 37202. (615)749-6301. Book publisher. Children's Editor: Etta Wilson. Publishes 12 picture books/year; 4 young reader titles/year; 6 middle reader titles/year; 2 young adult titles/year. 20% of books by first-time authors; 40% of books from agented writers.
Fiction: Picture books: contemporary. Young readers: easy-to-read. Middle readers: history, problem novels. Average word length: picture books—1,000; young readers—4,000; middle readers—12,000; young adults—25,000-30,000. Recently published *Culligan Man Can*, by Susan Kirby (grades 4-6, contemporary); *Wasted Space*, by Judie Gulley (grades 6-9, problem novel); *KaRawa*, by George Koehler (grades 5-8, fantasy).
Nonfiction: Picture books, young readers, middle readers, young adults: religion. Average word length: picture books—1,000; young readers—4,000. Recently published *My Very Own Book of the Lord's Prayer*, by Turner (grades 2-4, religion); *God Makes Us Different*, by Caswell (ages 5-8, religion).
How to Contact/Writers: Fiction/nonfiction: Query. Unsolicited manuscripts are not accepted without a prior query letter. SASE (IRC) for return of ms. Reports on queries in 2 months; on mss in 3 months. Publishes a book 10 months after acceptance. Will consider simultaneous; photocopied, computer printout, and electronic submissions via disk or modem.
Illustration: Number of illustrations used for fiction: picture books—14; young readers—8; middle readers—4; young adults—1. Editorial will review ms/illustration packages submitted by authors/artists. Art Director, Roy Wallace, will review illustrator's work done for possible use in author's texts.
How to Contact/Illustrators: Submit 3 chapters of ms with 1 piece of final art. "All art to be done on flexible boards (or peelable) for scanning; avoid using very lightweight paper for artwork (tends to warp, tear); do not use white tape to touch up art; keep art as clean as possible. No dirt or smudges on art (scanners will pick up & reproduce any imperfections and touch-up areas); avoid using fluorescent inks (these do not reproduce

well); all art should be prepared in same proportion (if not done actual size); indicate trim marks on all boards with non-photographic blue pen or blue pencil (also include gutter marks); if lightweight board is used for art, mount to heavier board when mailing to avoid bending art; all art should be covered individually before mailing." Illustrations only: Submit resume, tear sheets. Reports on art samples in 3 weeks. Original artwork returned at job's completion.

Terms/Writers & Illustrators: Pays authors in royalties of 5% based on retail price. Buys ms for "negotiable" fee. Offers average advance payment of "½ of first year's royalty." Factors used to determine payment for ms/illustration package "depends on credentials." Sends galleys to authors. Book catalog/manuscript guidelines free on request.

Tips: "Know the market, the developmental stages of children and the publisher to whom you are submitting. Study the classic picture books and practice integrating art with story." Looks for "a strong story line or unique situation involving a child and illustrated in a style and medium that supports the text." There is "too much fluff and emphasis on art without good stories. Abingdon Press continues its long tradition of publishing for children those works that emphasize Christian values and that promote child development. We believe books have the power to shape the attitudes, values and behavior of children in a positive way, and we are seeking manuscripts with that potential."

ADVOCACY PRESS, div. of The Girls Club of Santa Barbara, Box 236, Santa Barbara CA 93102. (805)962-2728. Book publisher. Editorial Contact: Kathy Araujo. Publishes 3-5 picture books/year; 2-4 young reader titles/year. 25% of books by first-time authors.

Fiction/Nonfiction: "We are, at present only allowed to publish books that speak to Equity (equal opportunity) issues. Length is immaterial." Recently published *My Way Sally*, by P. Paine and M. Bingham (ages 3-6, picture book); *Kylie's Song*, by Patty Sheehan (ages 3-6, picture book); *Tonia The Tree*, by Sandy Stryker (ages 3- 6, picture book).

How to Contact/Writers: Fiction/nonfiction: Submit outline/synopsis and sample chapters. SASE (IRC) for return of ms. Reports on queries/mss in 2 weeks. Publishes a book 6 months after acceptance. Will consider simultaneous, photocopied, and computer printout submissions.

Illustration: Number of illustrations used for fiction/nonfiction: picture books—30; middle readers—200; young adults—200. Editorial will review ms/illustration packages submitted by authors/artists and ms/illustration packages submitted by authors with illustrations done by separate artists. Marketing Director, Penny Paine, will review an illustrator's work for possible use in author's texts.

How to Contact/Illustrators: Ms/illustration packages: query first. Reports on art samples in 2 weeks.

Terms/Writers & Illustrators: Illustrators paid by the project. Sends galleys to authors; dummies to illustrators. Book catalog/manuscript guidelines available for legal-size SAE.

Tips: "Make your package look as professional as possible."

AEGINA PRESS/UNIVERSITY EDITIONS, INC., 59 Oak Lane, Spring Valley, Huntington WV 25704. (304)429-7204. Book publisher. Managing Editor: Ira Herman. Publishes 1 picture book/year; 1-2 young reader titles/year; 2 middle reader titles/year; 2-3 young adult titles/year. 50% of books by first-time authors; 5% of books from agented writers; 40% of books are subsidy published.

Fiction: Picture books: animal. Young readers: animal, easy-to-read, fantasy. Middle readers: history, sports. Young adults: problem novels, romance, science fiction. "Will consider most categories." Average word length: picture books—1,000; young readers—2,000; middle readers—10,000; young adults—20,000. Recently published *Oscar Crab and Rallo Car*, by Andrea Ross (picture book, easy-to-read); *The Sometimes Invisible*

Spaceship, by Charles Bowles (middle readers, fantasy); *Boots, The Story of a Saint*, by Nancy Ball (young readers, animal).

Nonfiction: "We have not previously published any juvenile nonfiction. We may consider doing so in the future, however."

How to Contact/Writers: Fiction/nonfiction: Submit complete ms. SASE (IRC) for answer to query and/or return of ms. Reports on queries in 1 week; on mss in 1 month. Publishes a book 5-6 months after acceptance. Will consider simultaneous, photocopied, and computer printout submissions.

Illustration: Number of illustrations used for fiction: picture books—15-20; young readers—10; middle readers—5-6. Editorial will review ms/illustration packages submitted by authors/artists and ms/illustration packages submitted by authors with illustrations done by separate artists.

How to Contact/Illustrators: Ms/illustration packages: Query first. "We generally use our own artists. We will consider outside art only as a part of a complete ms/illustration package." Reports on art samples in 1 month. Original artwork returned at job's completion.

Terms/Writers & Illustrators: Pays authors in royalties of 10-15% based on retail price. Payment "negotiated individually for each book." Sends galleys to authors. Book catalog available for SAE + 4 first-class stamps; manuscript guidelines for #10 envelope and 1 first-class stamp.

Tips: "Focus your subject and plot-line. For younger readers, stress visual imagery and fantasy characterizations. A cover letter should accompany the manuscript, which states the approximate length (not necessary for poetry). A brief synopsis of the manuscript and a listing of the author's publishing credits (if any) should also be included. Queries, sample chapters, synopses, and completed manuscripts are welcome".

AFRICAN AMERICAN IMAGES, 9204 Commercial, Chicago IL 60617. (312)375-9682. Book publisher. Editor: Lawanza Kunjufu. Publishes 2 picture books/year; 1 young reader title/year; 1 middle reader title/year; 1 young adult title/year. 90% of books by first-time authors.

Fiction: Picture books: contemporary, easy-to-read, history. Young readers, middle readers, young adults: contemporary, history.

Nonfiction: Picture books, young readers, middle readers, young adults: education, history.

How to Contact/Writers: Fiction/nonfiction: Submit complete ms. Reports on queries in 1 week; on mss in 3 weeks. Publishes a book 9 months after acceptance. Will consider simultaneous submissions.

Illustration: Number of illustrations used for fiction/nonfiction: picture books—20; young readers—15; middle readers—12; young adults—7. Editorial will review ms/illustration packages submitted by authors/artists; ms/illustration packages submitted by authors with illustrations done by separate artists; illustrator's work for possible use in author's texts.

How to Contact/Illustrators: Ms/illustration packages: Send 3 chapters of ms with 1 piece of final art. Illustrations only: Send tear sheets. Reports on art samples in 2 weeks. Original artwork returned at job's completion.

Terms/Writers & Illustrators: Buys ms outright. Factors to determine final payment: Color art vs. black-and-white and number of illustrations used. Pay for separate authors and illustrators: Authors get royalty; illustrator is paid for purchase of work outright. Illustrator paid by the project. Book catalog, manuscript/artist's guidelines free on request.

ALADDIN BOOKS/COLLIER BOOKS FOR YOUNG ADULTS, imprint of Macmillan Children's Book Group, 24th floor, 866 Third Avenue, New York NY 10022. (212)702- 9043. Book publisher. Associate Editor: Sharyn November. Publishes 30 picture books/year;

5 young reader titles/year; 15 middle reader titles/year; 15 young adult titles/year. 20% of books by first-time authors; 40% of books from agented writers.

Fiction: Young readers: easy-to-read. Middle readers: contemporary, fantasy, problem novels, romance, science fiction, sports, spy/mystery/adventure. Young adults: contemporary, fantasy, problem novels, romance, science fiction, sports, spy/mystery/adventure. Recently published *The Leaving*, by Lynn Hall (young adults, contemporary); *The View From the Cherry Tree*, by Willo Roberts (middle readers, mystery/suspense).

Nonfiction: Middle readers, young adults: sports, self-help. Recently published *The Teenager's Survival Guide to Moving*, by Pat Nida (young adults); *What's Going to Happen to Me?*, by Eda Le Shan (middle readers, self-help).

How to Contact/Writers: Fiction/nonfiction: Query; submit outline/synopsis and sample chapters. SASE (IRC) for answer to query and/or return of ms. Reports on queries in 2-6 weeks; on mss in 12-16 weeks. Publishes a book 12 months after acceptance. Will consider simultaneous, photocopied, and computer printout submissions.

Illustration: Editorial will review ms/illustration package submitted by authors/artists and ms/illustration packages submitted by authors with illustrations done by separate artists. Associate Editor, Sharyn November, will review illustrator's work for possible use in author's texts.

How to Contact/Illustrators: Submit ms/illustration packages: 3 chapters of ms with 1 piece of final art. Illustrations only: submit resume/tear sheets. Reports on art samples only if interested. Original artwork returned at job's completion. Pay for illustrators: by the project. Book catalog/manuscript guidelines available for SAE.

Tips: "We are currently concentrating on reprinting successful titles originally published by the hardcover imprints of the Macmillan Children's Book Group. However, we do occasionally publish original material. We prefer that longer manuscripts be preceded by a query letter and two or three sample chapters. We do not generally consider picture book manuscripts. Please do not submit more than two short (under 15 typed pages) or one longer manuscript at one time. If you wish to confirm that your manuscript has arrived safely, please include a self-addressed stamped postcard, or send the manuscript via registered mail. Read children's books—and talk to children, get a sense of their world. Learn something about the business of publishing—that way you can have an idea as to what editors are looking for and why they make the decisions that they do. Be clear-eyed and professional" Regarding illustrations: "Remember that what appears to adults may not necessarily appeals to children." (See also Atheneum Publishers, Bradbury Press, Four Winds Press, Margaret K. McElderry Books.)

ARCHWAY/MINSTREL BOOKS, Pocket Books, 1230 Ave. of the Americas, New York NY 10020. (212)698-7000. Book publisher. Editorial contact: Patricia McDonald. Publishes 12-15 young reader titles/year; 12 middle reader titles/year; 24 young adult titles/year.

Fiction: Middle readers: animal. Young adults: contemporary, fantasy, romance, sports, suspense/mystery/adventure, humor, funny school stories.

Nonfiction: Middle readers: sports. Young adults: animal, sports.

How to Contact/Writers: Fiction/nonfiction: Query, submit outline/synopsis and sample chapters. SASE (IRC) for answer to query and/or return of ms.

Terms/Writers & Illustrators: Pays authors in royalties.

ATHENEUM PUBLISHERS, Macmillan Children's Book Group, 866 Third Ave., New York NY 10022. (212)702-2000. Book Publisher. Editorial Director: Jonathan Lanman. Editorial Contacts: Gail Paris, Marcia Marshall. Publishes 15-20 picture books/year; 4-5 young reader titles/year; 20-25 middle reader titles/year; 10-15 young adult titles/year. 15-25% of books by first-time authors; 50% of books from agented writers.

Fiction: Picture books: animal, contemporary, fantasy. Young readers: contemporary, fantasy. Middle readers: animal, contemporary, fantasy. Young adults: contemporary, fantasy. Recently published *One of the Third Grade Thonkers*, by Phyllis Reynolds Naylor (ages 8-12, middle grade fiction); *Coyote Dreams*, by Susan Nunes (ages 4-8, picture book); *The Changeling Sea*, by Patricia McKillip (ages 10 and up, young adult fantasy novel).

Nonfiction: Picture books: animal, biography, education, history. Young readers: animal, biography, education, history. Middle readers: animal, biography, education, history. Young adults: animal, biography, education, history. Recently published *Born Different*, by Frederick Drimmer (ages 10-14, biography); *The Smithsonian Book of Flight for Young People*, by Walter Boyne (ages 8-12, history); *Heads*, by Ron and Nancy Goor (ages 7-11, science photo essay).

How to Contact/Writers: Fiction/nonfiction: Query; submit outline/synopsis and sample chapters. SASE (IRC) for answer to query and/or return of ms. Reports on queries 4-6 weeks; on mss 6-8 weeks. Publishes a book 18 months after acceptance. Will consider simultaneous, photocopied submissions from previously unpublished authors; "we request that the author let us know it is a simultaneous submission."

Illustration: Editorial will review ms/illustration packages submitted by authors/artists and ms/illustration packages submitted by authors with illustrations done by separate artists.

How to Contact/Illustrators: Ms/illustration packages: query first, 3 chapters of ms with 1 piece of final art. Illustrations only: resume, tear sheets. Reports on art samples only if interested. Original artwork returned at job's completion.

Terms/Writers & Illustrators: Pays authors in royalties of 8-12½% based on retail price. Illustrators paid royalty or flat fee depending on the project. Sends galleys to authors; proofs to illustrators. Book catalog available for 9×12 SAE and 5 first-class stamps; manuscript guidelines for #10 SAE and 1 first-class stamp. (See also Aladdin Books/Collier Books for Young Adults, Bradbury Press, Four Winds Press, Margaret K. McElderry Books.)

AVON BOOKS/BOOKS FOR YOUNG READERS (AVON FLARE AND AVON CAMELOT), div. of The Hearst Corporation, 105 Madison Ave., New York NY 10016. (212)481-5609. Book publisher. Editorial Director: Ellen Krieger. Editorial Contact: Gwen Montgomery. Editorial Assistant: Rachel Pine. Publishes 25-30 middle reader titles/year; 20-25 young adult titles/year. 10% of books by first-time authors; 20% of books from agented writers.

Fiction: Middle readers: contemporary, problem novels, sports, spy/mystery/adventure, comedy. Young adults: contemporary, problem novels, romance, spy/mystery/adventure. Average length: middle readers— 100-150 pages; young adults—150-250 pages. Recently published *The Plant That Ate Dirty Socks*, by Nancy McArthur (middle readers, comedy); *Cross Your Heart*, by Bruce and Carole Hart (young adults, contemporary); *At the Edge*, by Michael Behrens (young adults, coming of age).

Nonfiction: Middle readers: hobbies, music/dance, sports. Young adults: music/dance, "growing up". Average length: middle readers— 100-150 pages; young adults—150-250 pages. Recently published *Why Am I So Miserable If These Are the Best Years of My Life?*, by A. B. Eagan (young adults, growing up); *Dead Serious*, by Jane Mersky Leder (young adults, suicide); *Go Ask Alice*, Anonymous (young adults, drug abuse).

How to Contact/Writers: Fiction: Submit complete ms. Nonfiction: Submit outline/synopsis and sample chapters. SASE (IRC) for answer to query and/or return of ms. Reports on queries in 2 weeks; on mss in 4-8 weeks. Publishes book 18-24 months after acceptance. Will consider simultaneous, photocopied, and computer printout submissions.

Illustration: Number of illustrations used for fiction: middle readers 6-8. Number of illustrations used for nonfiction: middle readers 8-10; young adults 6-8. Very rarely will review ms/illustration packages submitted by authors/artists and ms/illustration packages submitted by authors with illustrations done by separate artists.

How to Contact/Illustrators: "We prefer to use our own illustrators. Submit ms without art."

Terms/Writers & Illustrators: Pays authors in royalties of 6% based on retail price. Average advance payment is "very open." Sends galleys to authors; sometimes sends dummies to illustrators. Book catalog available for 9x12 SAE and 4 first-class stamps; manuscript guidelines for letter-size SAE and 1 first-class stamp.

Tips: "We have two Young Readers imprints, Avon Camelot books for the middle grades, and Avon Flare for young adults. Out list is weighted more to individual titles than to series, with the emphasis in our paperback originals on high quality recreational reading—a fresh and original writing style; identifiable, three dimensional characters; a strong, well-paced story that pulls readers in and keeps them interested." Writers: "Make sure that you really know what a company's list looks like before you submit work. Is your work in line with what they usually do? Is your work appropriate for the age group that this company publishes for? Most of all, make sure that you hand in something that is well done—check spelling, grammar, punctuation, etc. Keep aware of what's in your bookstore (but not what's in there for too long!)" Illustrators: "Submit work to art directors and people who are in charge of illustration at publishers. This is usually not handled entirely by the editorial department."

BALLANTINE/DEL REY/FAWCETT BOOKS (See Fawcett Juniper.)

BANTAM BOOKS INC. (See Skylark Books for Young Readers, Starfire.)

BANTAM DOUBLEDAY, DELL PUBLISHING GROUP INC. (See Doubleday.)

BARRONS EDUCATIONAL SERIES, 250 Wireless Blvd., Hauppauge NY 11788. (516)434-3311. Book publisher. Acquisitions Editor (picture books): Grace Freedson. Editorial contact (young/middle readers, young adult titles): Don Reis. Publishes 20 picture books/year; 20 young reader titles/year; 20 middle reader titles/year; 10 young adult titles/year. 25% of books by first-time authors; 25% of books from agented writers.

Fiction: Picture books: animal, easy-to-read, sports. Recently published *A Giant Problem*, by Richard Fowler (ages 6-9); *It's Mine*, by Rod Campbell (ages 2-5); *The Dinosaur Eggs*, (ages 3-7).

Nonfiction: Picture books: animal. Young readers: biography, sports. Recently published *Journey Through History Series*, by Veres (ages 7-9); *Play Mozart/Play Beethoven*, by Alison Sage; *First Aid for Kids*, by Gary Fleisher, M.D.

How to Contact/Writers: Fiction: Query. Nonfiction: Submit outline/synopsis and sample chapters. Reports on queries in 3-8 weeks; on mss in 3-12 weeks. Publishes a book 6 months after acceptance. Will consider simultaneous submissions.

Illustration: Number of illustrations used for fiction/nonfiction: picture books—16. Editorial will review ms/illustration packages submitted by authors/artists; ms/illustration packages submitted by authors with illustrations done by separate artists; and illustrator's work for possible use in author's texts.

How to Contact/Illustrators: Ms/illustration packages: Query first; 3 chapters of ms with 1 piece of final art, remainder roughs. Illustrations only: Tear sheets or slides plus resume. Reports in 3-8 weeks.

Terms/Writers & Illustrators: Pays authors in royalties based on retail price. Illustrators paid by the project based on retail price. Sends galleys to authors; dummies to illustrators. Book catalog, manuscript/artist's guidelines free on request.

Tips: Writers: "We are predominately on the lookout for preschool storybooks and concept books." Illustrators: "We are happy to receive a sample illustration to keep on file for future consideration. Periodic notes reminding us of their work is acceptable." Children's book themes "are becoming much more contemporary and relevant to a child's day to day activities."

Carolynn Roche, Niwot, Colorado, was selected to illustrate The Stolen Appaloosa *because she "is extremely detail-oriented and also maintains an affinity as well as a strong educational background for the American Indian," Barbara J. Ciletti, Bookmaker's Guild publisher, explains. "It (the artwork) was designed to present a realistic view of the life and culture of the Northwest Indians in the 1800s." Roche provided Ciletti with drawings of authentically illustrated garments, buildings, and tribal art true to each Native American featured. This illustration is a graphite sketch; other pieces in the book are rendered in watercolor and colored pencil.*

© Bookmakers Guild, Inc. 1988

BOOKMAKER'S GUILD, INC., subsidiary of Dakota Graphics, Inc., 9655 W. Colfax Ave., Lakewood CO 80215. (303)235-0203. Book publisher. Publisher: Barbara J. Ciletti. Publishes 2-4 young reader titles/year; 2- 4 middle reader titles/year. 5-10% of books by first-time authors; 5% of books from agented writers.

Fiction: Picture books: animal, fantasy "require strong myth and fable storylines," history. Young readers: animal, contemporary, history, adventure. Middle readers: history, adventure. Young adults: adventure. Average word length: picture books—5,000-10,000; young readers—30,000+; middle readers—30,000+; young adults—40,000+. Recently published *The Stolen Appaloosa*, by Levitt & Guralnick (ages 9-12, Northwest Indian legends); *Roxane, The Blue Dane*, by Alice LaChevre (ages 9-12, mini saga); *Weighty Word Book*, by Levitt et al (ages 8-12, vocabulary through fable and pun).

Nonfiction: Picture books: animal, biography, education, history, nature/environment. Young readers: animal, biography, education, history, nature/environment. Middle readers: animal, biography, education, history, nature/environment. Young adults: animal, biography, education, history, nature/environment. Average word length: picture books—5,000-10,000; young readers—30,000; middle readers—30,000; young adults—30,000+. Recently published *Call to Adventure*, by Hillary Hauser (ages 10 and up, adventure and biography).

How to Contact/Writers: Fiction/nonfiction: Query; submit outline/synopsis and sample chapters. SASE (IRC) for answer to query and/or return of mss; include Social Security number with submission. Reports on queries in 4 weeks; on mss 4-12 weeks. Publishes a book 12-18 months after acceptance. Will consider simultaneous, photocopied, and computer printout submissions.

Illustration: Number of illustrations used for fiction: picture books—30; young readers—30. Number of illustrations used for nonfiction: picture books—30; young readers—30; middle readers—30-40; young adults—50+. Editorial will review ms/illustration packages submitted by authors/artists; ms/illustration packages submitted by authors with illustrations done by separate artists. Publisher, Barbara J. Ciletti will review an illustrator's work for possible use in author's texts.

How to Contact/Illustrators: Ms/illustration packages: Query first. Illustrations only: Resume and tear sheets. Reports only if interested.

Terms/Writers & Illustrators: Pays authors in royalties of 8-15% based on wholesale price. Additional payment for ms/illustration packages: Illustrators receive their own contract or their own agreement of work for hire; final payment is made after final art is approved. We pay (illustrators working on author's titles) by project. The price ranges depending on the intended audience, number of illustrations and their complexity. Sends galleys to authors; dummies to illustrators. Books catalog free on request; manuscript guidelines/artist's guidelines available for #10 SAE and 1 first-class stamp.

Tips: Writers: "Research. Conduct a thorough study on what has been done and who has done it. Use Bowker's *Literary Marketplace* and read *Publishing: What It Is* by John Dessauer." Illustrators: "It's important to show versatility and personality in your images. Different books may have a combination of requirements." Looks for: "Fresh, wholesome stories and illustrations that reflect some educational value."

BRADBURY PRESS, imprint of Macmillan Publishing Company, 866 Third Ave., New York NY 10022. (212)702-9809. Book publisher. Editorial Contact: Barbara Lalicki. Publishes 15-20 picture books/year; 5 young reader titles/year; 5 middle reader titles/year; 3 young adult titles/year. 30% of books by first-time authors; 60% of books from previously published or agented writers.

Fiction: Picture books: animal, contemporary, history. Young readers: animal, contemporary, easy-to-read, history. Middle readers: contemporary, fantasy, history, science fiction, spy/mystery/adventure. Young adults: contemporary, fantasy, history, science fiction, spy/mystery/adventure. Average length: picture books—32-48 pages; young readers—48 pages; middle readers—128 pages; young adults—140-160 pages. Recently published *Hatchet*, by Gary Paulsen (ages 11-13, adventure/survival); *Her Seven Brothers*, by Paul Goble (all ages, picture book); *Henry and Mudge in the Sparkle Days*, by Cynthia Rylant (ages 6-8, easy-to-read).

Nonfiction: Picture books: animal, history, music/dance, nature/environment. Young readers: animal, biography, education, history, hobbies, music/dance, nature/environment, sports. Middle readers: animal, biography, education, history, hobbies, music/dance, nature/environment, sports. Average length: picture books—32-48 pages; young readers—48 pages; middle readers—128 pages; young adults—140-160 pages. *African Journey*, by John Chiasson (8 and up, photoessay); *Dinosaurs Walked Here*, by Patricia Lauber (8 and up, photoessay/nature/history); *When I See My Doctor*, by Susan Kuklin (ages 3-5, photoessay).

How to Contact/Writers: Fiction: Query. Nonfiction: Submit outline/synopsis and sample chapters. SASE (IRC) for answer to query and/or return of ms. Reports on queries in 2-3 weeks; on mss in 6-8 weeks. Publishes a book 18 months after acceptance. Will consider photocopied and computer printout submissions.

Illustration: Number of illustrations used for fiction and nonfiction: picture books—30; young readers—1; middle readers—1; young adults—1. Art Director, Julie Quan, will review illustrator's work for possible use in author's texts.

How to Contact/Illustrators: Submit ms with color photocopies of art. Illustrations only: Portfolio drop off last Thursday of every month. Reports on art samples only if interested. Original artwork returned at job's completion.

Terms/Writers & Illustrators: Pays author in royalties based on retail price. Average advance: "% of estimated sales." Additional payment for ms/illustration packages. Pay for separate authors and illustrators: "advance, royalty." Sends galleys to authors; dummies to illustrators. Book catalog available for 8×10 SAE and 4 first-class stamps; manuscript and/or artist's guidelines for business-size SAE and 1 first-class stamp.

Tips: Writers: "Write about what you know about, think about plot, real conversations."

Illustrators: "Know how to draw and paint children." Looks for "a strong story, nothing gimmicky, no pop-ups." Trends include "nonfiction for pre-schoolers." (See also Aladdin Books/Collier Books for Young Adults, Atheneum Publishers, Four Winds Press, Margaret K. McElderry Books.)

BRANDEN PUBLISHING CO., 17 Station St., Box 843, Brookline Village MA 02147. (617)734-2045. Book publisher. Editorial Contact: Mr. Caso. Publishes 2 picture books/year; 2 young adult titles/year. 100% of books by first-time authors.
Fiction: Middle readers: history. Young adults: sports. Recently published *Pilgrims*, by Cauper (grade 1, illustrated).
Nonfiction: Recently published *Young Rocky*, by Kinney (young adults, biography).
How to Contact/Writers: Fiction/nonfiction: Query. All unsolicited ms returned unopened. SASE (IRC) for answer to query and/or return of ms. Reports on queries in 2 weeks; on mss in 8 weeks. Publishes a book 10 months after acceptance. Will consider photocopied, computer printout and electronic submissions via disk or modem.
Illustration: Editorial will review ms/illustration packages submitted by authors/artists and ms/illustration packages submitted by authors with illustrations done by separate artists.
How to Contact/Illustrators: Ms/illustration packages: Query only with SASE. Illustrations only: resume. Reports in 2 weeks.
Terms/Writers & Illustrators: Pays authors in royalties of 10%. Pay for separate authors and illustrators: by agreement between author and illustrator. Sends galleys to authors; dummies to illustrators. Book catalog available for 4 × 9½ SAE and 1 first-class stamp.
Tips: "Describe, in first paragraph, what the book is about; include brief resume; enclose SASE." Illustrators: "Do not send originals."

BREAKWATER BOOKS, Box 2188, St. John's Newfoundland, A1C 6E6 Canada. (709)722-6680. Book publisher. Marketing Manager: Catherine Hogan. Publishes 3 middle reader titles/year; 2 young adult titles/year.
Fiction: Recently published *Smoke Over Grand Pré*, by Davison/Marsh (young adults, historical); *Fanny for Change*, by Jean Feather (middle reader); *Borrowed Black*, by Ellen B. Obed (young reader, fantasy).
Nonfiction: Recently published *A Viking Ship*, by Niels Neerso (young adults).
How to Contact/Writers: Fiction/nonfiction: Submit outline/synopsis and sample chapters; submit complete ms. Publishes a book 2 years after acceptance. Will consider simultaneous and photocopied submissions.
Illustration: Number of illustrations used per fiction/nonfiction title "varies." Editorial will review ms/illustration packages submitted by authors/artists, ms/illustration packages submitted by authors with illustrations done by separate artists, and illustrator's work for possible use in author's text.
How to Contact/Illustrators: Submit 3 chapters of ms with 1 piece of final art, remainder roughs. Reports on art samples within weeks. Original artwork returned at job's completion.
Terms/Writers & Illustrators: Royalties 10% based on retail price. "Amount varies" for mss purchased outright. Sends galleys to authors; dummies to illustrators. Book catalog free on request.

CALICO BOOKS (The Kipling Press), Contemporary Books, Inc., 180 N. Michigan Ave., Chicago IL 60601. (312)782-9181. Book publisher. Independent book producer/packager. Managing Editor: Wendy Wax. Editor: Nancy Crossman. Publishes 15 picture books/year; 15 young reader titles/year; 10 middle reader titles/year. 30% of books by first-time authors; 5% of books from agented writers.
Fiction: Picture books: animal, easy-to-read. Young readers: animal, fantasy, history,

science fiction, spy/mystery/adventure. Recently published Miss Baba—*The Caribbean Foul Ball Caper*, by Rich & Winslow Pels (ages 10 and up, fantasy/mystery/adventure); *Cinderella* retold by Peter Elwell (ages 6 and up, fairy tale); *Itty Bitty Kiddie's*, by Russ Shorto (ages 2 and up, first skills).

Nonfiction: Picture books: animal, education, nature/environment. Young readers: education, history. Recently published *Albert's Riddle*, by Seth McEvoy (ages 10 and up, science thriller); *Brer Rabbit*, by Mark Davies (ages 6 and up, American folk tale); *The Secret History of Grammar*, by Russ Shorto/Bob Cuiklik (ages 10 and up, story/text).

How to Contact/Writers: Fiction/nonfiction: Query. Include Social Security number with submission. Publishes a book 6-10 months after acceptance. Will consider simultaneous, photocopied, and computer printout submissions.

Illustration: Number of illustrations used for fiction: picture books—20; young readers—20. Number of illustrations used for nonfiction: picture books—25; young readers—10. Editorial will review ms/illustration packages submitted by authors/artists and ms/illustration packages submitted by authors with illustrations done by separate artists. Editor, Nancy Crossman, will review an illustrator's work for possible use in author's texts.

How to Contact/Illustrators: Ms/illustration packages: Query first. Illustrations only: Resume, tear sheets.

Terms/Writers & Illustrators: Pays authors in royalties based on retail price. Illustrators paid by the project. Book catalog, manuscript/artist's guidelines free on request.

CARNIVAL ENTERPRISES, Box 19087, Minneapolis MN, 55419. (612)820-0169. Independent book producer/packager. Editor: Rosemary Wallner. Publishes 1-3 picture books/year; 1-3 young reader titles/year; 50 middle reader titles/year. 40% of books by first-time authors; 0% of books from agented writers.

Fiction: Picture books: animal, easy-to-read. Young readers: history. Middle readers: animal, contemporary, history, sports, spy/mystery/adventure. Average word length: picture books—600; young readers—"varies"; middle readers—5,000. Recently published *Shy Charlene*, by C. Nobens (young readers); *All Through the Night*, illustrated by G. & S. Fasens (picture book); *Tracks in the Northwoods*, by Dana Brenford (middle readers, mystery).

Nonfiction: Middle readers: animal, biography, history, hobbies, music/dance, nature/environment. Average word length: middle readers—5,000. Recently published *Stuntpeople*, by G. Stewart (middle readers); *Yellowstone National Park*, by C. Marron (middle readers); *AIDS*, by M. Turck (middle readers).

How to Contact/Writers: Fiction/nonfiction: Submit query. SASE (IRC) for answer to query. Reports on queries in 3-4 weeks.

Illustration: Number of illustrations used for fiction: middle readers—10. Editorial will review ms/illustration packages submitted by authors/artists and ms/illustration packages submitted by authors with illustrations done by separate artists. Art director, Gloria Blockey, will review illustrator's work for possible use in author's texts.

Terms/Writers & Illustrators: Methods of payment: "Varies too much. Depends on the publisher who hires us and the writer." Sends galleys to authors; dummies to illustrators.

CAROLINA WREN PRESS/LOLLIPOP POWER BOOKS, Box 277, Carrboro NC 27510. (919) 560-2738 (office). (919)376-8152 (main editor). Book publisher. Editor-in-Chief: Judy Hogan. Publishes 2 picture books/year; 1 young reader title in '88. 100% of books by first-time authors.

Fiction: Picture books: contemporary, easy-to-read, fantasy, history, problem novels, science fiction, black family, "especially interested in non-sexist, multi-racial." Average length: picture books—30 pages. Recently published *The Boy Toy*, by Phyllis Johnson (grade 1, picture book); *I Like You to Make Jokes*, by Ellen Bass (grades 1-2, picture book); *In Christina's Toolbox*, by Dianne Homan (grades 1-2, picture book).

Nonfiction: Picture books: biography, education, history, hobbies, music/dance, "children of divorce and lesbian homes and black families." Average length: picture books—30 pages.

How to Contact/Writers: Fiction/nonfiction: Query and request guidelines. SASE (IRC) for answer to query and/or return of ms. Reports on queries/ms in 12 weeks. Publishes a book 24-36 months after acceptance "at present."

Illustration: Number of illustrations used for fiction and nonfiction: picture books—12. Editorial will review ms/illustration packages submitted by authors/artists and ms/illustration packages submitted by authors with illustrations done by separate artists. Designer, Martha Lange (215 Monmouth St., Durham NC 27701) will review illustrator's work for possible use in author's texts.

How to Contact/Illustrators: Query first to Martha Lange. Reports on art samples only if interested. Original artwork returned at job's completion.

Terms/Writers & Illustrators: Pays authors in royalties of 5% of print-run based on retail price, or cash, if available. Additional payment for ms/illustration packages: Author gets 5%; illustrator gets 5%. Pays illustrators in royalties of 5% "of print-run based on retail price, or cash, if available." Sends galleys to authors; dummies to illustrators. Book catalog free on request; manuscript guidelines for business-size SAE and 1 first-class stamp; artist's guidelines free on request.

Tips: "Our books aim to show children that: girls and women are self-sufficient; boys and men can be emotional and nurturing; families may consist of one parent only, working parents, extended families; families may rely on daycare centers or alternative child care; all children, whatever their race, creed or color, are portrayed often and fairly in ways true to their own experience. We require that childhood be taken seriously. Children's lives can be no less complex than adults'; we expect that their problems are presented honestly and completely. The validity of their feelings must be recognized as children will benefit from reading of others coping with emotions or conflicts and finding solutions to their own problems. Current publishing priorities: strong female protagonists, especially Black, Hispanic, or Native-American girls and women; friendship and solidarity among girls; children working to change values and behavior; non-traditional family situations; stories with evident concern for the world around us." Writers: "Be sure you can hold the attention of a child. Practice stories on real children and become a good writer."Beginning illustrators: "Try to get classes with someone who understands illustration professionally. We are seeking new illustrators for our files. Please send us your name and current address and we will notify you when we have a manuscript ready for illustration. Keep us notified of any address change, as it may be a while before we contact you."

CAROLRHODA BOOKS, INC., Lerner Publications, 241 First Ave. N., Minneapolis MN 55401. (612)332-3344. Book publisher. Submissions Editor: Rebecca Poole. Publishes 10 picture books/year; 7 young reader titles/year; 10 middle reader titles/year. 20% of books by first-time authors; 10% of books from agented writers.

Fiction: Picture books: animal. Young readers: animal, contemporary, easy-to-read. Average word length: picture books—1,000-1,500; young readers—2,000. Recently published *Gift of the Willows*, by Helena Clare Pittman (young readers, story book); *Why the Crab Has No Head*, by Barbara Knutson (young readers, folktale); *Giant Story/Mouse Tale*, by Annegert Fuchshuber (young readers, story book).

Nonfiction: Young readers: history, hobbies, music/dance, nature/environment. Middle readers: animal, biography, history, music/dance, nature/environment. Average word length: young readers— 2,000; middle readers—6,000. Recently published *Go Free or Die*, by Jeri Ferris (young reader-middle reader, biography); *Wild Boars*, by Darrel Nicholson (young reader-middle reader, nature); *Farming the Land*, by Jerry Bushey (young reader, photo book).

How to Contact/Writers: Fiction/nonfiction: Submit complete ms. SASE (IRC) for return of ms. Reports on queries in 3 weeks; on mss in 12 weeks. Publishes a book 12 months after acceptance. Will consider simultaneous and photocopied submissions.

Illustration: Number of illustrations used for fiction: picture books—15-20; young readers—20. Number of illustrations used for nonfiction: young readers—15-20; middle readers—10-12. Editorial will review ms/illustration packages submitted by authors/ artists; ms/illustration packages submitted by authors with illustrations done by separate artists and illustrator's work for possible use in author's texts.

How to Contact/Illustrators: Ms/illustration packages: At least one sample illustration (in form of photocopy, slide, duplicate photo) with full ms. Illustrations only: resume/slides. Reports on art samples only if interested.

Terms/Writers & Illustrators: Buys ms outright for varied amount. Factors used to determine final payment: color vs. black-and-white, number of illustrations, quality of work. Sends galleys to authors; dummies to illustrators. Book catalog available for 9 × 12 SAE and 2 first-class stamps; manuscript guidelines for letter-size SAE and 1 first-class stamp.

Tips: Writers: "Research the publishing company to be sure it is in the market for the type of book you're interested in writing. Familiarize yourself with the company's list. We specialize in beginning readers, photo essays, and books published in series. We do very few single-title picture books, and only 3-6 novels a year, most of them for 7-11 year olds. For more detailed information about our publishing program, consult our catalog. We do not publish any of the following: textbooks, workbooks, songbooks, puzzles, plays, and religious material. In general, we suggest that you steer clear of alphabet books; preachy stories with a moral to convey; stories featuring anthropomorphic protagonists ('Amanda the Amoeba,' 'Frankie the Fire Engine,' 'Tonie the Tornado'); and stories that revolve around trite, hackneyed plots: Johnny moves to a new neighborhood and is miserable because he can't make any new friends; Steve and Jane find a sick bird with a broken wing, and they nurse it back to health; lonely protagonist is rejected by his peers—usually because he's 'different' from them in some way—until he saves the day by rescuing them from some terrible calamity; and so on. You should also avoid racial and sexual stereotypes in your writing, as well as sexist language." Illustrators: "Research each company and send appropriate samples for their files." (See also Lerner Publications.)

CHILDRENS PRESS, 5440 N. Cumberland, Chicago Il 60656. (312)693-0800. Book publisher. Publishes 20-30 picture books/year; 20 young reader nonfiction titles/year; 10 middle reader nonfiction titles/year; 40 young adult nonfiction titles/year. "Nonfiction comprises 80% of our list." 5% of books by first-time authors; 1% of books from agented writers.

Fiction: Picture books: easy-to-read. Young readers: animal, history, sports. Average word length: picture books—60-500; young readers—800-2,000. Recently published *Bugs*, by Pat McKissack (picture book, rookie reader); *A Minute is A Minute*, by B. Neasi (young readers, picture book).

Nonfiction: Picture books, young readers: nature/environment. Middle readers: biography, history, hobbies, nature/environment. Young adults: history, nature/environment. Average word length: picture books—600; young readers—1,800; young adults—14,000. Recently published *Benjamin Franklin*, by Carol Greene (young readers, biography); *Vietnam War (4 vol.)*, by David Wright (young adults, history); *Illinois*, by R. Conrad Stein (young adults, social studies).

How to Contact/Writers: Fiction/nonfiction: Submit outline/synopsis and sample chapters. SASE (IRC) for return of ms. Reports on queries in 8 weeks; on mss in 12 weeks. Publishes a book 6 months after acceptance. Will consider simultaneous submissions.

Illustration: Number of illustrations used for fiction: picture books—25; young readers—18. Editorial will review ms/illustration packages submitted by authors/artists and ms/illustration packages submitted by authors with illustrations done by separate artists. Creative Director, Margrit Fiddle, will review illustrator's work for possible use in author's texts.

How to Contact/Illustrators: Ms/illustration packages: Query first. Illustrations only: Resume. Reports in 4 weeks.

Terms/Writers & Illustrators: Offers average advance payment of $1,000. Pay for illustrators: By the project; royalties based on wholesale price. Sends galleys to authors sometimes. Books catalog, manuscript guidelines free on request.

Tips: Writers: "Do research in the children's section of the library. Not all children's books are fiction. Be persistent but realistic. If a publisher does nonfiction, do not send them a young adult novel." Illustrators: "Try to find out what a publisher is looking for and then propose a title or art style that covers the subject in a fresh and lively manner." Looks for "nonfiction—using primary or secondary source materials quotes from experts." Trends include "titles that fit into existing series. CP publishes the 'True' Book series; more than 198 titles published on topics ranging from science to government."

THE CHILD'S WORLD, INC., Box 989, Elgin IL 60121. (312)741- 7591. Book publisher. Editorial Contact: Jane Buerger. Publishes 50 picture books/year. 5% of books by first time authors.

Fiction: Picture books: animal, easy-to-read, history, sports, spy/mystery/adventure. Recently published *A Dragon in a Wagon*, by Jane Moncure (preschool-2, early reader); *What's So Special About Me? I'm One of a Kind*, by Janet McDonnell (preschool-2, early reader); *Talk-Along, Count the Possums*, by Dick Punnett (grades K-2, teachers concepts).

Nonfiction: Picture books: animal, biography, nature/environment. Recently published *Apatosaurus*, by Janet Riehecky (grades 1-4, reader); *Friendship*, by Beverly Fiday (grades K-3, reader); *A Visit to the Dairy Farm*, by Sandra Ziegler (grades K-3, reader).

How to Contact/Writers: Fiction/nonfiction: Query. SASE (IRC) for answer to query and/or return of ms. Reports on queries in 3-4 weeks; on mss in 4-12 weeks. Publishes a book 6 months after acceptance. Will consider simultaneous and photocopied submissions.

Illustration: Number of illustrations used for fiction and nonfiction: picture books— 16+. Will review ms/illustration packages submitted by authors/artists.

How to Contact/Illustrators: Ms/illustration packages: Query first. Reports on art samples up to 3 months.

Terms/Writers & Illustrators: "Price differs on job" for outright purchases. Factors used to determine final payment for ms/illustration package includes "number of illustrations used." Pay for illustrators: "sometimes" by the project. Book catalog/manuscript guidelines/artist's guidelines free on request.

Tips: Looks for "preschool-grade 2—easy-to-read or 'read-to-me' 32 pages."

CHINA BOOKS, 2929 24th St., San Francisco CA 94110. (415)282-2994. Book publisher. Independent book producer/packager. Managing Editor: Bob Schildgen. 10% of books by first-time authors; 10% of books from agented writers.

Nonfiction: Young readers, middle readers: hobbies, nature/environment. Average word length: young readers—2,000; middle readers—4,000. Recently published *Paper Pandas and Jumping Frogs*, by Florence Temko (young adults, hobby).

How to Contact/Writers: Fiction/nonfiction: Query; submit outline/synopsis and sample chapters. SASE for answer to query and/or return of ms. Publishes a book 9 months after acceptance. Will consider simultaneous, photocopied, computer printout and electronic submissions via disk or modem.

Illustration: Editorial will review ms/illustration packages submitted by authors/artists; ms/illustration packages submitted by authors with illustrations done by separate artists; and illustrator's work for possible use in author's texts.

Terms/Writers & Illustrators: Pays authors in royalties of 8-10% based on retail price; buys ms outright for $100-$500. Offers average advance payment of "1/3 of total royalty." Pay for illustrators: by the project $100-$500; royalties of 8% based on retail price. Sends galleys to authors; dummies to illustrators. Book catalog free on request; manuscript/artist's guidelines for SAE.

Tips: Looks for "something related to China or to Chinese-Americans."

CHRONICLE BOOKS, 275 Fifth St., San Francisco CA 94103. (415)777-7240. Book publisher. Editor: Victoria Rock. Publishes 12-16 picture books/year; 0-6 young reader titles/year; 0-4 middle reader titles/year; 0-2 young adult titles/year.

Fiction: Picture books: animal, contemporary, fantasy, history. Young readers: animal, contemporary, easy-to-read, fantasy, history, sports, adventure. Middle readers: animal, contemporary, fantasy, history, problem novels, sports, adventure. Young adults: contemporary, fantasy, history, adventure.

Nonfiction: Picture books: animal, biography, history, nature/environment. Young readers: animal, biography, history, nature/environment. Middle readers: animal, biography, history, music/dance, nature/environment. Young adults: biography, history, nature/environment.

How to Contact/Writers: Fiction/nonfiction: Query; submit outline synopsis and sample chapters; submit complete ms. SASE (IRC) for answer to query and/or return of ms. Reports on queries in 2 weeks; on mss in 6 weeks. Publishes a book 1-2 years after acceptance. Will consider simultaneous and photocopied submissions.

Illustration: Number of illustrations used for fiction and nonfiction: picture books—12-20; young readers—10-20; middle readers—5-10; young adults—jacket illustrations. Editorial will review ms/illustration packages submitted by authors/artists and ms/illustration packages submitted by authors with illustrations done by separate artists. Editor, Victoria Rock, will review illustrator's work for possible use in author's texts.

How to Contact/Illustrators: Picture book, young readers: complete ms and sample finished art (need not be from book itself as long as it is representative of style), slides of varied work. Middle readers/young adults: sample chapters and sample art. Illustrations only: resume and tear sheets and/or slides and/or photocopies. Reports on art samples only if interested or if artist requests response. Original artwork returned at job's completion.

Terms/Writers & Illustrators: In most cases, pays author in royalties . . . although there are instances when work is commissioned on a flat-fee basis. Pays authors in royalties based on retail price. Average advance payment "varies." Additional payment for ms/illustration packages. Factors used to determine final payment "vary according to type of book." Sends galleys to authors. Book catalog available for SAE.

Tips: Writers: "Try to write a story that is your story—not the story you think you should be writing. Try not to be condescending to your readers." Illustrators: "Send samples that vary in style. The wider range you demonstrate, the more likely you are to strike a note with an editor or art director. Again, as with writing, imbue your work with individual personality. Artwork must be graphically outstanding."

CLARION BOOKS, Houghton Mifflin Company, 52 Vanderbilt Ave., New York NY 10017. (212)972-1190. Book publisher. Editor and Publisher: James C. Giblin (picture books and fiction titles). Contact: Ann Troy (nonfiction titles). Publishes 10 picture books/year; 7 young reader titles/year; 14 middle reader titles/year; 4 young adult titles/year. 10% of books by first-time authors; 15% of books from agented writers.

Fiction: Picture books: animal, contemporary, fantasy, history, problem novels. Young readers: animal, contemporary, fantasy, history, problem novels. Middle readers: animal, contemporary, fantasy, history, problem novels, sports, spy/mystery/adventure. Young adults: history, problem novels, spy/mystery/adventure. Average word length: picture books—750-1,000; young readers—1,000-2,500; middle readers—10,000-30,000;

young adults—20,000—30,000. Recently published *Saying Good-bye to Grandma*, by Jane Resh Thomas (ages 7-10, young fiction); *Always and Forever Friends*, by C. S. Adler (ages 9-12, contemporary); *December Stillness*, by Mary Downing Hahn, (ages 10- 14, contemporary).

Nonfiction: Picture books: animal. Young readers: animal, history, nature/environment. Middle readers: biography, history, nature/environment. Average word length: picture books—750-1,000; young readers—1,000-2,500; middle readers—10,000-30,000. Recently published *Guppies in Tuxedos*, by Marvin Terban (ages 6-9, word play); *Trapped in Tar*, by Caroline Arnold (ages 8-12, natural history); *Lincoln: A Photobiography*, by Russell Freedman (ages 9-up, biography).

How to Contact/Writers: Fiction: Query on all ms over 50 pages. Nonfiction: Query. SASE (IRC) for answer to query and/or return of ms. Reports on queries in 4 weeks; mss in 8-12 weeks. Publishes a book 18 months after acceptance. Will consider photocopied and computer printout submissions.

Illustration: Number of illustrations used for fiction: picture books—20; young readers—15. Number of illustrations used for nonfiction: picture books—20; young readers—40; middle readers—20-50. Editorial will review ms/illustration packages submitted by authors/artists and ms/illustration packages submitted by authors with illustrations done by separate artists. Art Director, Carol Goldenberg, will review illustrator's work for possible use in author's texts.

How to Contact/Illustrators: Ms/illustration packages: "query first." Illustrations only: "tear sheets, photos or photocopies of samples." Reports on art samples only if interested. Original artwork returned at job's completion.

Terms/Writers & Illustrators: Pays authors in royalties of 10-12½% based on retail price. Offers average advance payment of $2,500-$5,000. Pay for separate authors and illustrators: "Separately, on an advance and royalty basis." Sends galleys to authors; dummies to illustrators. Book catalog, manuscript/artist's guidelines free on request.

Tips: Writers: "Discover the unique things that you have to say, and say them in the most effective way possible." Illustrators: "Discover the unique things that you have to draw/paint, and say them in the most effective way possible." Looks for: "A fresh, imaginative story or nonfiction text, written and/or illustrated in a distinctive voice and style." There is "a growing book store market for quality books, especially at the younger age levels."

COACH HOUSE PRESS, INC., Box 109, Dept. CW, Woodstock IL 60098. (815)338-7170. Play publisher. 65% of plays by first-time authors; 5% of plays from agented writers.
Fiction: Plays: young readers, middle readers, young adults. Recently published *Friday's Child*, by Sterling (middle-young adults, full length play); *Shoemaker and the Elves*, by Dorn (young reader, one-act play); *Alien Equation*, by Maccoby/Church (middle reader, full length play).

How to Contact/Writers: Submit complete ms. SASE (IRC) for return of ms. Reports on queries in 2 weeks; on mss in 8 weeks. Publishes a book 10 months after acceptance. Will consider simultaneous, photocopied and electronic submissions via disk or modem.

Terms/Writers & Illustrators: Pays authors in royalties of 10% based on retail price; 25-50% of production royalty. Sends galleys to authors. Book catalog available for 9 × 12 SAE and $1.25 postage; manuscript guidelines for #10 SAE and 1 first-class stamp.

Tips: "If you want your plays published, get them produced by independent theaters. Use the production experience to strengthen your script." Looks for: "plays that have been tested before young audiences."

CONSUMER REPORT BOOKS, Consumer Union, 51 East 42nd St., New York NY 10017. (212)983-8250. Book publisher. Editorial Contact: Sarah Uman. Publishes 2 young adult titles/year. 50% of books from agented writers.
Nonfiction: Young adults: education, nature/environment, health. Average word

length: young adults—50,000. Recently published *How and Why?*, by Catherine O'Neill (young adults, health); *AIDS: Trading Fears for Facts*, by Karen Hein, M.D. and Theresa DiGeronimo (young adults, health).

How to Contact/Writers: Nonfiction: Submit outline/synopsis and sample chapters; submit complete ms; submit table of contents. SASE (IRC) for answer to query. Reports on queries/mss in 6 weeks. Publishes a book 24 months after acceptance. Will consider simultaneous, photocopied and computer printout submissions.

Illustrations: Number of illustrations used for nonfiction: young adults—50. Editorial will review ms/illustration packages submitted by authors/artists and ms/illustration packages submitted by authors with illustrations done by separate artists.

How to Contact/Illustrators: Ms/illustration packages: query first.

Terms/Writers & Illustrators: Pays authors in royalties based on retail price. Factors used to determine payment for ms/illustration packages include "number of illustrations." Pay for separate authors and illustrators: Pay for "author—advance against royalty; illustrator—flat fee by the project." Sends galleys to authors. Book catalog/manuscript guidelines free on request.

COTEAU BOOKS LTD., Thunder Creek Publishing Co-op Ltd., 209-1945 Scarth St., Regina SK, S4P 2H2 Canada. (306)352-5346. Book publisher. Managing Editor: Shelley Sopher. Publishes 1 picture book/year. 85% of books by first-time authors. Subsidy publishes "8 books per year."

Fiction: Picture books: animal, contemporary, fantasy, spy/mystery/adventure. Average word length: picture books—500. Recently published *What Holds Up the Moon*, by Lois Simmie (grades 1-2, picture); *Monster Cheese*, by Steve Wolfson (grades 2-4, picture); *Prairie Jungle*, edited (various grades, anthology of song, poems and stories).

How to Contact/Writers: Fiction: Submit complete ms. SASE (IRC) for answer to query and/or return of ms. Reports on queries in 2 weeks; on mss in 6 weeks. Publishes a book 12-24 months after acceptance. Will consider photocopied and computer printout submissions.

Illustration: Number of illustrations used for fiction: picture books—30. Editorial will review ms/illustration packages submitted by authors/artists and ms/illustration packages submitted by authors with illustrations done by separate artists. Managing Editor, Shelley Sopher, will review illustrator's work for possible use in author's texts.

How to Contact/Illustrators: Ms/illustration packages "roughs." Reports on art samples within 6 weeks. Original artwork returned at job's completion.

Terms/Writers & Illustrators: Pays authors in royalties of 5-12% based on retail price. Other method of payment: "signing bonus." Pay for illustrators: by the project $500-$2,000; royalty 5% maximum based on retail price. Sends galleys to authors; dummies to illustrators. Book catalog free on request.

COUNCIL FOR INDIAN EDUCATION, 517 Rimrock Rd., Billings MT 59102. (406)252-7451. Book publisher. Editor: Hap Gilliland. Publishes 1 picture book/year; 1 young reader title/year; 3 middle reader titles/year; 1 young adult title/year. "Have done only one shared expense book but may do one a year—larger books that we can't afford alone."

Fiction: Picture books: animal, easy-to-read. Young readers: animal, easy-to-read, history. Middle readers: animal, history. Young adults: animal, history. Other: Native American life, past and present. Recently published *Fire Mate*, by Olga Cossi (grades 4-10, story of Indian girl and her dog); *Navajo Magic of Hunting*, (grades 3-8, narrative poem of boy's first hunt); *Many Horses*, by Stormy Rodolph (grades 7-12, Blackfeet Indian novel).

Nonfiction: Picture books: animal, nature/environment. Young readers: animal, biography, history, hobbies, nature/environment. Middle readers: animal, biography, history, hobbies, music/dance, nature/environment. Young adults: animal, biography, history, hobbies, music/dance, nature/environment, sports. Other: related to American Indian life and culture, past and present. Recently published *Indian Canoeing*, by Pierre Pulling (grades 4-adult, how to paddle a canoe).

How to Contact/Writers: Fiction: Submit complete ms. Nonfiction: Submit outline/synopsis and sample chapters, or submit complete ms. SASE (IRC) for return of ms. Reports on queries in 2 months; mss in 3 months. "We accept ⅓ to ⅙ of the manuscripts received. Those with potential must be evaluated by all the members of our Indian Editorial Board who make the final selection. This board makes sure the material is true to the Indian way of life and is the kind of material they want their children to read." Publishes a book 4 months after acceptance. Will consider simultaneous, photocopied, and computer printout submissions.

Illustration: Number of illustrations used for fiction: picture books—25; young readers—12; middle readers—10; young adults—10. Number of illustrations used for non-fiction: picture books—20; young readers—10; middle readers—10; young adults—10. Editorial will review ms/illustration packages submitted by authors/artists and ms/illustration packages submitted by authors with illustrations done by separate artists. Editor, Hap Gilliland, will review illustrator's work for possible use in author's texts. "Black and white art work only."

How to Contact/Illustrators: Ms/illustration packages: "samples sent with manuscript." Illustrations only: "samples." Reports on art samples in 3 months "when we report back to author on ms." Original artwork returned at job's completion "if requested."

Terms/Writers & Illustrators: Pays authors in royalties of 10% based on wholesale price. Buys ms outright for "1½¢ per word." Additional payment for ms/illustration packages "sometimes." Factors used to determine payment for ms/illustration package include "number of illustrations used." Sends galleys to authors. Book catalog/manuscript guidelines available for SAE and 1 first-class stamp.

Tips: "For our publications write about one specific tribe or group and be sure actions portrayed are culturally correct for the group and time period portrayed. What kind of material can we use? These are our preferences, in the order listed: Contemporary Indian Life—Exciting stories that could happen to Indian children now. (Be sure the children act like present-day Indians, not like some other culture.) Indians of the old days—Authentically portrayed. Be specific about who, where, and when. How-to—Indian arts, crafts, and activities. Biography—Indians past and present. History and culture—Factual material of high interest only. If you are Indian express your ideas and ideals. Folk stories and legends—High interest expressing Indian ideas. Name the specific tribe. Poetry—possibly—if it expresses real Indian ideals. Instructional material and information for teachers of Indian children."

CROSSWAY BOOKS, imprint of Good News Publishers, 9825 W. Roosevelt Rd., Westchester IL 60153. (312)345-7474. Book publisher. Managing Editor: Ted Griffin. Publishes 2-4 middle reader titles/year; 2-4 young adult titles/year. 50% of books by first-time authors; 10% of books from agented writers.

Fiction: Middle readers: contemporary, sports. Young adults: fantasy, science fiction, sports, spy/mystery/adventure. Recently published *Trapped at the Bottom of the Sea*, by Frank Peretti (middle-young adults, adventure); *Sadie Rose and the Daring Escape*, by Hilda Stahl (middle readers, adventure); *The Janis Project*, by Nancy Rue (young adults, contemporary).

How to Contact/Writers: Fiction: Submit outline/synopsis and sample chapters. SASE (IRC) for answer to query. Report on queries in 6 weeks. Publishes a book 12-18 months after acceptance. Will consider simultaneous, photocopied, and computer printout submissions.

Illustration: Number of illustrations used for fiction: picture books—1. Editorial will review ms/illustration packages submitted by authors/artists and ms/illustration packages submitted by authors with illustrations done by separate artists.

Terms/Writers & Illustrators: Pays authors in royalties based on wholesale price. Illustrators paid by the project. Sends galleys to authors. Book catalog/manuscript guidelines available for 8½ × 11 SAE and $1.25 postage.

Tips: "Please do as thorough a job of research and writing as possible before submitting your manuscript. We do not wish to receive manuscripts hastily thrown together, or in such rough-draft form that we cannot discern their true quality. Part of your research as well should include a visit to your local Christian bookstore to familiarize yourself with our catalog and our book line."

MAY DAVENPORT, PUBLISHERS, 26313 Purissima Rd., Los Altos Hills CA 94022. (415)948-6499. Book publisher. Independent book producer/packager. Editor: May Davenport. Publishes 1-2 picture books/year; 2-3 young adult titles/year. 99% of books by first-time authors. Subsidy publishes 20% of books.

Fiction: Young adults: fantasy, plays for teens. Average length: plays — 30 minutes stage or TV performance; young adult fantasy — 20,000-30,000 words. Recently published *Pompey Poems*, by Ellen Langill (grades 7-12, paper and hardcover); *Comic Tale Anthology #1*, Editor, May Davenport (grades 7-12, paper); *Comic Tale Anthology #2*, Editor, May Davenport (grades 7-12, paper and hardcover).

Nonfiction: Picture books: animal. Recently published *Willie, Zilly and the Bantams*, by Grace Collins (preschool-1, hardcover); Reprint *ABC of Ecology*, by Frances Wosmek (preschool-2, paper).

How to Contact/Writers: Fiction/nonfiction: Query. SASE for answer to query. Reports on queries in 2-3 weeks. Publishes a book 6-12 months after acceptance. Will consider simultaneous, photocopied, and computer printout submissions.

Illustration: Editorial will review ms/illustration packages submitted by authors/artists and ms/illustration packages submitted by authors with illustrations done by separate artists, if the "story or play" is meaningful to young adult teenagers. "If illustrators send samples, I keep those on file and get in touch with them if I need extra help."

How to Contact/Illustrators: Ms/illustration packages: Query first. Illustrations only: Sample spontaneous art — thumbnail sketches. Reports on art samples only if interested.

Terms/Writers & Illustrators: Pays authors in royalties based on retail price. Pays "by mutual agreement, no advances." Pay for separate authors and illustrators: "Prefer writer to agree to share with his illustrator 50-50. Usually my illustrators are paid as work-for-hire, so there is no writer-illustrator problem." Pay for illustrators: By the project $4.50-$7.50. Sends galleys to authors. Book listing, manuscript guidelines free on request with SASE.

Tips: "Be yourself. You either can use words readily as a medium of expression, so it's not so much what you are saying, but how poetically you say it."

DIAL BOOKS FOR YOUNG READERS, Penguin/USA (NAL Penguin, Inc.), 2 Park Ave., New York NY 10016. (212)725-1818. Editor: Arthur Levine. Publishes 40-50 picture books/year; 10 young reader titles/year; 5 middle reader titles/year; 10 young adult titles/year.

Fiction: Picture books: animal, contemporary, fantasy, history, sports, spy/mystery/adventure. Young readers: animal, contemporary, easy-to-read, fantasy, history, sports, spy/mystery/adventure. Middle readers, young adults: contemporary, fantasy, history, problem novels, science fiction, sports, spy/mystery/adventure.

Nonfiction: Uses very little nonfiction. Interested in only artistic and literary content.

How to Contact/Writers: Fiction: Query, submit outline/synopsis and sample chapters for longer work, submit complete ms for short material. SASE (IRC) for answer to query and/or return of ms. SASE must be able to hold your ms if returned.

Illustration: Editorial will review ms/illustration packages submitted by authors/artists;

ms/illustration packages submitted by authors with illustrations done by separate artists (prefers to use own artists); will review an illustrator's work for possible use in author's texts.

How to Contact/Illustrators: Ms/illustration packages: Query first or 1 piece of final color art and sketches. Illustrations only: Resume, tear sheets.

Terms/Writers & Illustrators: Pays authors in royalties based on retail price. Average advance payment "varies." Manuscript guidelines for SAE.

DILLON PRESS, INC., 242 Portland Ave. S., Minneapolis MN 55415. (612)333-2691. Book publisher. Nonfiction: Tom Schneider. Fiction: Lora Lee Polack. Publishes 15-20 young reader titles/year; 15-20 middle reader titles/year. 50% of books by first-time authors; 10% of books from agented writers.

Fiction: Young readers: history—refers to a specific series of books titled *It Really Happened.* Average word length: young readers—4,000-5,000. Recently published *Day of Darkness,* by Cathy Martin (grade 3, fiction based on actual event); *Carlos the Camel,* by Ann Shaffer (grade 3, fiction based on actual event).

Nonfiction: Young readers and middle readers: animal, biography, history, nature/ environment, sports. Average word length: young readers—2,000; middle readers— 5,000-7,000. Recently published *San Francisco,* by Patricia Haddock (ages 8-12, social studies - American city); *The Llama,* by Gail LaBonte (ages 8-12, natural history-wildlife); *Señor Alcalde: Henry Cisneros,* by John Gillies (ages 11-18, biography).

How to Contact/Writers: Nonfiction: Query, plus writing sample (refers to *It Really Happened* series). SASE (IRC) for answer to query and/or return of ms. Reports on queries in 2-3 weeks; on mss in 6-8 weeks. Publishes a book 12-15 months after acceptance. Will consider simultaneous, photocopied, and computer printout submissions.

Illustration: Number of illustrations used for fiction: young readers—6-8 (refers to *It Really Happened* books). Number of illustrations used for nonfiction: young readers—20; middle readers—25. Editorial will review ms/illustration packages submitted by authors/ artists and ms/illustration packages submitted by authors with illustrations done by separate artists. Editorial Director, Uva Dillon, will review an illustrator's work for possible use in author's texts.

How to Contact/Illustrators: Ms/illustration packages: Query with sample chapters and art sample. Illustrations only: Slides and/or samples. Reports on art samples only if interested.

Terms/Writers & Illustrators: Pays authors in royalties of 5-10%. Outright purchase "negotiated." Average advance: "negotiated." Additional payment for ms/illustration packages: "negotiated." Factors to determine final payment: number of illustrations or photos—quality. Pay for separate authors and illustrators: "negotiated." Illustrators paid by the project via negotiation. Sends galleys to authors. Book catalog for 9x12 SAE; manuscript guidelines for 4x9 SAE.

Tips: Writers: "Research competitive books and ideas and submit a complete well-organized proposal with sample chapters or complete manuscript." Illustrators: "Provide evidence of artistic ability and knowledge of book publishing." Looks for a book: "that matches our current publishing plans for existing or new series of educational books (nonfiction) for young readers K-12, with an emphasis on 2nd grade through 7th grade."

DOUBLE M PRESS, 16455 Tuba St., Sepulveda CA 91343. (818)360-3166. Book publisher. Publisher: Charlotte Markman Stein. Publishes young reader titles, middle reader titles, and young adult titles. 50% of books by first-time authors.

Fiction: Middle readers: contemporary, fantasy, historical. Young readers: contemporary. Young adults: contemporary, problem novels. Average word length: young adults—40,000-60,000. "We are trade publishers, who, starting in 1989, are concentrating on children's books, all ages."

Nonfiction: Young readers: biography, education, history, mythology. Middle readers: biography, education, history, mythology. Young adults: biography, education, history, mythology. Recently published *10 Minutes With ME*, by Joanne Cohn-Gilletly (preschool, 20 projects); *Spectrum of Visual Arts for Young Children*, by Blond & Janusz (preschool, crafts); *Child Celebrates the Jewish Holidays*, by Anne Geffner (middle readers, cultural).

How to Contact/Writers: Fiction/nonfiction: Query. SASE (IRC) for answer to query and/or return of mss. Reports on queries in 2 weeks; on mss in 4-6 weeks. Publishes a book 12 months after acceptance. Will consider photocopied submissions.

Illustration: Number of illustrations used for fiction/nonfiction: middle readers—3-4; young adults—3-4. Editorial will review ms/illustration packages submitted by authors/artists and ms/illustration packages submitted by authors with illustrations done by separate artists "query first." Michele P. Bodenheimer, will review an illustrator's work for possible use in author's texts.

How to Contact/Illustrators: Ms/illustration packages: Query first. Illustrations only: Tear sheets, slides. Reports on art samples in 4 weeks.

Terms/Writers & Illustrators: Pays authors in royalties based on retail price. Buys ms outright "based on work." Additional payment for ms/illustration packages. Factors used to determine final payment include color art, number of illustrations. Pay for separate authors and illustrators: "royalties to each." Pay for illustrators: by the project; "we also pay royalties, depends on work." Sends galleys to authors; dummies to illustrators. Manuscript/artist's guidelines available for SAE.

Tips: In writers looks for: "Stories that pertain and are relevant to children's and young adult's lives. They must be well written. Imaginative handling of contemporary problems and a constructive outlook." Looks for: "Illustrations that appeal to the imaginative, or fantasy in children. Good technique."

DOUBLEDAY, div. of Bantam Doubleday Dell, 666 Fifth Ave., New York NY 10103. (212)492-9772. Book publisher. Publisher: Wendy Barish. Publishes 10-20 picture books/year; 20 young reader titles/year; 20 middle reader titles/year. 10% of books by first-time authors; 30% of books from agented writers.

How to Contact/Writers: Fiction/nonfiction: Query. SASE (IRC) for answer to query. Reports on queries in 3 weeks; on mss in 6-8 weeks. Publishes a book 24 months after acceptance. Will consider simultaneous, photocopied, and computer printout submissions.

Illustration: Editorial will review ms/illustration packages submitted by authors/artists; ms/illustration packages submitted by authors with illustrations done by separate artists and an illustrator's work for possible use in author's texts.

How to Contact/Illustrators: Ms/illustration packages: Query. Illustrations only: "Previous books, slides, tear sheets." Reports on art samples only if interested. Original art work returned at job's completion.

Terms/Writers & Illustrators: Pays authors in royalties based on retail price. Buys ms outright. Additional payment for ms/illustration packages. Separate writers and illustrators paid separately. Illustrators paid by the project. Sends galleys to authors; dummies to illustrators. Book catalog, manuscript guidelines free on request.

Tips: Writers: "Learn the marketplace and fill a need." Illustrators: "Do a sample dummy and sample art for an available well-known, text to show ability."

DUTTON CHILDREN'S BOOKS, NAL-Penguin, 2 Park Ave., New York NY 10016. (212)725-1818. Book publisher. Editor-in-Chief: Lucia Monfried. Publishes approximately 40 picture books/year; 4 young reader titles/year; 10 middle reader titles/year; 8 young adult titles/year. 15% of books by first-time authors.

Fiction: Picture books: animal, fantasy, spy/mystery/adventure. Young readers: easy-to-read, fantasy, science fiction. Middle readers: animal, contemporary, fantasy, history, science fiction, spy/mystery/adventure. Young adults: animal, contemporary, fantasy, history, romance, science fiction, spy/mystery/adventure. Recently published *Digby and Kate*, by Barbara Baker (young readers, easy-to-read); *The Jedera Adventure*, by Lloyd Alexander (middle readers/young adults, fantasy); *Almost Fifteen*, by Marilyn Sachs (young adults, contemporary).

Nonfiction: Picture books: animal, nature/environment. Young readers: nature/environment. Middle readers and young adults: animal, nature/environment. Recently published *Animal Faces*, by Pierre Marie Valat (all levels, punch-out novelty); *Sir Dana, A Knight*, by Dana Fradon (picture book, historical); *Blimps*, by Roxie Munro (picture book, science/aviation).

How to Contact/Writers: Fiction/nonfiction: query. SASE (IRC) for answer to query and/or return of ms. Reports on queries in 2 months; on mss in 2-3 months. Publishes a book 12-18 months after acceptance. Will consider simultaneous, photocopied, computer printout and electronic submissions via disk or modem.

Illustration: Number of illustrations used for fiction: picture books—14-28; easy readers—30; middle readers—15. Editorial will review ms/illustration packages submitted by authors/artists and ms/illustration packages submitted by authors with illustrations done by separate artists. Design department will review illustrator's work for possible use in author's texts.

How to Contact/Illustrators: Ms/illustration packages: Query first. Illustrations only: Resume, tear sheets, slides—no original art please. Reports on art samples in 2 months. Original artwork returned at job's completion.

Terms/Writers & Illustrators: Pays authors in royalties based on retail price. Book catalog, manuscript guidelines for SAE.

Tips: Writers: "We publish high-quality trade books and are interested in well-written manuscripts with fresh ideas and child appeal. We recommend spending time in bookstores and libraries to get an idea of the books on the market. Find out what topics have been treated again and again and should thus be avoided. Dutton has a complete publishing program—we are looking for good writing and strong quality in all categories of fiction. We would be interested in nonfiction including preschool and middle grade nonfiction, including U.S. history, general biography (ages 7-10), science, and photo essays." Illustrators: "Spend time in bookstores and libraries to familiarize yourself with the market. Be aware of which style of illustration would be of interest to which publishing house—is your work best suited for mass market or trade? We're interested in seeing samples or portfolios from potential illustrators of picture books (full color), young novels (black and white), and jacket artists."

EAKIN PUBLICATIONS, INC., Eakin Press, Box 23069, Austin TX 78735. (512)288-1771. Book publisher. President: Ed Eakin. Publishes 2 picture books/year; 3 young reader titles/year; 10 middle reader titles/year; 2 young adult titles/year. 50% of books by first-time authors; 5% of books from agented writers.

Fiction: Picture books: animal. Middle readers: history, sports. Young adults: history, sports. Average word length: picture books—3,000; young readers—10,000; middle readers—15,000-20,000; young adults—20,000-30,000.

Nonfiction: Picture books: animal. Middle readers: history, sports. Young adults: history, sports.

How to Contact/Writers: Fiction/nonfiction: Query. SASE (IRC) for answer to query. Reports on queries in 2 weeks; on mss in 6 weeks. Publishes a book 1 year after acceptance. Will consider simultaneous, photocopied, computer printout and electronic submissions via disk or modem.

Illustration: Number of illustrations used for fiction/nonfiction: picture books—40; young readers—40; middle readers—5; young adults—5. Editorial will review ms/illustration packages submitted by authors/artists; ms/illustration packages submitted by authors with illustrations done by separate artists and an illustrator's work for possible use in author's texts.

How to Contact/Illustrators: Ms/illustration packages: Query. Illustrations only: Tear sheets. Reports on art samples in 2 weeks.

Terms/Writers & Illustrators: Pays authors in royalties of 10-15% based on wholesale price. Buys ms outright for $50-$150. Offers average advance payment of $500. Pay for separate authors and illustrators: "Usually share royalty." Pay for illustrators: Royalty 10-15% based on wholesale price. Sends galleys to authors. Book catalog, manuscript/artist's guidelines for SAE.

Tips: Writers: "Always include SASE—be sure all elements of manuscript are included—include vitae of author or illustrator." Illustrators: "Team up with good writer." Looks for: "books relating to Texas and the Southwest or ethnic groups."

ENSLOW PUBLISHERS INC., Bloy St. & Ramsey Ave., Box 777, Hillside NJ 07205. (201)964-4116. Vice President: Mark Enslow. Publishes 15 middle reader titles/year; 15 young adult titles/year. 30% of books by first-time authors; 10% of books from agented writers.

Nonfiction: Middle readers: biography, history, sports. Young adults: biography, history, sports. Average word length: middle readers—14,000; young adults—14,000. Recently published *Human Rights*, by S.Totten (young adults, nonfiction); *Archbishop Tutu*, by J. Haskins (young adults, biography); *Birds—Right Before Your Eyes*, by J. Wiessinger (middle readers, nature).

How to Contact/Writers: Nonfiction: Query. SASE (IRC) for answer to query. Reports on queries/mss in 2 weeks. Publishes a book 12 months after acceptance. Will consider simultaneous and photocopied submissions.

Illustration: Number of illustrations used for nonfiction: middle readers—28; young adults—28.

Terms/Writers & Illustrators: Pays authors in royalties of 6-10% based on retail price. Sends galleys to authors. Book catalog/manuscript guidelines available for SAE.

Tips: "Know about competing books already published."

EXPOSITION PHOENIX PRESS, 1620 South Federal Highway, Pompano FL 33062. (305)943-7165. Editorial Contact: Allan Taber. Publishes 12-20 picture books/year; 12-20 young reader titles/year; 50 middle reader titles/year; 50 young adult titles/year. 90% of books by first-time authors; 1% of books from agented writers. Subsidy publishes 99%.

Fiction: Picture books: animal. Young readers: easy-to-read, fantasy, sports. Middle readers: contemporary, history, romance, science fiction, sports. Average length: "64 page minimum."

How to Contact/Writers: Fiction/nonfiction: Submit through agent only. SASE (IRC) for answer to query. Publishes a book 7 months after acceptance. Will consider simultaneous, photocopied, and computer printout submissions.

Illustration: Editorial will review ms/illustration packages submitted by authors/artists; ms/illustration packages submitted by authors with illustrations done by separate artists; and an illustrator's work for possible use in author's texts.

How to Contact/Illustrators: Original artwork returned at job's completion.

Terms/Writers & Illustrators: Pays authors in royalties of 40% based on wholesale price. Illustrators "usually" paid by the project. Sends galleys to authors. Book catalog, manuscript/artist's guidelines free on request.

Tips: "The 'PPP' plan—Publish, Present & Push plus the PAG plan—Personal Attention Guaranteed!" Looks for "children's and how-to books."

FACTS ON FILE, 460 Park Ave. S., New York NY 10016. (212)683-2244. Book publisher. Editorial Contact: James Warren. Editorial Assistant: Barbara Levine. Publishes 8-10 middle reader titles/year; 18-20 young adult titles/year. 5% of books by first-time authors; 45% of books from agented writers. Subsidy publishes 35%.

Nonfiction: Middle readers: animal, biography, education, history, music/dance, nature/environment, religion, sports. Young adults: animal, biography, education, history, music/dance, nature/environment, religion, sports. Recently published *Amelia Earhart*, by Carol Pearce (ages 10 and up, biography); *World of Music: Rock & Roll*, by Richard Carlin (ages 10-14, historical survey); *Jewish-American Heritage*, by David Brownstone (ages 9-13, history).

How to Contact/Writers: Nonfiction: Submit outline/synopsis and sample chapters. Reports on queries in 4 weeks. Publishes a book 10 months after acceptance. Will consider simultaneous, photocopied, and computer printout submissions. Sends galleys to authors. Book catalog free on request.

Tips: "Nothing too cutesy. Prepare a very thorough, carefully written proposal. We do a lot of series books."

FARRAR, STRAUS & GIROUX, 19 Union Square West, New York NY 10003. (212)741-6934. Book publisher. Editor-in-Chief: Margaret Ferguson. Publishes 18 picture books/year; 10 young reader titles/year; 4 middle reader titles/year; 2 young adult titles/year. 5% of books by first-time authors; 5% of books from agented writers.

Fiction: "Original and well-written material for all ages." Recently published *Dear Mili*, pictures by Maurice Sendak (all ages, fantasy); *Tales for a Winter's Eve*, by Wendy Watson (ages 3 and up); Don't Call Me Little Bunny, by Gregoire Solotareff (ages 3 and up); *Sweet Creek Holler*, by Ruth White (ages 10 and up).

How to Contact/Writers: Fiction/nonfiction: Query; submit outline/synopsis and sample chapters. SASE (IRC) for answer to query and/or return of mss. Reports on queries in 6 weeks; on mss in 12 weeks. Publishes a book 18 months after acceptance. Will consider simultaneous, photocopied, and computer printout submissions.

Illustration: Number of illustrations used for fiction: picture books—32; middle readers—10. Number of illustrations used for nonfiction: middle readers—15. Will review ms/illustration packages submitted by authors/artists and an illustrator's work for possible use in author's texts.

How to Contact/Illustrators: Ms/illustration packages: Ms with 1 piece of final art, remainder roughs. Illustrations only: Tear sheets. Reports on art samples only if interested. Original artwork returned at job's completion.

Terms/Writers & Illustrators: "We offer an advance against royalties for both authors and illustrators." Sends galleys to authors; dummies to illustrators. Book catalog available for SAE and 56¢ postage; manuscript guidelines for 1 first-class stamp.

Tips: "Study our catalog before submitting. We will see illustrator's portfolios by appointment."

FAWCETT JUNIPER, imprint of Ballantine/DelRey/Fawcett Books, 201 E. 50 St., New York NY 10022. (212)751-2600. Book publisher. Editor-in-Chief; Vice President: Leona Nevler. Publishes 36 young adult titles/year.

Fiction: Middle readers: contemporary, romance, science fiction (boys). Young adults: contemporary, romance, science fiction. Publishes five lines: First Kiss—middle reader, Sugar and Spice—middle reader, Roommates—young adults, Endless Summer—young adults, Planet Builders—young adults.

How to Contact/Writers: Fiction: Query. SASE (IRC) for answer to query and/or return of ms.

Terms/Writers & Illustrators: Pays authors in royalties.

FLEET PRESS CORPORATION, Ste. 719, 160 Fifth Ave., New York NY 10010. (212)243-6100. Book publisher. Editor: P. Scott. Publishes "various" number of middle reader and young adult titles/year. 50% of books by first-time authors.

Nonfiction: Young adults: biography, history, nature/environment. Average word length: young adults—20,000.

How to Contact/Writers: Nonfiction: Query. All unsolicited mss returned unopened. SASE (IRC) for answer to query. Reports on queries in 2-4 weeks. Publishes a book 12 months after acceptance. Will consider simultaneous and photocopied submissions.

Illustration: Number of illustrations used for nonfiction: young adults—10-15. Editorial will review ms/illustration packages submitted by authors/artists and ms/illustration packages submitted by authors with illustrations done by separate artists.

Terms/Writers & Illustrators: Pays authors in royalties of 10% (% varies) based on wholesale or retail prices. Average advance payments "varies." Pay for separate authors and illustrators: "Artist must make arrangements directly with author." Sends galleys to authors.

Tips: "Work with agent."

FOUR WINDS PRESS, imprint of Macmillan Publishing Co., 866 Third Ave., New York NY 10022. (212)702-2180. Book publisher. Editor-in-Chief: Cindy Kane. Publishes 10-12 picture books/year; 3-5 middle reader titles/year; 2-5 young adult titles/year. 15-20% of books by first-time authors; 80% of books from agented writers.

Fiction: Picture books: animal. Young readers: animal, contemporary, easy-to-read. Middle readers: animal, history, sports, spy/mystery/adventure. Young adults: contemporary, fantasy, history, problem novels, science fiction, sports, spy/mystery/adventure. Average word length: picture books—750-1,500; young readers—5,000-6,000; middle readers—10,000-30,000; young adults—37,500-50,000. Recently published *Step Into The Night*, by Joanne Ryder (ages 5-8, grades K-3, picture book/nature); *How's Business*, by Alison Prince (ages 9-12, grades 4-7, historical novel); *Return to Morocco*, by Norma Johnston (ages 12 & up, grades 7 & up, suspense novel).

Nonfiction: Picture books: animal, nature/environment. Young readers: animal, nature/environment. Middle readers: animal, biography, history, hobbies, music/dance, nature/environment, sports. Young adults: biography, history, music/dance, religion, sports. Average word length: picture books—750-1,500; young readers—5,000-6,000; middle readers—10,000-30,000; young adults—37,500-50,000. Recently published *Dinosaurs, Dragonflies & Diamonds*, by Gail Gibbons (ages 5-8, grades K-3, picture book); *The One-Room School at Squabble Hollow*, by Rosmarie Hauserr (ages 8-11, photo essay); *Drugged Athletes*, by Jonathan Harris (ages 10-14, nonfiction).

How to Contact/Writers: Fiction: Submit outline/synopsis and sample chapters (middle readers, young adults); submit complete ms (picture books). Nonfiction: Query. SASE (IRC) for answer to query and/or return of ms. Reports on queries/mss in 6-8 weeks. Publishes a book 18-24 months after acceptance. Will consider simultaneous, photocopied and computer printout submissions.

Illustration: Number of illustrations used for fiction and nonfiction: picture books—24-40 full page illustrations; young readers—15-20 mostly full page illustrations; middle readers—10-20 ¼, ½ and full page illustrations. Editorial will review ms/illustration packages submitted by authors/artists and ms/illustrations packages submitted by authors with illustrations done by separate artists. Art Director, Cecilia Yung, will review illustrator's work for possible use in author's texts.

How to Contact/Illustrators: Picture books: submit full ms with art samples (not originals!). Illustrations only: "Illustration portfolios are reviewed every Thursday on a drop-off basis. If you cannot drop off your portfolio, you should mail tear sheets. Your portfolio should contain samples of work that best reflect your technical and creative ability to illustrate a text for children. These samples should include two or three different scenes of animals and/or children rendered in a setting. These should show your ability to handle composition, create interesting characters, and maintain consistency between scenes. Use whatever medium is best suited to your technique. Generally, still life, three dimensional artwork and abstract compositions do not translate well to children's book illustrations." Reports on ms/art samples in 4-6 weeks; art samples only if interested. Original artwork returned at job's completion.

Terms/Writers & Illustrators: Pays authors in royalties of 5-10% based on retail price (depends on whether artist is sharing royalties). Factors used to determine payment for ms/illustration package include "complexity of artwork, number of pieces, color vs. black-and-white." Pay for separate authors and illustrators: "Each has separate contract and is paid by royalty or flat fee." Pay for illustrators: by the project; royalties range from 2-5%; "fees and royalties vary widely according to budget for book." Sends galleys to authors; dummies to illustrators. Book catalog available for 7½×10½ SAE; manuscript and/or artist's guidelines for 1 first-class stamp and a business-size envelope.

Tips: The length of your story depends on the age of the child for whom it is intended. There are no fixed lengths. A good story is almost always the right length or can easily be made so. (See also Aladdin Books/Collier Books for Young Adults, Atheneum Publishers, Bradbury Press, Margaret K. McElderry Books.)

FREE SPIRIT PUBLISHING, Ste. 716, 123 N. 3rd St., Minneapolis MN 55401. (612)338-2068. Book publisher. Publisher/President: Judy Galbraith. Publishes 1-2 middle reader titles/year; 1-2 young adult titles/year. 80% of books by first-time authors.

Nonfiction: Young readers: education, psychology/self-help, reference. Middle readers: education, psychology/self-help, reference. Young adults: education, psychology/self-help, reference. Recently published *Directory of American Youth Organizations*, by Judith Erickson (grades 3-12, reference); *Perfectionism: What's Bad About Being Too Good*, by Miriam Adderholdt-Elliott (young adults, psychology/self-help).

How to Contact/Writers: Nonfiction: Submit outline/synopsis and sample chapters. SASE (IRC) for return of mss. Reports on queries in 3 months. Publishes a book 12-18 months after acceptance. Will consider photocopied and computer printout submissions.

Illustration: Number of illustrations for nonfiction: young readers—15; middle readers—15; young adults—10. Editorial will review ms/illustration packages submitted by authors/artists; ms/illustration packages submitted by authors with illustrations done by separate artists; illustrator's work for possible use in author's title.

How to Contact/Illustrators: Submit 3 chapters of ms with 1 piece of final art. Prefers to see: "B&w cartoon illustrations, graphic treatments." Illustrations only: resume, tear sheets. Reports on art samples only if interested. Original artwork returned at job's completion if requested.

Terms/Writers & Illustrators: Pays authors in royalties of 8-12% based on wholesale price. Offers advance payment of $500-$1,000. Factors used to determine final payment for ms/illustration is color art vs. black-and-white and number of illustrations used. Pay for illustrations: by the project, $50-$500. Sends galleys to authors; dummies to illustrators. Book catalog free on request.

Tips: Writers: "Research publisher interests *before* sending anything." Illustrations: "Hustle your work as much as possible. I've hired illustrators 'off the street.' " Looks for: "A truly helpful, informative, pro-kid, and good-humored book."

GALLAUDET UNIVERSITY PRESS (See Kendall Green Publications.)

THE GIRLS CLUB OF SANTA BARBARA (See Advocacy Press.)

DAVID R. GODINE, PUBLISHER, 300 Massachusetts, Boston MA 02115. (617)536-0761. Book publisher. Editor: Audrey Bryant. Publishes 3-4 picture books/year; 2 young reader titles/year; 3-4 middle reader titles/year. 10% of books by first-time authors; 20% of books from agented writers.

Fiction: Picture books: animal. Young readers: animal, easy-to-read, fantasy, spy/mystery/adventure, folk or fairy tales. Middle readers: animal, fantasy, folk or fairy tales. Recently published *The Cuckoo Clock*, by M. Stolz (ages 10-12, middle readers); *Too*

Many Eggs, by M. Butler (ages 4-8, picture book); *A Natural Man*, by S. Sanfield (ages 8-11, early readers).

How to Contact/Writers: Fiction: Submit complete ms. Reports on queries in 2 weeks; on mss in 3 weeks. Publishes a book 18 months after acceptance. Will consider simultaneous, photocopied, and computer printout submissions.

Illustration: Number of illustrations used for fiction: picture books—16; young readers—12; middle readers—10. Editorial will review ms/illustration packages submitted by authors/artists; ms/illustration packages submitted by authors with illustrations done by separate artists and illustrator's work for possible use in author's texts.

How to Contact/Illustrators: Ms/illustration packages: "roughs and 1 finished art plus either sample chapters for very long works or whole ms for short works." Illustrations only: "slides, with one full-size blow-up of art." Reports on art samples in 3 weeks. Original artwork returned at job's completion.

Terms/Writers & Illustrators: Pays authors in royalties based on retail price. Factor used to determine final payment: number of illustrations. Pay for separate authors and illustrators: "differs with each collaboration." Illustrators paid by the project. Sends galleys to authors; dummies to illustrators. Book catalog/manuscript guidelines free on request.

KENDALL GREEN PUBLICATIONS, imprint of Gallaudet University Press, 800 Florida Ave. NE, Washington DC 20002. (202)651-5488. Book publisher. Managing Editor: Ivey B. Pittle. Publishes 2-3 picture books/year; 2-3 young reader titles/year; 1-2 middle reader titles/year; 1-2 young adult titles/year. 75% of books by first-time authors.

Fiction: Picture books, young readers: contemporary. Middle readers, young adults: contemporary, problem novels, spy/mystery/adventure. Average word length: picture books—50; young readers—1,300; middle readers—26,000; young adults—52,000. Recently published *The Flying Fingers Club*, by Jean Andrews (middle readers, mystery); *A Season of Change*, by Lois Hodge (young adults, problem); *Things Change*, forthcoming, by Ada Litchfield (middle readers, contemporary).

Nonfiction: Picture books; young readers: sign language. Middle readers; young adults: biography, history, sign language. Average word length: picture books—50; young readers—1,300; middle readers—26,000; young adults—52,000. Recently published *Chris Gets Ear Tubes*, by Betty Pace (young readers, practical); *My Signing Book of Numbers*, by Patricia Bellan Gillen (picture book, sign language); *Buffy's Orange Leash*, by Stephen Golder and Lise Memling (young readers, informational).

How to Contact/Writers: Fiction/nonfiction: submit outline/synopsis and sample chapters; submit complete ms. Reports on queries/mss in 4-8 weeks. Publishes a book 10-12 months after acceptance. Will consider simultaneous, photocopied, and computer printout submissions.

Illustration: Number of illustrations used for fiction: young readers—32; middle readers—1-5; young adults—1-5. Number of illustrations used for nonfiction: picture books—30-40; young readers—32; middle readers—20; young adults—5. Editorial will review ms/illustration packages submitted by authors/artists; ms/illustration packages submitted by authors with illustrations done by separate artists; and illustrator's work for possible use in author's texts.

How to Contact/Illustrators: Ms/illustration packages: Full ms with 2 finished pieces, remainder roughs. Illustrations only: Tear sheets, finished art, resume. Reports on art samples in 4 weeks. Original artwork returned at job's completion.

Terms/Writers & Illustrators: Pays authors in royalties of 10-15% based on net price. Factors used to determine final payment: number of illustrations, color vs. black and white. Pay for separate authors and illustrators: Split royalty. Pay for illustrators: by the project; royalties of 5% based on net price. Sends galleys to authors; sometimes dummies to illustrators. Book catalog, manuscript guidelines free on request.

Tips: "All books published by Kendall Green Publications have to be related to hearing loss. This includes sign language books, books explaining hearing loss, and fiction with hearing-impaired character(s)."

GOOD NEWS PUBLISHERS (See Crossway Books.)

GREENHAVEN PRESS, 10907 Technology Place, San Diego CA 92127. (619)485-7424. Book publisher. Senior Editor: Terry O'Neill, Greenhaven Press, 573 Shoreview Park Rd., St. Paul MN 55126. Publishes 8 young adult titles/year. 25% of books by first-time authors.
Nonfiction: Middle readers: biography, history. Young adults: animal, biography, history, nature/environment. Other titles "to fit our specific series." Average word length: young adults – 15,000-18,000. Recently published *Great Mysteries: Opposing Viewpoints Pearl Harbor*; *Great Mysteries: Opposing Viewpoints The Bermuda Triangle*; *Great Mysteries: Opposing Viewpoints Animal Communication* (young adults). Explore multiple views of the topic.
How to Contact/Writers: Nonfiction: Query; submit outline/synopsis and sample chapters. SASE (IRC) for answer to query and/or return of mss. Reports on queries (with SASE) generally in 1-2 weeks. Publishes a book 12-15 months after acceptance.
Illustration: Number of illustrations used for nonfiction: young adults – 50-75. Senior Editor, Terry O'Neill, will accept query letters with a couple of examples of illustrations to keep on file – no portfolios. Preference: photos; line art.
How to Contact/Illustrators: Ms/illustration packages: Query first. Illustrations only: Resume, tear sheets, 1 or 2 samples we can keep. Reports on art samples only if interested. Original artwork returned at job's completion, "varies."
Terms/Writers & Illustrators: Buys ms outright for $1,500-$2,500. Offers average advance payment of ⅓-½. Factors used to determine final payment include number of illustrations used. Sends galleys to authors. Books catalog available for 9 × 12 SAE and 65¢ postage.
Tips: "Always send SASE; find out about publishers before submitting – don't waste their time and your time by submitting inappropriate material; submit material in proofread, clean, legible copies."

GREENWILLOW BOOKS, imprint and div. of William Morrow and Co., 105 Madison Ave., New York NY 10016. (212)889-3050. Book publisher. Editor-in-Chief: Susan Hirschman. Publishes 40 picture books/year; 5 young reader titles/year; 5 middle reader titles/year; 10 young adult titles/year. 10% of books by first-time authors; 15% of books from agented writers.
Fiction: Picture books: animal, history. Young readers: animal, easy-to-read, history. Middle readers: animal, history. Young adults: animal, contemporary, fantasy, history, problem novels, science fiction, sports, spy/mystery/adventure. Recently published *Running Loose*, by Chris Crutcher (young adults, novel); *Four Brave Sailors*, by Mirra Ginsburg (ages 3-6, picture book); *Dinosaurs are 568*, by Jean Rogers (mid-level, reader).
Nonfiction: Picture books: animal, history. Young readers: animal, history. Middle readers: animal, history. Young adults: animal, biography, history. Recently published *Bugs*, by Nancy W. Parker (ages 5-8); *Alcohol: What it is, What it does*, by J. Seixas (ages 5-8).
How to Contact/Writers: Fiction/nonfiction: Submit complete ms. SASE (IRC) for return of ms. Reports on mss in 1 month. Publishes a book 1 year after acceptance. Will consider simultaneous, photocopied, and computer printout submissions.
Illustration: Number of illustrations used for fiction/nonfiction: picture books – 20; young readers – 10; middle readers – 10. Editorial will review ms/illustration packages submitted by authors/artists and ms/illustration packages submitted by authors with illustrations done by separate artists.
How to Contact/Illustrators: Ms/illustration packages: "full ms with 1 piece finished

art and very rough dummy." Reports on art samples only if interested. Original artwork returned at job's completion.

Terms/Writers & Illustrators: Pays authors in royalties. Pay for separate authors and illustrators: "royalty basis." Pay for illustrators: "depends on book—some receive flat fee, others on royalty basis." Sends galleys to authors; dummies to illustrators. Book catalog available for 9½ × 12 SAE and 2 first-class stamps; manuscript/artist's guidelines for letter-size SAE and 1 first-class stamp. (See also Lothrop, Lee & Shepard Books.)

GULLIVER BOOKS (See Harcourt Brace Jovanovich.)

HARBINGER HOUSE, INC., Ste. 106, 3131 N. Country Club, Tucson AZ 85716. (602)326-9595. Publisher: Laurel Gregory. Editor-in-Chief: Linnea Gentry. Publishes 3 picture books/year; 3 young reader titles/year; 2-3 middle reader titles/year; 2 young adult titles/year. 40% of books by first-time authors; 10% of books from agented writers.
Fiction: Picture books: "all kinds." Young readers: adventure, fantasy, history. Middle readers: animal, fantasy, problem novels, science fiction, sports, spy/mystery/adventure. Young adults: fantasy, history, problem novels, science fiction, sports, spy/mystery/adventure. Recently published *The Marsh King's Daughter,* by Andersen/Gentry (ages 11 and up, classic fantasy); *Jason in the Land of the Dragons,* by Kuninori (ages 6-9, adventure fantasy); *One Green Mesquite Tree,* by Jernigan (ages 3-5, counting rhyme).
Nonfiction: Picture books: "all kinds." Young Readers: animal, history, nature/environment, geography. Middle readers: animal, biography, history, music/dance, nature/environment, space science, geography. Young adults: biography, history, music/dance, nature, religion, space science, geography. Recently published *The Reef & the Wrasse,* by Steere & Ring (ages 8-11, natural history); (in progress) *Out in the Night,* by Liptak (ages 8-11, natural history); (in progress) *Planet Seekers,* by Corrick (ages 12 and up, space science).
How to Contact/Writers: Fiction/nonfiction: Submit outline/synopsis and sample chapters. SASE (IRC) for answer to query. Reports on queries in 3-4 weeks; on mss in 6-8 weeks. Publishes a book 12-18 months after acceptance. Will consider simultaneous, photocopied, and computer printout submissions.
Illustration: Average number of illustrations used for fiction: picture books—14; young readers—12; middle readers—12; young adults—11. Number of illustrations used for nonfiction: picture books—14; young readers— 20; middle readers—18; young adults— "varies greatly." Editorial will review ms/illustration packages submitted by authors/artists; ms/illustration packages submitted by authors with illustrations done by separate artists and illustrator's work for possible use in author's texts.
How to Contact/Illustrators: "For picture books and young readers only: Minimum of 3 pieces of finished art." Illustrations only: "Tear sheets and slides." Reports on art samples in 4 weeks. Original artwork returned at job's completion.
Terms/Writers & Illustrators: Pays authors in royalties based on retail price. Average advance payment "varies widely." Factors used to determine final payment for ms/illustration package include "color art vs. black-and-white, and number of illustrations for outright purchase of illustrations for young adult and middle titles." Pay for separate authors and illustrators: "royalties split between author and artist." Pay for illustrators: "royalties based on quantity of each edition." Sends galleys to authors; "sometimes" sends dummies to illustrators. Book catalog free on request.
Tips: Writers: "Study writing and the field of children's literature beforehand." Looks for "manuscripts with a particular, well-articulated message or purpose." Illustrators: "Study illustration and the field of children's literature beforehand." Looks for "art of imagination and skill that has something special." In children's book publishing there has been "a gradual improvement in the standards of quality in both the ideas and their presentation."

HARCOURT BRACE JOVANOVICH, Children's Books Division which includes: HBJ Children's Books, Gulliver Books, Voyager Paperbacks, Odyssey Paperbacks, Jane Yolen Books, 1250 Sixth Ave., San Diego CA 92101. (619)699-6810. Book publisher. Attention: Manuscript Submissions, Children's Books Division. Publishes 40-45 picture books/year; 15-20 middle reader titles/year; 8-12 young adult titles/year. 20% of books by first-time authors; 50% of books from agented writers.
Fiction: Picture books: animal, contemporary, fantasy, history. Young readers: animal, contemporary, fantasy, history. Middle readers: animal, contemporary, fantasy, history, problem novels, romance, science fiction, sports, spy/mystery/adventure. Young adults: animal, contemporary, fantasy, history, problem novels, romance, science fiction, sports, spy/mystery/adventure. Average word length: picture books—"varies greatly;" middle readers—20,000-50,000; young adults—35,000-65,000. Recently published *Elbert's Bad Word*, by Audrey and Don Wood (ages 4-8, picture book); *Zelda Strikes Again*, by Lynn Hall (ages 8-12, middle grades); *A Sudden Silence*, by Eve Bunting (ages 12-17, young adults).
Nonfiction: Picture books, young readers: animal, biography, history, hobbies, music/dance, nature/environment, religion, sports. Middle readers, young adults: animal, biography, education, history, hobbies, music/dance, nature/environment, religion, sports. Average word length: picture books—"varies greatly;" middle readers—20,000-50,000; young adults—35,000-65,000. Recently published *Small Energy Sources: Choices that Work*, by Augusta Goldin (ages 12 and up, young adults); *Planting a Rainbow*, by Lois Ehlert (ages 4-8, picture book/concept book).
How to Contact/Writers: Fiction/nonfiction: Query; submit outline/synopsis and sample chapters; submit complete ms for picture books only. "Only HBJ Children's Books accepts unsolicited manuscripts." SASE (IRC) for answer to query and/or return of mss. Reports on queries/mss in 6-8 weeks. Will consider photocopied and computer printout submissions.
Illustration: Number of illustrations used for fiction and nonfiction: picture books—25-30; middle readers—6-12; young adults—jacket. Editorial will review ms/illustration packages submitted by authors/artists and ms/illustration packages submitted by authors with illustrations done by separate artists. Art Director, Children's Books, Joy Chu, will review an illustrator's work for possible use in author's texts.
How to Contact/Illustrators: Ms/illustration packages: picture books ms—complete ms acceptable. Longer books—outline and 2-4 sample chapters. Send several samples of art; no original art. Illustrations only: Resume, tear sheets, color xeroxes, color stats all accepted. Please DO NOT send original artwork or transparencies. Include SASE for return, please. Reports on art samples in 6-10 weeks. Original artwork returned at job's completion.
Terms/Writers & Illustrators: Pays authors in royalties based on retail price. Pay for separate writers and illustrators: "separately, usually on advance/royalty basis. Situations vary according to individual projects." Pay for illustrators: by the project. Sends galleys to authors; dummies to illustrators. Book catalog available for 8½×11 SASE; manuscript/artist's guidelines for business-size SASE.
Tips: "Study the field of children's books—go to your local library and book stores. Become acquainted with HBJ's books in particular if you are interested in submitting proposals to us. Our current needs include young adult fiction, nonfiction for all ages, and picture books for the very young."

HARVEST HOUSE PUBLISHERS, 1075 Arrowsmith, Eugene OR 97402. (503)343-0123. Book publisher. Manuscript Coordinator: LaRae Weikert. Publishes 5-6 picture books/year; 3 young reader titles/year; 3 young adult titles/year. 25% of books by first-time authors.
Fiction: Christian theme. Picture books: animal, easy-to-read. Young readers: contemporary, easy-to-read. Middle readers: contemporary, fantasy. Young adults: fantasy,

problem novels, romance. Recently published *The Rumpoles and the Barleys*, by Karen Mezek (ages 2-8, picture book); *Grumbleweeds*, by Gil Beers (ages 3-6, picture book); *Bedtime Hugs*, by Debby Boone (ages 2-6, picture book).

Nonfiction: Religion: picture books, young readers, middle readers, young adults.

How to Contact/Writers: Fiction/nonfiction: Query; submit outline/synopsis and sample chapters; submit complete ms. SASE (IRC) for return of mss. Publishes a book 12 months after acceptance. Will consider simultaneous, photocopied, and computer printout submissions.

Illustration: Number of illustrations used for fiction: picture books — 32. Editorial will review ms/illustration packages submitted by authors/artists; ms/illustration packages submitted by authors with illustrations done by separate artists and illustrator's work for possible use in author's texts.

How to Contact/Illustrators: Ms/illustration packages: "3 chapters of ms with 1 piece of final art and any approximate rough sketches." Illustrations only: "resume, tear sheets." Reports on art samples in 2 months. Original artwork returned at job's completion.

Terms/Writers & Illustrators: Pays authors in royalties of 10-15%. Average advance payment: "negotiable." Additional payment for ms/illustration packages. Factors used to determine final payment for ms/illustration package include "color art vs. black-and-white, number of illustrations used, experience of the illustrator, time-frame for completion of work." Pay for separate authors and illustrators: "Shared royalty with illustrator oftentimes receiving an advance." Pay for illustrators: "Sometimes paid by project." Sends galleys to authors; sometimes dummies to illustrators. Book catalog, manuscript/artist's guidelines free on request.

HBJ CHILDREN'S BOOKS (See Harcourt Brace Jovanovich.)

THE HEARST CORPORATION (See Avon Books/Books for Young Readers.)

HENRY HOLT & CO., INC., 115 W. 18th St., New York NY 10011. (212)886-9200. Book publisher. Editor-in-Chief: Brenda Bowen. Publishes 15-20 picture books/year; 40-60 young reader titles/year; 6 middle reader titles/year; 6 young adult titles/year. 5% of books by first-time authors; 40% of books from agented writers.

Fiction: Recently published *Here Are My Hands*, by Bill Martin, illustrated by Ted Rand (ages 4-7, picture book); *Moon Tiger*, by Phyllis Root/Ed Young (ages 4-7, picture book).

How to Contact/Writers: Fiction/nonfiction: Submit complete ms. SASE (IRC) necessary for answer to query and/or return of mss. Reports on queries/mss in 2 months. Publishes a book 12-18 months after acceptance. Will consider simultaneous, photocopied, and readable computer printout submissions.

Illustration: Editorial will review ms/illustration packages submitted by authors/artists; ms/illustration packages submitted by authors with illustrations done by separate artists; and illustrator's work for possible use in author's texts.

How to Contact/Illustrators: Ms/illustration packages: "Random samples OK." Illustrations only: Tear sheets, slides. Reports on art samples only if interested. Original art work returned at job's completion.

Terms/Writers & Illustrators: Pays authors in royalties based on retail price. Pay for illustrators: royalties based on retail price. Sends galleys to authors; dummies to illustrators.

HOMESTEAD PUBLISHING, Box 193, Moose WY 83012. Book publisher. Editor: Carl Schreier. Publishes 8 picture books/year; 2 young reader titles/year; 2 middle reader titles/year; 2 young adult titles/year. 30% of books by first-time authors; 1% of books from agented writers.

Fiction: Picture books: animal. Young readers: animal. Middle readers: animal. Average word length: young readers—1,000; middle readers—5,000; young adults—5,000. Recently published *The Great Plains: A Young Reader's Journal*, by Bullock (ages 1-8, nature); *Yellowstone's Geyser's Hot Springs and Fumaroles*, by Schreier (ages 1-adult, nature).

Nonfiction: Picture books: animal, biography, history, nature/environment. Young readers: animal, nature/environment. Middle readers: animal, biography, history, nature/environment. Young adults: animal, history, nature/environment. Average word length: young readers—1,000; middle readers—5,000; young adults—5,000. Recently published *Yellowstone: Selected Photographs 1870-1960*, by Simpson (ages 1-adult, history); *Looking at Flowers*, by O'Connor (ages 1-adult, nature).

How to Contact/Writers: Fiction/nonfiction: Query; submit outline/synopsis and sample chapters. SASE (IRC) for answer to query and/or return of ms. Reports on queries/mss in 4 weeks. Publishes a book 1 year after acceptance. Will consider simultaneous and photocopied submissions.

Illustration: Number of illustrations used for fiction: picture books—70; young readers—50; middle readers—50; young adults—50. Number of illustrations used for nonfiction: picture books—150; young readers—50; middle readers—50; young adults—50. Editorial will review ms/illustration packages submitted by authors/artists; ms/illustration packages submitted by authors with illustrations done by separate artists and illustrator's work for possible use in author's texts. Prefers to see "watercolor, opaque, oil" illustrations.

How to Contact/Illustrators: Ms/illustration packages: "Query first with sample writing and art style." Illustrations only: "Resumes, style samples." Reports on art samples in 4 weeks. Original artwork returned at job's completion.

Terms/Writers & Illustrators: Pays authors in royalties of 5-10% based on wholesale price. Outright purchase: "depends on project." Average advance payment: "depends on project." Factors used to determine final payment: "quality and price." Pay for separate authors and illustrators: "split." Pay for illustrators: $50-$10,000/project; 3-10% royalty based on wholesale price. Sends galleys to authors; dummies to illustrators.

Tips: Provide "good quality, top rate, original idea, thought out."

HOUGHTON MIFFLIN CO., Children's Trade Books, 2 Park St., Boston MA 02108. Book publisher. VP/Director: Walter Lorraine. Senior Editor: Matilda Welter; Editor: Mary Lee Donovan. Averages 45-50 titles/year. Publishes hardcover originals and trade paperback reprints (some simultaneous hard/soft).

How to Contact/Writers: Fiction: Submit complete ms. Nonfiction: Submit outline/synopsis and sample chapters. SASE (IRC) for answer to query and/or return of mss. Reports on queries in 1 month; on mss in 2 months. Will consider computer printout submissions (no dot matrix).

How to Contact/Illustrators: Review artwork/photos as part of ms package.

Terms/Writers & Illustrators: Pays standard royalty; offers advance. Book catalog free on request.

HUMANICS CHILDREN'S HOUSE, Humanics Limited, 1389 Peachtree St., Atlanta GA 30309. (404)874-1930. Book publisher. Acquisitions Editor: Robert Grayson Hall. Publishes 4 picture books/year; 4 young reader titles/year. 85% of books by first-time authors; 30% subsidy published.

Fiction: Picture books: contemporary, easy-to-read, fantasy, spy/mystery/adventure, self-image concentration. Average word length: picture books—250-350. Recently published *Home at Last*, by Mauro Magellan (ages 1-7, fantasy/fiction); *Max the Apt. Cat*, by Mauro Magellan (ages 1-7, self-image); *Creatures of an Exceptional Kind*, by Dorothy Whitney (ages 1-7).

Nonfiction: "Educational materials, Author-Ph.D, M.A. level, activities, project books." Average word length: picture books—500-600. Recently published *Folder Game*

Festival, by E. Commins (grades 1-6, teacher's aid); *Projects, Patterns and Poems*, by M. Rupert (grades 1-6, teacher's aid).

How to Contact/Writers: Fiction: Submit outline/synopsis and sample chapters; submit complete ms. Nonfiction: Query; submit outline/synopsis and sample chapters; submit complete ms. SASE (IRC) for answer to query and/or return of mss. Reports on queries/mss in 6 months. Publishes a book 12-18 months after acceptance. Will consider simultaneous, photocopied, computer printout and electronic submissions via disk or modem.

Illustration: Number of illustrations used for fiction: picture books—16. Number of illustrations used for nonfiction: picture books—25-80. Editorial will review ms/illustration packages submitted by authors/artists; ms/illustration packages submitted by authors with illustrations done by separate artists; and illustrator's work for possible use in author's texts.

How to Contact/Illustrators: Ms/illustration packages: Preferably complete ms with 3-4 illustrations. Illustrations only: Resume, tear sheets. Original artwork returned at job's completion "depending on contract."

Terms/Writers & Illustrators: Pays authors in royalties of 3-10% based on wholesale price. Outright purchase "dependent on ms, previous work." Factors used to determine final payment: "overall ms quality." Pay for separate authors and illustrators: "equally, or through prior agreement between the two." Sends galleys to authors; dummies to illustrators. Book catalog free on request; manuscript/artist's guidelines for regular SAE and 1 first-class stamp.

Tips: Writers: "Have some academic educational background. Ms should be creative, innovative, and have an approach geared toward self-image social, and intellectual development." Illustrators: "Take chances! I like abstract, thought provoking illustrations as well as simple line drawings. (Actually, we prefer the more fantastic, abstract illustrations)." Trends in children's book publishing includes "A general movement toward self-image, holism, creativity, and anti-ethnocentrism."

HUNTER HOUSE PUBLISHERS, Box 847, Claremont CA 91711. (714)624-2277. Book publisher. Independent book producer/packager. Editorial Manager: Jennifer D. Trzyna. Publishes 1 young adult title/year. 80% of books by first-time authors; 5% of books from agented writers; 50% subsidy published.

Nonfiction: Young adults: self-help. Recently published *Getting High in Natural Ways*, by Rocklin/Levinson (young adults, alternatives to drug use); *Raising Each Other*, by Brondino et al. (young adults, parent/teen relationships); *PMS: A Guide for Young Women* (young adults, health/menstruation).

How to Contact/Writers: Nonfiction: Query; submit outline/synopsis and sample chapters. SASE (IRC) for answer to query and/or return of ms. Reports on queries in 3-4 weeks; on mss in 8-16 weeks. Publishes a book 18 months after acceptance. Will consider simultaneous and photocopied submissions.

Illustration: Number of illustrations used for nonfiction: young adults—5-25.

Terms/Writers & Illustrators: Pays authors in royalties "depends on individual case." Sends galleys to authors. Book catalog available for 9 × 12 SAE and 65¢ postage; manuscript guidelines for standard SAE and 1 first-class stamp.

IDEALS PUBLISHING CORPORATION, Box 140300, Nashville TN 37214. (615)885-8270. Book publisher. Children's Book Editor: Peggy Schaefer. Publishes 50-60 picture books/year; 15-20 young reader titles/year. 5-10% of books by first-time authors; 5-10% of books from agented writers.

Fiction: Picture books: animal, contemporary, easy-to-read, fantasy, history, problem novels, science fiction, sports, spy/mystery/adventure. Young readers: animal, contemporary, easy-to-read, fantasy, history, problem novels, science fiction, sports, spy/mystery/adventure. Average word length: picture books—200-1,200; young readers—1,200-

2,400. Recently published *A Star in the Pasture*, by Zwers/Tobin Heyer (ages 4-7, 10×9 hardcover with dust jacket); *Chores*, by Cosgrove (ages 3-6, 10×9 hardcover with dust jacket); *Snarly Snuffin*, by Cosgrove (ages 3-8, 8½×11 softcover).

Nonfiction: Picture books: animal, biography, history, hobbies, music/dance, nature/environment, religion, sports. Young readers: animal, biography, history, hobbies, music/dance, nature/environment, religion, sports. Average word length: picture books—200-1,000; young readers—1,000-2,400. Recently published *Daniel Boone*, by Gleiter/Thompson (ages 5-8, 8×9 softcover); *Trucks*, by Stickland (ages 3-5, 6×6 hardcover); *The Deer*, by Royston (ages 5-8, 8×8 softcover).

How to Contact/Writers: Fiction/nonfiction: Submit complete ms. SASE (IRC) for answer to query and/or return of ms. Report on queries/mss in 6-8 weeks. Publishes a book 18-24 months after acceptance. Will consider photocopied and computer printout submissions.

Illustration: Number of illustrations used for fiction and nonfiction: picture books—12-18; young readers—12-18. Editorial will review ms/illustration packages submitted by authors/artists; ms/illustration packages submitted by authors with illustrations done by separate artists; and an illustrator's work for possible use in author's texts. Preference: No cartoon—tight or loose, but realistic watercolors, acrylics.

How to Contact/Illustrators: Ms/illustration packages: Ms with 1 piece final art and remainder roughs. Illustrations only: Resume and tear sheets showing variety of styles. Reports on art samples only if interested.

Terms/Writers & Illustrators: "All terms vary according to individual projects and authors/artists."

Tips: Writers: "Know the type of book the publisher you are approaching is interested in. Trend is placing more value on nonfiction and packaging." (i.e., We are not interested in young adult romances.) Illustrators: "Be flexible in contract terms—and be able to show as much final artwork as possible."

KAR-BEN COPIES, INC., 6800 Tildenwood Lane, Rockville MD 20852. (301)984-8733. Book publisher. Editor: Madeline Wikler. Publishes 10 picture books/year. 20% of books by first-time authors.

Fiction: Picture books: Jewish Holiday, Jewish storybook. Average word length: picture books—1,500. Recently published *Rachel & Mischa*, by Steve/Ilene Bayar (grades K-5, picture/photo essay); *Justin's Hebrew Name*, by Ellie Gellman (grades K-5, picture book).

Nonfiction: Picture books: religion-Jewish interest. Average word length: picture books—1,500. Recently published *All About Hanukkah*, by Groner/Wickler (grades K-5, picture book); *Kids Love Israel*, by Barbara Sofer (adult, family travel guide).

How to Contact/Writers: Fiction/nonfiction: Submit complete ms. SASE (IRC) for answer to query and/or return of mss. Reports on queries in 6 weeks. Publishes a book 6 months after acceptance. Will consider simultaneous, photocopied, and computer printout submissions.

Illustration: Number of illustrations used for fiction: picture books—15. Number of illustrations used for nonfiction: picture books—10. Editorial will review ms/illustration packages submitted by authors/artists; ms/illustration packages submitted by authors with illustrations done by separate artists; and illustrator's work for possible use in author's texts.

How to Contact/Illustrators: Ms illustration packages: Query first. Illustrations only: Tear sheets. Reports on art samples in 6 weeks. Original artwork returned at job's completion.

Terms/Writers & Illustrators: Pays authors in royalties of 4-8% based on net sales. Buys ms outright for $250-$2,500. Offers average advance payment of $1,000. Pay for separate authors and illustrators: "both get advance and royalty." Sends galleys to authors; dummies to illustrators. Book catalog/manuscript guidelines free on request.

"I wanted to portray the era when the story takes place as accurately and elegantly as possible," explains Rosalyn Schanzer, Fairfax Station, Virginia. "The Temple as it existed at that time period, the seven-branched menorah, the fruits, and the battle dress of Antiochus' army are examples of a few items researched for this book." This illustration, one of many used in All About Hanukkah *by Kar-Ben Copies, Inc., was drawn using luma-colored inks with sepia penline. Schanzer was paid an advance plus royalties for her book illustrations.*

© Rosalyn Schanzer 1988

Tips: Looks for "books for young children with Jewish interest and content, modern, non-sexist, not didactic."

KRUZA KALEIDOSCOPIX, INC., Box 389, Franklin MA 02038. (508)528-6211. Book publisher. Picture Books Editor: Jay Kruza. Young/middle readers editorial contact: Russ Burbank. Publishes 8 picture books/year; 1 young reader title/year; 1 middle reader title/year. 50% of books by first-time authors.

Fiction: Picture books: animal, fantasy, history. Young readers: animal, fantasy, history. Average word length: picture books—200-500; young readers—500-2,000; middle readers—1,000-10,000. Recently published *Petey the Pelican*, by Cox (ages 4-8, picture book); *Long Sleep*, by Blackman (ages 4-8, picture book); *ABC's Sports*, by Carole Iverson (ages 4-8, picture book).

Nonfiction: Picture books: animal, history, nature/environment. Young readers: animal, history, nature/environment, religion. Middle readers: biography, sports.

How to Contact/Writers: Fiction/nonfiction: Query; submit outline/synopsis and sample chapters; submit complete ms. SASE (IRC) for answer to query and/or return of mss. Reports on queries/mss in 2-8 weeks. Publishes a book 15 months after acceptance.

Illustration: Number of illustrations used for fiction: picture books—20-36; young readers—20-36; middle readers—20-36. Number of illustrations used for nonfiction: picture books—20; young readers—36; middle readers—20. Editorial will review ms/illustration packages submitted by authors/artists and ms/illustration packages submitted by authors with illustrations done by separate artists. Art Editor, Brian Sawyer, will review an illustrator's work for possible use in author's texts. Prefers to see "realistic" illustrations.

How to Contact/Illustrators: Illustrations only: "actual work sample and photos." Reports on art samples only if interested.

Terms/Writers & Illustrators: Pays authors in royalties of 3-5% based on wholesale price; buys ms outright for $250-$500. Additional payment for ms/illustrations package includes a 5-10% royalty. Pay for illustrators: $25-$200/illustration. Manuscript/artist's guidelines available for #10 SAE.

Tips: Writers: "Rework your story several times before submitting it without grammatical or spelling mistakes. Our company charges a $3 reading fee per manuscript to reduce unprepared manuscripts." Illustrators: "Submit professional looking samples for file. The correct manuscript may come along." Wants ms/illustrations "that teach a moral. Smooth prose that flows like poetry is preferred. The story will be read aloud. Vocabulary and language should fit actions. Short staccato words connote fast action; avoid stories that solve problems by the "wave of a wand" or that condone improper behavior. Jack of Beanstalk fame was a dullard, a thief, and even a murderer. We seek to purchase all rights to the story and artwork. Payment may be a lump sum in cash. For stronger mss., a royalty arrangement based on actual books sold for a period of seven years may be the payment."

LAUBACH LITERACY INTERNATIONAL (See New Readers Press.)

LERNER PUBLICATIONS CO., 241 First Ave. N., Minneapolis MN 55401. (612)332-3344. Book publisher. Editor: Jennifer Martin. Publishes 15 young reader titles/year; 25 middle reader titles/year; 30 young adult titles/year. 20% of books by first-time authors; 5% of books from agented writers.
Fiction: Middle readers: contemporary, history, science fiction, sports, mystery. Young adults: contemporary, history, science fiction, sports, mystery. Recently published *Earthchange*, by Clare Cooper (grades 4-8, science fiction); *Hot Like the Sun*, by Mel Cebulash (grades 5 and up, mystery).
Nonfiction: Young readers: animal, biography, history, nature/environment, sports, science, social studies, geography, social issues. Middle readers: animal, biography, history, nature/environment, sports, science, social studies, geography, social issues. Young adults: animal, biography, history, nature/environment, sports, science, social studies, geography, social issues. Average word length: young readers—3,000; middle readers—7,000; young adults—12,000. Recently published *Understanding AIDS*, by Ethan Lerner (grades 3-6, social issues); *Be A Dinosaur Detective*, by Dougal Dixon (grades K-4, science); *Dwight Gooden-Strikeout King*, by Nate Aaseng (grades 4-9, sports).
How to Contact/Writers: Fiction: Submit outline/synopsis and sample chapters. Nonfiction: Query; submit outline/synopsis and sample chapters. SASE (IRC) for return of mss. Reports on queries in 1 month; on mss in 2 months. Publishes a book 12 months after acceptance. Will consider simultaneous, photocopied, and computer printout submissions.
Terms/Writers & Illustrators: Sends galleys to authors. Book catalog available for 9 × 12 SAE and $1 postage; manuscript guidelines for 4 × 9 SAE and 1 first-class stamp.
Tips: "Before you send your manuscript to us, you might first take a look at the kinds of books that our company publishes. We specialize in publishing high-quality educational books for children from preschool through high school. Avoid sex stereotypes (e.g., strong, aggressive, unemotional males/weak, submissive, emotional females) in your writing, as well as sexist language." (See also Carolrhoda Books, Inc.)

LIGUORI PUBLICATIONS, 1 Liguori Dr., Liguori MO 63057-9999. (314)464-2500. Book publisher. Managing Editor: Rev. Thomas Artz, C.SS.R. Publishes 1 middle reader title/year; 3 young adult titles/year. 15% of books by first-time authors.
Nonfiction: Young readers, Middle readers, Young adults: religion. Average word length: young readers—10,000; young adults—15,000. Recently published *Advent is for Children*, by Julie Kelemen (middle grades, religion); *10 Good Reasons to be Catholic*, by Jim Auer (young adults, religion); *ABC's of the Mass for Children*, by Francine O'Connor (ages 3-6, religion).
How to Contact/Writers: Nonfiction: Query; submit outline/synopsis and sample chapters. SASE (IRC) for return of ms; include Social Security number with submission. Reports on queries in 6 weeks; on mss in 6-8 weeks. Publishes a book 12 months after

acceptance. Will consider photocopied, computer printout and electronic submissions via disk or modem.

Illustration: Number of illustrations used for nonfiction: young readers—40. Editorial will review ms/illustration packages submitted by authors/artists and ms/illustration packages submitted by authors with illustrations done by separate artists.

How to Contact/Illustrators: Ms/illustration packages: Query first.

Terms/Writers & Illustrators: Pays authors in royalties of 9-11% based on retail price. Book catalog available for 9 × 12 SAE and 3 first-class stamps; manuscript guidelines for #10 SAE and 1 first-class stamp.

Tips: Ms/illustrations "must be religious and suitable to a Roman Catholic audience. Writers should note that children's/teen's books are a very small part of Liguori's book publishing endeavors."

LITTLE, BROWN AND COMPANY, 34 Beacon St., Boston MA 02108. (617)227-0730. Book publisher. Editor-in-Chief: Maria Modugno. Editorial contact: Stephanie O. Lurie. Publishes 30% picture books/year; 10% young reader titles/year; 30% middle reader titles/year; 10% young adult titles/year. 10% of books by first-time authors; 50% of books from agented writers.

Fiction: Picture books: animal, contemporary, fantasy, history, problem novels, sports, spy/mystery/adventure. Young readers: contemporary, fantasy, history, problem novels, sports, spy/mystery/adventure. Middle readers: animal, contemporary, fantasy, history, problem novels, sports, spy/mystery/adventure. Young adults: animal, contemporary, fantasy, history, problem novels, sports, spy/mystery/adventure. Average word length: picture books—1,000; young readers—6,000; middle readers—15,000-25,000; young adults—20,000-40,000. Recently published *A Job for Jenny Archer*, by Ellen Conford (young readers).

Nonfiction: Average word length: picture books—2,000; young readers—4,000-6,000; middle readers—15,000-25,000; young adults—20,000-40,000. Recently published *Splash! All About Baths*, by Gelman/Bev Buxmaum (young readers); *At the Edge of the Pond*, by Jennifer Dewey (young readers); *What Teenagers Want to Know About Sex*, by The Boston Children's Hospital (young adults).

How to Contact/Writers: Fiction: Submit complete ms. Nonfiction: Submit outline/synopsis and 3 sample chapters. SASE (IRC) for return of ms. Reports on queries in 6 weeks; on mss in 6-8 weeks. Publishes a book 18 months after acceptance. Will consider photocopied, computer printout and electronic submissions via disk or modem.

Illustration: Number of illustrations used for fiction: picture books—32; young readers—8-10; middle readers—1; young adults—1. Number of illustrations used for nonfiction: picture books—32; young readers—32-48; middle readers—1; young adults—1. Editorial will review ms/illustration packages submitted by authors/artists and ms/illustration packages submitted by authors with illustrations done by separate artists. Editor-in-Chief, Maria Modugno, will review illustrator's work for possible use in author's texts.

How to Contact/Illustrators: Ms/illustration packages: complete ms with 1 piece of final art. Illustrations only: Slides. Reports on art samples in 6-8 weeks. Original art work returned at job's completion.

Terms/Writers & Illustrators: Pays authors in royalties based on retail price. Offers average advance payment of $2,000-$10,000. Sends galleys to authors; dummies to illustrators. Book catalog, manuscript/artist's guidelines free on request.

LOTHROP, LEE & SHEPARD BOOKS, div. and imprint of William Morrow Co. Inc., Children's Fiction, 105 Madison Ave., New York NY 10016. (212)889-3050. Editor-in-Chief: Dorothy Briley. Publishes 60 total titles/year.

Fiction: Picture books: animal, easy-to-read, sports. Young readers: sports. Middle readers: contemporary, easy-to-read, fantasy, history, sports. Young adults: contemporary, fantasy, history, sports.

Nonfiction: Picture books, young readers, middle readers, young adults: animal, biography, education, history, hobbies, music/dance, nature/environment, religion, sports.
How to Contact/Writers: Fiction/nonfiction: Cover letter, query, submit outline/synopsis and sample chapters. SASE (IRC) for answer to query and/or return of ms.
Illustration: Editorial will review ms/illustration packages submitted by authors/artists and ms/illustration packages submitted by authors with illustrations done by separate artists.
How to Contact/Illustrators: Ms/illustration packages: Write for guidelines first.
Terms/Writers & Illustrators: Methods of payment: "varies." Manuscript/artist's guidelines free for SASE. (See also Greenwillow Books.)

MACMILLAN PUBLISHING CO. (See Aladdin Books/Collier Books for Young Adults, Atheneum Publishers, Bradbury Press, Four Winds Press, Margaret K. McElderry Books.)

MARYLAND HISTORICAL PRESS, 9205 Tuckerman St., Lanham MD 20706. (301)577-5308. Book publisher. Independent book producer/packager. Publisher: Mrs. Vera Rollo. Publishes 1 picture book/year; 1 young reader title/year; 1 middle reader title/year; 1 young adult title/year. 30% of books by first-time authors.
Nonfiction: Picture books, young readers, middle readers, young adults: biography, history. Recently published *What You Should Know About the American Flag*, by Earl P. Williams, Jr. (young adults); *Indians of the Tidewater Country of Maryland, Virginia, North Carolina, and Delaware*, by Thelma G. Ruskin (elementary students); *Maryland: Its Past and Present*, by Dr. Richard Wilson and Dr. E. L. Bridner, Jr. (4th-grade level).
How to Contact/Writers: Nonfiction: Query. Reports on queries in 1 month. Publishes a book 9 months after acceptance. Will consider simultaneous submissions.
Terms/Writers & Illustrators: Pays authors in royalties, buys artwork outright. Factors used to determine final payment: Time spent. Pay for illustrators: By the project. Sends galley to authors. Book catalog free on request.
Tips: "See what niche is not filled, ask: 'What do libraries and teachers need?' "

MARGARET K. McELDERRY BOOKS, imprint of Macmillan Publishing Co., 866 Third Ave., New York NY 10022. (212)702-7855. Book publisher. Publisher: Margaret K. McElderry. Publishes 10-12 picture books/year; 2-4 young reader titles/year; 8-10 middle reader titles/year; 3-5 young adult titles/year. 33% of books by first-time authors; 33% of books from agented writers.
Fiction: Picture books: animal, contemporary. Young readers: animal, contemporary, easy-to-read. Middle readers: animal, contemporary, fantasy, science fiction, spy/mystery/adventure. Young adults: contemporary, fantasy, science fiction. Average word length: picture books—500; young readers—2,000; middle readers—5,000-6,000; young adults—45,000-50,000. Recently published *A Family Project*, by Sara Ellis (ages 10-14, contemporary story involving crib death); *Memory*, by Margaret Mahy (ages 14 and up, contemporary story involving Alzheimer's Disease); *Another Shore*, by Nancy Bond (ages 12 and up, time travel story).
Nonfiction: Picture books: animal, history, nature/environment, science. Young readers: animal, history, nature/environment, science, sports. Middle readers: animal, biography, history, music/dance, nature/environment, science, sports. Young adults: biography, music/dance, nature/environment. Average word length: picture books—500-1,000; young readers—1,500-3,000; middle readers—5,000-7,500; young adults—30,000-45,000. Recently published *There was a Place*, by Myra Cohn Livingston (ages 8-12, poetry); *Story of a Main Street*, by John S. Goodall (all ages, pictorial social history).
How to Contact/Writers: Fiction/Nonfiction: Submit complete ms. SASE (IRC) for return of ms. Reports on queries in 2-3 weeks; on mss in 8 weeks. Publishes a book 12-

18 months after acceptance. Will consider simultaneous (only if indicated as such), and computer printout submissions.

Illustration: Number of illustrations used for fiction: picture books—"every page"; young readers—15-20; middle readers—15-20. Number of illustrations used for nonfiction: picture books—"every page"; young readers—20-30; middle readers—15-25. Editorial will review ms/illustration packages submitted by authors/artists; ms/illustration packages submitted by authors with illustrations done by separate artists; and an illustrator's work for possible use in author's texts.

How to Contact/Illustrators: Ms/illustration packages: Ms (complete) and 2 or 3 pieces of finished art. Illustrations only: Resume and slides or sketches. Reports on art samples in 6-8 weeks. Original artwork returned at job's completion.

Terms/Writers & Illustrators: Pays authors in royalties based on retail price. Pay for separate authors and illustrators: "50-50 as a rule for picture books." Pay for illustrators: by the project. Sends galleys to authors; dummies to illustrators, "they make the dummies for picture books." Book catalog, manuscript/artist's guidelines free on request.

Tips: Writers: "Read widely in the field and write constantly." Illustrators: "Look at books already published and go to exhibitions of all sorts, sketch constantly." There is an "emphasis on books for babies and young children; on nonfiction; on poetry." (See also Aladdin Books/Collier Books for Young Adults, Atheneum Publishers, Bradbury Press, Four Winds Press.)

MERIWETHER PUBLISHING LTD., 885 Elkton Dr., Colorado Springs CO 80907. Book publisher. "We do most of our artwork in house; we do not publish for the children's elementary market." 85% of books by first-time authors; 5% of books from agented writers.

Nonfiction: Young adults: how-to, how-to church activities. Average length: 150 pages. Recently published *Fund Raising for Youth*, by Ross (jr. to sr. high, help book); *Winning Monologues for Young Actors*, by Litherland (jr. and sr. high, theatrical).

How to Contact/Writers: Nonfiction: Query; submit outline/synopsis and sample chapters. SASE (IRC) for answer to query and/or return of mss; include Social Security number with submission. Reports on queries in 4 weeks. Publishes a book 6-12 months after acceptance. Will consider simultaneous, photocopied, and computer printout submissions.

Illustration: Number of illustrations used for nonfiction: young adults—15. Art Director, Michelle Zapel, will review an illustrator's work for possible use in author's texts.

How to Contact/Illustrators: Ms/illustration packages: Query first. Illustrations only: Slides. Reports on art samples in 4 weeks.

Terms/Writers & Illustrators: Pays authors in royalties based on retail or wholesale price. Pay for illustrators: by the project; royalties based on retail or wholesale price. Sends galleys to authors. Book catalog for SAE and $1 postage; manuscript guidelines for SAE and 1 first-class stamp.

Tips: "For us—write good how-to nonfiction ideas—new approaches to old ideas."

JULIAN MESSNER, imprint of Simon & Schuster, Prentice Hall Bldg., Englewood Cliffs NJ 07632. Book publisher. Editorial Director: Jane Steltenpohl. Publishes 4 young reader titles/year; 15 middle reader titles/year; 6 young adult titles/year. 25% of books by first-time authors; 50% of books from agented writers.

Nonfiction: Middle readers: animal, biography, history, hobbies, nature/environment, general science. Young adults: animal, biography, history, nature/environment, general science. Average word length: middle readers—30,000; young adults—40,000-45,000. Recently published *Science Fun with Mud and Dirt*, by Rose Wyler (young readers-middle readers, general science); *Mikhail Gorbachev*, by George Sullivan (young adults, biography); *Step into China*, by Neil Johnson (middle readers, photo essay).

How to Contact/Writers: Nonfiction: Query. Reports on queries in 2 months; on mss in 3 months. Publishes a book 8 months after acceptance. Will consider simultaneous inquiries.

Illustration: Number of illustrations used for nonfiction: middle readers—20; young adults—12. Editorial will review ms/illustration inquiries submitted by authors with illustrations done by separate artists. Art Director, Carol Kuchta, will review an illustrator's work for possible use in author's texts.

How to Contact/Illustrators: Ms/illustration packages: Query first. Illustrations only: "Resume and xeroxes." Reports on art samples only if interested. Original artwork returned at job's completion.

Terms/Writers & Illustrators: Pays authors in royalties. Additional payment for ms/illustration packages. Sends galleys to authors.

METAMORPHOUS PRESS, Box 10616, Portland OR 97210. (503) 228-4972. Book publisher. Editorial Contact: Anita Sullivan. Publishes 1 picture book/year; 1 young reader title/year; 1 middle reader title/year; 1 young adult title/year. 90% of books by first-time authors; 10% of books from agented writers. Subsidy publishes 10%.

Fiction: "Metaphors for positive change."

Nonfiction: Picture books: education. Young readers: education, music/dance. Middle readers: education, music/dance, self help/esteem. Young adults: education, music/dance, self-help/esteem. Recently published *Thinking, Changing, Rearranging*, by Anderson (ages 10 and up, workbook to improve self-esteem); *Classroom Magic*, by Lloyd (lesson plans for elementary grades).

How to Contact/Writers: Fiction: Query. Nonfiction: Query; Submit outline/synopsis and sample chapters. SASE (IRC) for return of mss. Reports on queries in 3-4 months; on mss in 4-6 months. Publishes a book 12-24 months after acceptance. Will consider simultaneous, photocopied, computer printout and electronic submissions via disk or modem.

Illustration: Number of illustrations used for fiction/nonfiction: "varies." Editorial will review ms/illustration packages submitted by authors/artists and ms/illustration packages submitted by authors with illustrations done by separate artists. Children's Editor, Janele Gantt, will review an illustrator's work for possible use in author's texts.

How to Contact/Illustrators: Ms/illustrations: Query. Illustrations only: "vitae with samples of range and style." Reports on art samples only if interested.

Terms/Writers & Illustrators: Other methods of pay: "varies, negotiable." Pay for separate authors and illustrators: "Individually negotiated usually between author and illustrator." Sends galleys to authors; dummies to illustrators. Book catalog free on request.

Tips: Looks for "Books that relate and illustrate the notion that we create our own realities, self-reliance and positive outlooks work best for us—creative metaphors and personal development guides given preference."

MISTY HILL PRESS, 5024 Turner Rd., Sebastopol CA 95472. (707)823-7437. Book publisher. Editor-in-Chief: Sally Karste. Publishes 2 middle reader titles/year. 100% of books by first-time authors.

Fiction: Middle readers: history. Young adults: history.

Nonfiction: Middle readers: history. Young adults: history. Recently published *Trails to Poosey*, by Olive Cooke (young adults, historical fiction).

How to Contact/Writers: Fiction/nonfiction: Submit outline/synopsis and sample chapters. SASE (IRC) for answer to query and/or return of ms. Reports on queries in 1 week; on mss in 4 weeks. Publishes a book 8 months after acceptance. Will consider simultaneous submissions.

Terms/Writers & Illustrators: Illustrators paid by the project. Sends galleys to authors.

Tips: "Historical fiction: substantial research, good adventure or action against the historical setting. Historical fiction only."

MOREHOUSE-BARLOW, 78 Danbury Rd., Wilton CT 06897. (203)762-0721. Book publisher. Juvenile Books Editor: Stephanie Oda. Publishes 6 picture books/year. 75% of books by first-time authors. Subsidy publishes 25%.

Fiction: Picture book, young readers, middle readers, young adults: religion.

Nonfiction: Picture books: religion, moral message, family values. Young readers: religion, moral message, family values. Middle readers: religion, moral message, family values. Young adults: moral message, family values.

How to Contact/Writers: Fiction/nonfiction: Submit outline/synopsis and sample chapters. Include Social Security number with submission. Reports on queries in 4-6 weeks. Publishes a book 12 months after acceptance. Will consider computer printout and electronic submissions via disk or modem. Editorial will review ms/illustration packages submitted by authors/artists; ms/illustration packages submitted by authors with illustrations done by separate artists; and illustrator's work for possible use in author's texts.

How to Contact/Illustrators: Ms/illustration packages: 3 chapters of ms with 1 piece of final art. Illustrations only: Resume, tear sheets. Reports on art samples in 4-6 weeks. Original artwork returned at job's completion.

Terms/Writers & Illustrators: Pays authors "both royalties and outright." Offers average advance payment of $500. Additional payment for ms/illustration packages. Sends galleys to authors. Book catalog free on request.

Tips: Writers: "Prefer authors who can do own illustrations. Be fresh, be fun, not pedantic, but let your work have a message." Currently expanding juvenile list. Illustrators: "Work hard to develop original style." Looks for ms/illustrations "with a religious or moral value while remaining fun and entertaining."

WILLIAM MORROW & CO. INC. (See Greenwillow Books; Lothrop, Lee & Shepard Books.)

MOSAIC PRESS, 358 Oliver Rd., Cincinnati OH 45215. (513)761-5977. Miniature book publisher. Publisher: Miriam Irwin. Publishes less than 1 young reader title/year. 50% of books by first-time authors.

Fiction: Middle readers: animal, contemporary, history, problem novels, sports, spy/mystery/adventure. Average word length: middle readers—under 2,000.

Nonfiction: Middle readers: animal, biography, education, history, hobbies, music/dance, nature/environment, religion, sports. Average word length: middle readers—2,000. Recently published *Scrimshaw*, by Carolyn Orr (adult, factual history). "We have done 4 children's books in 10 years. None of our recent books were for children (out of 87 titles)."

How to Contact/Writers: Fiction: Query; submit complete ms. Nonfiction: Submit complete ms. SASE (IRC) for answer to query and/or return of mss. Reports on queries/mss in 2 weeks. Publishes a book 4 years after acceptance. Will consider simultaneous, photocopied, and computer printout submissions.

Illustration: Number of illustrations used for fiction: middle readers—12. Number of illustrations used for nonfiction: middle readers—8. Editorial will review ms/illustration packages submitted by authors/artists; ms/illustration packages submitted by authors with illustrations done by separate artists; and illustrator's work for possible use in author's texts. Prefers to see "pen and ink under 5" tall."

How to Contact/Illustrators: Illustrations only: "photocopies of pen and ink work with SASE." Reports on art samples in 2 weeks. Original artwork returned at job's completion "after several years if requested."

Terms/Writers & Illustrators: Buys ms outright for $50 and 5 copies of book. Additional payment for ms/illustration package is $50 and 5 copies of book. Factors used to determine final payment: "flat fee." Pay for separate authors and illustrators: "by check when the book goes to press. The first completed copies are sent to artist and author."

Pay for illustrators: $50 and 5 copies. Book catalog is available for $3. Manuscript/artist's guidelines for legal SAE and 45¢.

Tips: Looks for "any type of writing that has something to say worth preserving in the form of a miniature book; that says it beautifully in very few words."

NATIONAL PRESS INC., 7201 Wisconsin Ave., Bethesda MD 20814. (301)657-1616. Book publisher. Contact: Submissions Editor. Publishes 3 picture books/year. "We are currently building up our children's market in all categories." 75% of books by first-time authors; 25% of books from agented writers.

Fiction: Picture books: animal, contemporary, easy-to-read, fantasy, history, problem novels, romance, science fiction, sports, spy/mystery/adventure. Young readers: animal, contemporary easy-to-read, fantasy, history, problem novels, romance, science fiction, sports, spy/mystery/adventure. Middle readers: animal, contemporary easy-to-read, fantasy, history, problem novels, romance, science fiction, sports, spy/mystery/adventure. Young adults: animal, contemporary easy-to-read, fantasy, history, problem novels, romance, science fiction, sports, spy/mystery/adventure. Recently published *Planet of Trash*, by Poppel (young readers, picture book); *Battle of the Dinos*, by Poppel (young readers, picture book); *Winnie the Blue Whale*, (young readers, picture book).

Nonfiction: Picture books: animal, biography, history, sports. Young readers: animal, biography, history, sports. Middle readers: animal, biography, history, sports. Young adults: animal, biography, history, sports.

How to Contact/Writers: Fiction/nonfiction: Submit outline/synopsis and sample chapters. SASE (IRC) for answer to query and/or return of mss. Reports on queries in 6 weeks; on mss in 8 weeks. Publishes a book 12 months after acceptance. Will consider simultaneous, photocopied, computer printout and electronic submissions via disk or modem.

Illustration: Editorial will review ms/illustration packages submitted by authors/artists and ms/illustration packages submitted by authors with illustrations done by separate artists. Editor, K. McComas, will review an illustrator's work for possible use in author's texts.

How to Contact/Illustrators: Reports on art samples in 6 weeks.

Terms/Writers & Illustrators: Factors used to determine final payment: color art vs. black-and-white and number of illustrations used. Sends dummies to illustrators. Book catalog, manuscript guidelines free on request.

Tips: "Well-conceived submissions are extremely rare. Good ideas fall through the cracks of meandering query letters and amateurish material. Writers' naiveté, in most cases, is astonishing—and unproductive. However, good material will always filter through." Trends in children's book publishing include: "Return to the classics, which hopefully means more discriminating parents."

NEW DAY BOOKS, Sister Company to Greenhaven Press, Box 289009, San Diego CA 92128-9009. (619)485-7424. Book publisher. Editor: Carol O'Sullivan. We are new. We project 40+ middle reader titles/year. 50% of books by first-time authors; 50% of books from agented writers.

Nonfiction: Middle readers: animal, education, history (if it's a history of a topic), music/dance, nature/environment, religion, sports, "any overviews of specific topics—i.e., political, social, cultural, economic, criminal, moral issues." Average word length: middle readers—12,000-15,000. Presently issuing *Garbage*, by Karen O'Connor (grades 5-8, overview); *Self-Esteem*, by Diane Chalfant (grades 5-8, self-help, overview); *Special Effects - Movies*, by Tom Powers (grades 5-8, overview).

How to Contact/Writers: Nonfiction: Query. Reports on queries in 2 weeks. Publishes a book 6 months after acceptance. Will consider simultaneous, photocopied, and computer printout submissions.

Illustration: "We use photos, mostly." Will review ms/illustration packages submitted by authors with illustrations done by separate artists. Preference: "7 × 9 format — 4-color cover."

How to Contact/Illustrators: Ms/illustration packages: Query first.

Terms/Writers & Illustrators: "Fee negotiated upon review of manuscript." Sends galleys to authors. Manuscript guidelines free on request.

Tips: "Know the publisher's needs and requirements. Books must be written at a 7-9 grade reading level. There's a growing market for quality nonfiction. Tentative Titles: Free Speech, Tobacco, Alcohol, Discrimination, Immigration, Poverty, The Homeless in America, Space Weapons, Drug Abuse, Terrorism, MAD (Arms Race), Animal Experimentation, etc. We are currently working on books addressing Endangered Species, AIDS, Pollution, Gun Control, etc. Both the above lists are presented to give writers an example of the kinds of titles we are seeking. If you are interested in writing about a specific topic, please query us by mail before you begin writing to be sure we have not assigned a particular topic to another author. The author should strive for objectivity. There obviously will be many issues on which a position should be taken — e.g. discrimination, tobacco, alcoholism, etc. However, moralizing, self-righteous condemnations, maligning, lamenting, mocking, etc. should be avoided. Moreover, where a pro/con position is taken, contrasting viewpoints should be presented. Certain moral issues such as abortion and euthanasia, if dealt with at all, should be presented with strict objectivity."

NEW DAY PRESS, 2355 E. 89, Cleveland OH 44106. (216)795-7070. Book publisher. Editorial Contact: Carolyn Gordon. Publishes 1 middle reader title/year; 1 young adult title/year. 75% of books by first-time authors.

Fiction: Middle readers, young adults: history. Recently published *Walk In My Footsteps*, by Martha Grooms (young adults, fictionalized memoirs).

Nonfiction: Middle readers, young adults: biography, history. Recently published *Black Image Makers*, by E. Gaines et al. (middle readers-young adults, biographical narratives).

How to Contact/Writers: Fiction/nonfiction: Query. SASE (IRC) for return of mss. Reports on queries in 4 weeks; on mss in 12 weeks. Publishes a book a year or more after acceptance.

Illustration: Number of illustrations used for fiction and nonfiction: middle readers — 5; young adults — 5. Editorial will review ms/illustration packages submitted by authors/ artists and ms/illustration packages submitted by authors with illustrations done by separate artists.

How to Contact/Illustrators: Reports on art samples in 3 months. Buys ms outright for $100. Book catalog free on request.

Tips: Looks for "black history/biography/achievement" ms/illustrations.

NEW READERS PRESS, div. of Laubach Literacy International, Box 131, Syracuse NY 13210. (315)422-9121. Book publisher. Acquisitions Editor: Kay Koschnick. Publishes 2-3 young adult titles/year. 85% of books by first-time authors; 5% of books from agented writers.

Fiction: Young adults: easy-to-read. Average word length: young adults (16+ only) — 12,000-15,000. Recently published *Love Letters*, by Harriette Coret (young adults, 16+, easy-to-read novel); *Birthday Boy*, by Thomas Ogren (young adults, 16+, easy-to-read novel); *Don't Sell Me Short*, by Judith Bosley (young adults, 16+, easy-to-read novel).

Nonfiction: Young adults: biography. Average word length: young adults (16+ only) — 12,000-15,000.

How to Contact/Writers: Fiction/nonfiction: Query; submit outline/synopsis and sample chapters. SASE (IRC) for return of ms. Reports on queries in 3 weeks; on mss in 12 weeks. Publishes a book 12 months after acceptance. Will consider photocopied submissions.

Illustration: Number of illustrations used for fiction: young adults — 6-10.

Terms/Writers & Illustrators: Pays authors in royalties of 5-7.5% based on retail price.

Outright purchase "depends on nature of work." Offers average advance payment of $200. Book catalog, manuscript guidelines free on request.

Tips: Nonfiction: "Submissions most likely to fit our publishing program would be in the following areas: reading skills development, supplementary reading material, writing, listening skills, speaking skills, study skills, English as a second language, logical thinking and problem solving, math, social studies, science and health, practical life skills, career education, self-awareness and interpersonal relationships." Fiction: "Original fiction. We want stories in which it's clear that the author has something to say and is writing not merely to entertain but mostly to express something that will leave the reader with a new awareness. Fiction aimed at adults and older teenagers—main characters should be no younger than 15 or 16, however. Our audience does include teenagers, but young people generally prefer to read about characters their age or somewhat older."

NEW SEED PRESS, Box 9488, Berkeley CA 94709. (415)540-7576. Book publisher. Editor: Helen Chetin. Published 1 picture book in 1973, 1 in 1976; 3 young readers titles each in 1975, 1977, 1979; 1 middle reader title in 1974; 1 young adult title in 1982 and 1 in 1986. 90% of books by first-time authors.

Fiction: Picture books, young readers: contemporary. Middle readers, young adults: contemporary, history. Recently published *Green March Moons*, by Mary TallMountain (ages 12 and up, Native Alaskan life); *Angel Island Prisoner*, by Helen Chetin (ages 12 and up, Chinese/English, history).

How to Contact/Writers: Fiction/nonfiction: Query. SASE (IRC) for answer to query and/or return of mss. Reports on queries in 2 weeks; on mss in 8 weeks. Will consider simultaneous, photocopied, and computer printout submissions.

Illustration: Editorial will review ms/illustration packages submitted by authors/artists; ms/illustration packages submitted by authors with illustrations done by separate artists; and an illustrator's work for possible use in author's texts.

How to Contact/Illustrators: Ms/illustration packages: Query with sample. Illustrations only: Tear sheets. Reports on art samples only if interested. Original artwork returned at job's completion.

Terms/Writers & Illustrators: Pays authors in royalties of 10% based on retail price. Buys ms outright for "negotiable" price. Average advance payment "varies." Sends galleys to authors; dummies to illustrators. Book catalog free on request; manuscript guidelines for legal-size SAE and 1 first-class stamp.

Tips: "Know your publisher before submitting."

ODDO PUBLISHING, INC., Box 68, Fayetteville GA 30214. (404)461-7627. Book publisher. Contact: Editor. Publishes 3-6 picture books/year; 1-2 young reader titles/year; 1-2 middle reader titles/year. 25% of books by first-time authors.

Fiction: Picture books: animal, contemporary, easy-to-read, science fiction, sports, spy/mystery/adventure. Young readers: animal, contemporary, easy-to-read, fantasy, science fiction, sports, spy/mystery/adventure. Middle readers: animal, contemporary, fantasy, science fiction, sports, spy/mystery/adventure. Average word length: picture books— 500; young readers—1,000; middle readers—2,000. Recently published *Bobby Bear & Uncle Sam's Riddle*, by Dr. Lee Mountain (pre K-1, picture book); *Bobby Bear & The Kite Contest*, by Marilue (pre K-1, picture book); *Bobby Bear's Birthday*, by Rae Oetting (pre K-1, picture book).

Nonfiction: Picture books: animal, nature/environment, sports. Young readers: animal, biography, hobbies, nature/environment, sports. Middle readers: animal, biography, hobbies, nature/environment, sports. Average word length: picture books—500; young readers—1,000; middle readers—2,000.

How to Contact/Writers: Fiction/nonfiction: Query; submit outline/synopsis and sample chapters. SASE (IRC) for answer to query and/or return of mss. Reports on queries 1-2 weeks; on mss 8-12 weeks. Publishes a book 24 months after acceptance. Will con-

"This artwork represents well the type of work we seek," says Paul C. Oddo, chief executive officer of Oddo Publishing, Inc. These qualities include a cheerful and detailed style. Marilue Johnson, Santa Fe, New Mexico, developed this Bobby Bear character for the book, **Bobby Bear and Uncle Sam's Riddle.** *"Marilue has a special talent for imparting 'personality' into the characters she illustrates,"* Oddo explains. This book was the 1988 recipient of the Freedoms Foundation at Valley Forge award.

sider simultaneous, photocopied, and computer printout (excluding dot matrix) submissions.

Illustration: Number of illustrations used for fiction and nonfiction: picture books—33; young readers—33; middle readers—33. Editorial will review ms/illustration packages submitted by authors/artists; ms/illustration packages submitted by authors with illustrations done by separate artists; and an illustrator's work for possible use in author's texts.

How to Contact/Illustrators: Ms/illustration packages: Query first. Illustrations only: Sample art or slides. Reports on art samples only if interested, or if required to review slides.

Terms/Writers & Illustrators: Buys ms outright, "negotiable" price. Additional payment for ms/illustration packages "negotiable." Factors used to determine final payment include number of illustrations. Pay for separate authors and illustrators: separate contracts. Illustrators paid by the project. Sends galleys to authors "only if necessary." Book catalog available for 9×12 SAE and $2.25.

Tips: "Send simultaneous submissions. Do not be discouraged by 'no.' Keep sending to publishers." Looks for: "Books/art with a 'positive' tone. No immorality or risque subjects. Books must have an underlying theme or concept. 'Coping' subjects are accepted. We want children who read our books to learn something and feel good when they are finished."

ORCHARD BOOKS, div. and imprint of Franklin Watts, Inc., 387 Park Ave. S., New York NY 10016. (212)686-7070. Book publisher. Publisher and Editor-in-Chief: Norma Jean Sawicki. "We publish between 50 and 60 books, fiction, poetry, picture books, and photo essays." 10-25% of books by first-time authors.

Nonfiction: "We publish very selective nonfiction."

How to Contact/Writers: Fiction: Submit outline/synopsis and sample chapters; submit complete ms. Nonfiction: Submit outline/synopsis and sample chapters. SASE (IRC) for answer to query and/or return of mss. Reports on queries in 4 weeks; on mss in 4-8 weeks. Average length of time between acceptance of a book-length ms and publication of work "depends on the editorial work necessary. If none, about 8 months." Will consider simultaneous, photocopied, and computer printout submissions.

Illustration: Editorial will review ms/illustration packages submitted by authors/artists and ms/illustration packages submitted by authors with illustrations done by separate artists. "But it is better to submit ms and illustration separately unless they are by the same person, or a pairing that is part of the project such as husband and wife."

How to Contact/Illustrators: Ms/illustration packages: 3 chapters of ms with 1 piece of final art, remainder roughs. Illustrations only: "tear sheets or xerox copies or photo-stats of the work." Reports on art samples in 4 weeks. Original artwork returned at job's completion.

Terms/Writers & Illustrators: Pays authors in royalties "industry standard" based on retail price. Additional payment for ms/illustration packages. Factors used to determine final payment for ms/illustration package include number of illustrations, and experi-ence. "We never buy manuscripts outright. An author/illustrator gets the whole royalty. An author who needs the illustrator shares the royalty." Sends galleys to authors; dum-mies to illustrators. Book catalog free on request.

Tips: "Master your craft, be true to your highest aspirations, and persevere."

PADRE PRODUCTIONS (See The Press of MacDonald & Reinecke.)

PANDO PUBLICATIONS, 540 Longleaf Dr., Roswell GA 30075. (404)587-3363. Book publisher. Owner: Andrew Bernstein. Publishes 2-6 middle reader titles/year; 2-6 young adult titles/year. 20% of books by first-time authors.

Fiction: Middle readers: animal, contemporary, easy-to-read, fantasy, history, problem novels, romance, science fiction, sports, spy/mystery/adventure. Young adults: animal, contemporary, easy-to-read, fantasy, history, problem novels, romance, science fiction, sports, spy/mystery/adventure. Average length: middle readers—175 pages; young adults—200 pages. "New company, no children's fiction yet."

Nonfiction: Middle readers: animal, biography, education, history, hobbies, music/dance, nature/environment, religion, sports. Young adults: animal, biography, educa-tion, history, hobbies, music/dance, nature/environment, religion, sports. Average length: middle readers—175 pages; young adults—200 pages. Recently published *Teach Me to Play: A First Bridge Book*, by Jude Goodwin (ages 8-14, how-to, about card game of bridge).

How to Contact/Writers: Fiction/nonfiction: All unsolicited mss returned unopened. SASE (IRC) for return of ms. Reports on queries in 4 weeks; on mss in 6 weeks. Publishes a book 9 months after acceptance. Will consider simultaneous, photocopied, computer printout but "prefers" electronic submissions via disk or modem.

Illustration: Number of illustrations used for nonfiction: middle readers—125; young adults—125. Editorial will review ms/illustration packages submitted by authors/artists; ms/illustration packages submitted by authors with illustrations done by separate artists; and illustrator's work for possible use in author's texts.

How to Contact/Illustrators: Ms/illustrations: Query first. Illustrations only: Tear sheets. Reports on art samples in 1 month. Original artwork returned at job's comple-tion.

Terms/Writers & Illustrators: Method(s) of payment: "Whatever we agree on." Offers average advance payment of "⅓ royalty due on first run." Factors used to determine final payment: "Our agreement (contract)." Pay for separate authors and illustrators is "according to contract." Illustrators paid "according to contract." Sends galleys to au-thors; dummies to illustrators. "Book descriptions available on request." Manuscript/artist's guidelines are free on request.

Tips: Writers: "Find an untapped market then write to fill the need." Illustrators: "Find an author with a good idea and writing ability. Develop the book with the author. Join a professional group to meet people-ABA, publisher's groups, as well as writer's groups

© Paulist Press 1988

Georgia J. Christo, Paulist Press editor, purchased all rights to this illustration from Pamela T. Keating, Flushing, New York. It was used as a color cover and inside black-and-white illustration for the book I Never Do Anything Bad. *The cover illustration was rendered in water colors, and the inside piece in pen and ink. "This artist is able to convey movement," explains Christo. "Her art is full of energy. Pam is able to capture a feeling and can express this feeling with charm and wit."*

and publishing auxiliary groups. Talk to printers." Looks for "How-to books but will consider anything."

PAULIST PRESS, 997 Macarthur Blvd., Mahwah NJ 07430. (201)825-7300. Book publisher. Editor: Georgia J. Christo. Publishes 6 picture books/year; 2 young reader titles/year; 1 middle reader title/year; 1 young adult title/year. 60% of books by first-time authors; 10% of books from agented writers.
Fiction: Picture books, young readers, middle readers, young adults: religious/moral. Average length: picture books—24 pages; young readers—24-32 pages; middle readers—64 pages; young adults—64-80 pages. Recently published *I Never Do Anything Bad*, by Penny Colman (picture book and young readers, decision-making); *Rachel and the Rabbi Jesus*, by Rosario DeBello (picture book and young readers, biblical); *Willie of Church Street*, by Margaret N. Ralph (picture book and young readers, self-acceptance).
Nonfiction: Picture books, young readers, middle readers, young adults: religion. Recently published *Saint Therese of Liseux*, by Dorothy Smith (middle readers, spiritual); *Lectionary Coloring Stories*, by Judi Winkowski (young readers, catechetical); *Saint Francis of Assisi*, by Dorothy Smith (middle readers, spiritual).
How to Contact/Writers: Fiction/nonfiction: Submit complete ms. SASE (IRC) for return of ms. Reports on queries in 1-2 weeks; on mss in 4 weeks. Publishes a book 12-16 months after acceptance. Will consider simultaneous, photocopied, and computer printout submissions, "prefer original, typed, double-spaced ms."
Illustration: Number of illustrations used for fiction and nonfiction: picture books—12-16; young readers—12; middle readers—6-8; young adults—6. Editorial will review ms/illustration packages submitted by authors/artists; ms/illustration packages submitted by authors with illustrations done by separate artists; and an illustrator's work for possible use in author's texts.
How to Contact/Illustrators: Ms/illustration packages: Complete ms with 1 piece of final art, remainder roughs. Illustrations only: Resume, tear sheets. Reports on art

samples in 2-3 weeks. Original artwork returned at job's completion, "if requested by illustrator."

Terms/Writers & Illustrators: Outright purchase: $25-$40/illustration. Offers average advance payment of $350-$500. Factors used to determine final payment: Color art, b&w, number of illustrations, complexity of work. Pay for separate authors and illustrators: Author paid by royalty rate; illustrator paid by flat fee. Sends galleys to authors; dummies to illustrators. Book catalog available for SAE.

Tips: "Be patient and persistent. Don't be afraid to express yourself with your sense of humor. Books today are discussing adult issues; children are more sophisticated and are capable of understanding more in terms of current trends (because of television)." Looks for: "religious, manuscripts dealing with morals, heroes and heroines creative stories with a religious theme."

PENGUIN/USA (NAL Penguin Inc.) (See Dial Books for Young Readers, Dutton Children's Books.)

PERSPECTIVES PRESS, Box 90318, Indianapolis IN 46290. (317)872-3055. Book publisher. Publisher: Pat Johnston. Publishes total 2-6 children's titles of all ages. 95% of books by first-time authors.

Fiction: Picture books, young readers, middle readers, young adults: adoption, foster care. Recently published *Real For Sure Sister*, by Angel (middle readers); *The Mulberry Bird*, by Brodzinsky (young readers, middle readers).

Nonfiction: Picture books, young readers, middle readers, young adults: adoption, foster care. Recently published *Filling in the Blanks*, by Gabel (middle/young adults, self-help).

How to Contact/Writers: Fiction/nonfiction: Query. SASE (IRC) for answer to query and/or return of mss. Reports on queries in 2 weeks; on mss in 6 weeks. Publishes a book 6-9 months after acceptance. Will consider simultaneous and photocopied submissions.

Terms/Writers & Illustrators: Pays authors in royalties of 5-15% based on net sales. Sends galleys to authors; dummies to illustrators. Book catalog, manuscript guidelines available for #10 SAE and 2 first-class stamps.

Tips: "Do your homework! I'm amazed at the number of authors who don't bother to check that we have a very limited interest area and subsequently submit unsolicited material that is completely inappropriate for us. For children, we focus exclusively on issues of adoption and interim (foster) care; for adults we also include infertility issues."

PHILOMEL BOOKS, imprint of The Putnam & Grosset Group, 200 Madison Ave., New York NY 10016. (212)951-8700. Book publisher. Editor-in-Chief: Patricia Lee Gauch (picture books). Editorial Contact: Paula Wiseman (young reader titles). Publishes 20 picture books/year; 5-10 young reader titles/year. 50% of books by first-time authors; 20% of books from agented writers.

Fiction: Picture books: animal, fantasy, history. Young readers: animal, fantasy, history. Middle readers: fantasy, history. Young adults: contemporary, fantasy, history. "Any well written book." Average word length: "Books of quality varying length." Recently published *Mossflower*, by Brian Jacques (young adults); *Hear the Wind Blow*, by Patricia Pendergraft (middle readers).

Nonfiction: Picture books, young readers, middle readers, young adults: animal, biography, history. "Creative nonfiction on any subject." Average length: "not to exceed 150 pages." Recently published *Young Lions*, by Yoshida.

How to Contact/Writers: Fiction/nonfiction: Query; submit outline/synopsis and sample chapters; all other unsolicited mss returned unopened. SASE (IRC) for answer to query. Reports on queries/mss in 3 months. Publishes a book 2 years after acceptance. "Prefer type or daisy wheel electronic submissions."

Illustration: Number of illustrations used for fiction: picture books—24. Will review ms/

illustration packages submitted by authors/artists "if requested." Art Director, Nanette Stevenson, will review an illustrator's work for possible use in author's texts.

How to Contact/Illustrators: Ms/illustration packages: Query first. Illustrations only: "appointment to show portfolio." Reports on art samples in 2 months. Original art work returned at job's completion.

Terms/Writers & Illustrators: Pays authors in advance royalties. Average advance payment "varies." Illustrators paid by advance and in royalties. Sends galleys to authors; dummies to illustrators. Books catalog, manuscript/artist's guidelines free on request.

Tips: "Discover your own voice and own story—and persevere." Looks for "something unusual, original, well-written. Fine art. Our needs change, but at this time, we are interested in receiving young fiction for the 4- to 10-year-old child. The genre (fantasy, contemporary, or historical fiction) is not so important as the story itself, and the spirited life the story allows its main character. We are also interested in receiving adolescent novels, particularly novels that contain regional spirit, such as a story about a young boy or girl written from a southern, southwestern, or northwestern perspective."

PIPPIN PRESS, 229 E. 85th St., Gracie Station, Box 92, New York NY 10028. (212)288-4920. Book publisher. Publisher/President: Barbara Francis. Publishes 6-8 picture books/year; 3 young reader titles/year. "Not interested in young adult books. Pippin Press produced its first list in the fall of 1988."

Fiction: Picture books: animal, fantasy, humorous. Young readers: fantasy, spy/mystery/adventure, humorous. Middle readers: fantasy, spy/mystery/adventure, humorous. Average word length: picture books—750-1,500; young readers—2,000-3,000; middle readers—3,000+. Recently published *An Autumn Tale*, by David Updike, illustrator, Robert Andrew Parker (ages 7-10, fantasy, picture book); *Nanny Noony and the Magic Spell*, by Edward Frascino (ages 4-8, humor, picture book).

Nonfiction: Picture books: animal. Young readers: biography, humorous. Recently published *I Did it With My Hatchet: A Story of George Washington*, by Robert Quackenbush.

How to Contact/Writers: Fiction/nonfiction: Query. SASE (IRC) for answer to query; Include Social Security number with submission. Reports on queries in 2-3 weeks; on mss in 6-8 weeks. Publishes a book 9-18 months after acceptance. Will consider simultaneous and photocopied submissions.

Illustration: Number of illustrations used for fiction: picture books—25-30; young readers—15-20; middle readers—8-10. Number of illustrations used for nonfiction: picture books—25-30; young readers—15-20; middle readers—15-20. Editorial will review an illustrator's work for possible use in author's texts.

How to Contact/Illustrators: Illustrations only: "Tear sheets, or xeroxes would be fine. I see illustrations by appointment." Reports on art samples only if interested. Original artwork returned at job's completion.

Terms/Writers & Illustrators: Pays authors in royalties based on retail price. Pay for illustrators: Royalty based on retail price. Sends galleys to authors; dummies to illustrators. "The illustrator prepares the dummy on PB; dummies for longer books prepared by the designer are submitted to the illustrator." Book catalog available for 6×9 SAE; manuscript/artist's guidelines for #10 SAE.

Tips: "Be thoroughly familiar with the market, what is being published and what sells. Visits to children's room at local libraries and to children's bookstores would be helpful. Read reviews in *The New York Times Book Review*, *The Booklist*, *Publishers Weekly*, *School Library Journal*." Looks for "humorous picture book story, humorous fiction for young readers, middle group. Children's books almost across the board are the fastest growing segment of the publishing industry. Exceptions include problem young adult novels, historical fiction."

PLAYERS PRESS, INC., Box 1132, Studio City CA 91604. (818)789-4980. Book publisher. Vice President/Editorial: R. W. Gordon. Publishes 2-10 young readers dramatic plays and musicals titles/year; 2-10 middle readers dramatic plays and musicals titles/year; 4-20 young adults dramatic plays and musicals titles/year. 12% of books by first-time authors; 1% of books from agented writers.

Fiction: "We use all categories (young readers, middle readers, young adults) but only for dramatic plays and/or musicals." Recently published *Rapunzel n' The Witch*, by William-Alan Landes (grades 3-6, musical play).

Nonfiction: "Any children's nonfiction all pertaining to the entertainment industry, performing arts and how-to for the theatrical arts only."

How to Contact/Writers: Fiction/nonfiction: Submit plays or outline/synopsis and sample chapters of entertainment books. SASE (IRC) for answer or return of mss. Reports on queries in 2-4 weeks; on mss in 12-16 weeks. Publishes a book 10 months after acceptance. Will consider simultaneous submissions.

Illustration: Number of illustrations used for fiction: young readers—1-10; middle readers—1-8. Number of illustrations used for nonfiction: young readers—15; middle readers—2; young adults—20. Associate Editor, M.E. Clapper, will review an illustrator's work for possible use in author's texts.

How to Contact/Illustrators: Ms/illustration packages: Query first. Illustrations only: Resume, tear sheets, slides, "SASE." Reports on art samples only if interested.

Terms/Writers & Illustrators: Pays authors in royalties of 2-20% based on retail price. Other method(s) of payment: "Negotiable." Factors used to determine final payment include color art, number of illustrations used. Pay for illustrators: by the project; royalties range from 2-5%. Sends galleys to authors; dummies to illustrators. Book catalog available for $1.

Tips: Looks for "plays/musicals and books pertaining to the performing arts only."

POCKET BOOKS (See Archway/Minstrel Books.)

THE PRESS OF MACDONALD & REINECKE, imprint of Padre Productions, Box 840, Arroyo Grande CA 93420-0840. (805)473-1947. Book publisher. Editor: Lachlan P. MacDonald. 80% of books by first-time authors; 5% of books from agented writers.

Fiction: Middle readers: fantasy, history, nature. Average length: middle reader—120-140 pages. Recently published *Joel in Tananar*, by Robert M. Walton (ages 8-14, fantasy adventure).

Nonfiction: Middle readers: biography, history, hobbies, nature/environment. Average length: middle readers—120 pages. Recently published *Pioneer California*, by Margaret Roberts (grades 4-9, history).

How to Contact/Writers: Fiction: Submit outline/synopsis and sample chapters. Nonfiction: Submit complete ms. SASE (IRC) for answer to query and/or return of mss. Reports on queries in 2 weeks; on mss in 16 weeks. Publishes a book 36 months after acceptance. Will consider simultaneous submissions.

Illustration: Number of illustrations used for fiction: middle readers—8. Number of illustrations used for nonfiction: middle readers—12. Editorial will review ms/illustration packages submitted by authors/artists; ms/illustration packages submitted by authors with illustrations done by separate artists; and illustrator's work for possible use in author's texts.

How to Contact/Illustrators: Illustrations only: Tear sheets. Reports on art samples only if interested.

Terms/Writers & Illustrators: Pays authors in royalties based on retail price. Other method(s) of payment: "Advance plus royalty." Average advance payment "varies." Additional payment for ms/illustration packages. Factors used to determine final payment include color art vs. black-and-white. Pay for separate authors and illustrators: "Separate contracts." Illustrators paid by the project. Sends galleys to authors; dummies to illustrators. Book catalogs for 9×12 SAE and 45¢ in first-class stamps. Manuscript guidelines/artist's guidelines for #10 SASE.

Tips: Writers: "Concentrate on nonfiction that recognizes changes in today's audience and includes minority and gender considerations without tokenism. The Press of Mac-Donald & Reinecke is devoted to highly selected works of drama, fiction, poetry and literary nonfiction. Juveniles must be suitable for 140-page books appealing to both boys and girls in the 8-14 year range of readers." Illustrators: "There is a desperate lack of realism by illustrators who can depict proportionate bodies and anatomy. The flood of torn-paper and poster junk is appalling." Looks for: "A book of historical nonfiction of U.S. regional interest with illustrations that have 19th Century elegance and realistic character representations, about topics that still matter today."

PRICE STERN SLOAN, 360 N. LaCienega Blvd., Los Angeles CA 90048. (213)657-6100. Book publisher. Publishes 6 picture books/year; 10 young reader titles/year; 15 middle reader titles/year. 65-70% of books by first-time authors; 35% of books from agented writers.

Fiction: Picture books: animal, contemporary, easy-to-read, spy/mystery/adventure. Young readers: animal, contemporary, easy-to-read, spy/mystery/adventure. Middle readers: animal, contemporary, easy-to-read, spy/mystery/adventure. Recently published *Adventures in the Solar System*, by Geoffrey Williams (ages 7-12, space adventure book and cassette); *Elephant Ann & How the First Circus Began*, by Jon Madian (ages 0-7, storybook); *Good Night Sleep Tight*, by Mary Cron (ages 0-7, storybook).

Nonfiction: Picture books, young readers, middle readers: animal, educational, history, hobbies, nature/environment, sports. Young adults: biography. Recently published *Since 1776*, by Paul C. Murphy (ages 11 and up, history); *Collecting Bugs & Things*, by Julia Moutran (ages 5 and up, science activities).

How to Contact/Writers: Fiction/nonfiction: Query. SASE (IRC) for answer to query. Reports on queries/mss in 3 months. Publishes a book 6-8 months after acceptance. Will consider simultaneous, photocopied, and computer printout submissions.

Illustration: Editorial will review ms/illustration packages submitted by authors/artists and ms/illustration packages submitted by authors with illustrations done by separate artists. Art Director, John Beach, will review an illustrator's work for possible use in author's texts.

How to Contact/Illustrators: Ms/illustration: Query first. Illustrations only: Resume, tear sheets, slides. Reports on art samples only if interested.

Terms/Writers & Illustrators: Pays authors in royalties based on net price. Sends galleys to authors; dummies to illustrators. Book catalog available for 9×12 SAE and 6 first-class stamps; manuscript guidelines for legal-size SAE; artist's guidelines for letter-size SAE and 1 first-class stamp.

Tips: "Avoid writing stories with themes that have been done over and over again. We are looking for books that teach as well as entertain. Subject areas include nature, science, how-to, wordplay for early readers, book and cassette ideas, activity books, and original storybooks."

PROFORMA BOOKS, Q.E.D. Press of Ann Arbor, Inc., Box 4312, Ann Arbor MI 48106. (313)994-0371. Book publisher. Marketing Manager: Dan Fox. Publishes 1 young adult title/year. 80% of books by first-time authors. Subsidy publishes 15%.

Fiction: Young readers: fairy tale. Young adults: contemporary, history, problem novels, fairy tale. Average word length: young readers—2,000-5,000; young adults—5,000-10,000. Recently published *The Princess and the Unicorn*, by Michele Gallatin (young readers, young adults, fairy tale).

Nonfiction: Average word length: young readers—5,000-10,000; young adults—10,000-15,000.

How to Contact/Writers: Fiction/nonfiction: Query; submit outline/synopsis and sample chapters. Report on queries in 6 weeks; mss in 8 weeks. Publishes a book 6 months after acceptance. Will consider simultaneous, photocopied, computer printout submissions and electronic submissions via disk or modem (Macintosh format).

Illustration: Number of illustrations used for fiction: Young adults—6. Editorial will review ms/illustration packages submitted by authors/artists; ms/illustration packages submitted by authors with illustrations done by separate artists; and an illustrator's work for possible use in author's texts.

How to Contact/Illustrators: Ms/illustration packages: Query. Reports on art samples in 3 weeks. Original artwork returned at job's completion.

Terms/Writers & Illustrators: Pays authors in royalties of 6-15% based on retail price. Sends galleys to authors; dummies to illustrators. Book catalog free on request.

Tips: Looks for: "Fairy tales for young children to adult allegory types."

THE PUTNAM & GROSSET GROUP (See Philomel Books.)

THE ROSEN PUBLISHING GROUP, 29 E. 21st St., New York NY 10010. (212)777-3017. Book publisher. Editorial Contact: Ruth Rosen. Publisher: Roger Rosen. Publishes 8 middle reader titles/year; 50 young adult titles/year. 50% of books by first-time authors; 3% of books from agented writers.

Nonfiction: Young readers: contemporary, easy-to-read, sports. Middle readers: contemporary, easy-to-read, sports, psychological self-help. Young adults: contemporary, east-to-read, sports, careers, psychological self-help. Average word length: young readers—8,000; middle readers—10,000; young adults—40,000. Recently published *Careers in Trucking*, by Donald Schauer (grade 8, vocational guidance); *Coping with Date Rape*, by Andrea Panot (grade 8, psychology, self-help); *Everything You Need to Know About Teen Suicide*, by Jay Schliefer (grade 4, psychology, self-help).

How to Contact/Writers: Nonfiction: Submit outline/synopsis and sample chapters. SASE (IRC) necessary for answer to query. Publishes a book 9 months after acceptance. Will consider simultaneous, photocopied, and computer printout submissions.

Illustration: Number of illustrations used for nonfiction: young readers—20; middle readers—10. Editorial will review ms/illustration packages submitted by authors/artists and ms/illustration packages submitted by authors with illustrations done by separate artists. Roger Rosen, will review an illustrator's work for possible use in author's texts.

How to Contact/Illustrators: Ms/illustration packages: 3 chapters of ms with 1 piece of final art. Illustrations only: Resume, tear sheets. Original artwork returned at job's completion.

Terms/Writers & Illustrators: Pays authors in royalties. Sends galleys to authors. Book catalog free on request.

Tips: "Target your manuscript to a specific age group and reading level and write for established series published by the house you are approaching."

ST. PAUL BOOKS AND MEDIA, Daughters of St. Paul, 50 St. Paul's Ave., Jamaica Plain, Boston MA 02130. (617)522-8911. Book publisher. Editor: Sister Anne Joan, fsp. Publishes 4 picture books/year; 2 young reader titles/year; 2-3 middle reader titles/year; 2 young adult titles/year. 25% of books by first-time authors.

Fiction: Picture books: animal, contemporary. Young readers: contemporary, history. Middle readers: contemporary, fantasy, history, problem novels. Young adults: contemporary, fantasy, history, problem novels. Average word length: picture books—500; young readers—1,500-3,000; middle readers—12,000; young adults—21,000. Recently published *Narrow Bartholomew*, by Koenig (young readers, contemporary).

Nonfiction: Picture books: religion. Young readers, middle readers, young adults: religious biography, religion. Average word length: picture books—500-750; young readers—1,800-3,000; middle readers—14,000; young adults—21,000. Recently published *It's Important*, by J. Hutson (preschool, picture book, education-religion); *Wait For Me*, by M. H. Wallace (middle readers, religious biography); *Poland's Noble Son*, by M. Mayer (middle readers, religious biography).

How to Contact/Writers: Fiction/nonfiction: Submit outline/synopsis and sample chapters. SASE (IRC) for return of ms. Reports on queries in 3-4 weeks; on mss in 4-8 weeks. Publishes a book 9-12 months after acceptance. Will consider computer printout submissions.

Illustration: Number of illustrations used for fiction: picture books—14; young readers—10; middle readers—8; young adults—6. Number of illustrations used for nonfiction: picture books—14; young readers—10; middle readers—8; young adults—8. Editorial will review ms/illustration packages submitted by authors/artists; ms/illustration packages submitted by authors with illustrations done by separate artists; and illustrator's work for possible use in author's texts. Style/size of illustration "varies according to the title. Re: colors, our scanner will not take fluorescents."

How to Contact/Illustrators: Ms/illustration packages: "Outline, sample chapters, one piece finished art, remainder roughs." Illustrations only: "Resume and tear sheets." Reports on art samples in 2 weeks.

Terms/Writers & Illustrators: Pays authors in royalties of 8-12% based on gross sales. Additional payment for ms/illustrations packages: "negotiable." Pay for separate authors and illustrators: "Royalties (based on gross sales) are divided. Usually does not" send galleys to authors or dummies to illustrators. Book catalog available for 9×11½ SAE and 3 first-class stamps; manuscript guidelines for legal-size SAE.

Tips: "We are a Roman Catholic publishing house looking for manuscripts (whether fiction or nonfiction) that communicate high moral, religious and family values. Lives of saints, Bible stories welcome, as well as historical or contemporary novels for children. In Catholic circles, a renewed interest in Saints. In general, high interest in allegorical fantasy, as well as stories that reflect attitudes and life situations children are deeply familiar with."

SANDLAPPER PUBLISHING CO., INC., 281 Amelia St., Box 1932, Orangeburg SC 29116. (803)531-1658. Book publisher. Editor: Nancy M. Drake. 10% of books by first-time authors.

Fiction: Middle readers: easy-to-read, spy/mystery/adventure. Young adults: contemporary, history. Recently published *Whopper!*, by Idella Bodie (middle readers).

Nonfiction: Young adults: biography, education, history, hobbies, nature/environment, sports. Recently published *The South Carolina Story*, by Anne Osborne (young adults to adults, history); *SC's Lowcountry: A Past Preserved*, by Halcomb/Messmer (adults, pictorial/history); *Dorn: Of the People*, by Dorn/Derks (adults, political/history).

How to Contact/Writers: Fiction/nonfiction: Submit outline/synopsis and sample chapters. SASE (IRC) for answer to query. Reports on queries in 1 week; on mss in 24 weeks. Publishes a book 24 months after acceptance. Will consider simultaneous and photocopied submissions.

Illustration: Number of illustrations used for fiction: picture books, young readers, middle readers, young adults—6/category. Number of illustrations used for nonfiction: picture books, young readers, middle readers, young adults—20/category. Editorial will review ms/illustration packages submitted by authors/artists; ms/illustration packages submitted by authors with illustrations done by separate artists; and an illustrator's work for possible use in author's texts.

How to Contact/Illustrators: Illustrations only: Resume, tear sheets, slides. Reports on art samples in 2 weeks. Original artwork returned at job's completion.

Terms/Writers & Illustrators: Pays authors in royalties. Illustrator paid by the project. Sends galleys to authors. Book catalog, manuscript guidelines free on request.

Tips: Looks for: "regional works on the south; history, literature, cuisine and culture."

SCOJTIA, PUBLISHING CO., INC., The Lion, 6457 Wilcox Station, Box 38002, Los Angeles CA 90038. Book publisher. Managing Editor: Patrique Quintahlen. Publishes 2 picture books/year; 1 young reader title/year; 1 middle reader title/year; 1 young adult title/year. 90% of books by first-time authors; 50% of books from agented writers.
Fiction: Picture books: animal, contemporary, easy-to-read. Young adults: history, problem novels, romance, science fiction, sports, spy/mystery/adventure. Average word length: picture books—2,000; young readers—3,000; middle readers—2,500; young adults—20,000.
How to Contact/Writers: Fiction/nonfiction: Query; submit outline/synopsis and sample chapters. SASE (IRC) for answer to query and/or return of ms. Reports on queries/mss in 4 months. Publishes a book 12 months after acceptance. Will consider simultaneous, photocopied and electronic submissions via disk or modem.
Illustration: Number of illustrations used for fiction and nonfiction: picture books—25; young readers—25; middle readers—8; young adults—8. Editorial will review ms/illustration packages submitted by authors/artists; ms/illustration packages submitted by authors with illustrations done by separate artists; and an illustrator's work for possible use in author's texts.
How to Contact/Illustrators: Ms/illustration packages: Query first. Illustrations only: Resume, tear sheets. Reports on art samples in 4 months. Original artwork returned at job's completion.
Terms/Writers & Illustrators: Pays authors in royalties of 4-8% based on retail price. Buys ms outright for $20-$200. Offers average advance payment of $500. Factors used to determine final payment include number of illustrations. Pay for separate authors and illustrators: According to the terms of contract for each, author's contract, illustrator's contract, for project. Pay for illustrators: By the project, $60-$600. Sends galleys to authors; dummies to illustrators.
Tips: Writers: "Children love action, characters that touch on emotions that they feel but cannot explain, except by play; and by pretending to be, for a moment, such likeable characters. Create realistic characters that children will love, even the child in all of us. There is a growing need for children's books for 12 and up that deal more with acceptable roles for children in the new American family, which children in movies—morally—don't always exemplify." Illustrators: "Be original, here it is necessary to remember that with your imagination you can do anything; but it is also important to be organized with a stock of your best work that you perfect and keep in a portfolio, work from strength, your best of your work (drawings/illustrations). Originality will spring best from here."

HAROLD SHAW PUBLISHERS, 388 Gundersen Dr., Box 567, Wheaton IL 60189. (312)665-6700. Book publisher. Dir. of Editorial Services: Ramona Cramer Tucker. Publishes 4 middle reader titles/year; 8 young adult titles/year. 10% of books by first-time authors; 5% of books from agented writers.
Nonfiction: Middle readers: religion, Bible studies. Young adults: religion, Bible studies. Average length: middle readers—32-46 pages.; young adults—64-120 pages. Recently published *In the Middle*, by Mary Kehle (middle readers, general title on divorce); *It's a Jungle in Here*, by Sandy and Dale Larsen (young adults, teen devotional); *God's Special Creation*, by Marlene LeFever (middle readers, camp study guide).
How to Contact/Writers: Nonfiction: Query. SASE (IRC) necessary for answer to query and/or return of ms. Reports on queries in 2-4 weeks; on mss in 4-6 weeks. Publishes a book 12 months after acceptance. Will consider simultaneous and photocopied submissions.
Illustration: Number of illustrations used for nonfiction: middle readers—12; young adults—12. Editorial will review ms/illustration packages submitted by authors/artists; ms/illustration packages submitted by authors with illustrations done by separate artists and an illustrator's work for possible use in author's texts.
How to Contact/Writers: Ms/illustration packages: Query first. Illustrations only: Re-

sume, sample of work (2-3). Reports on art samples in 4 weeks. Original artwork returned at job's completion.

Terms/Writers & Illustrators: Pays authors in royalties of 5-10% based on retail price. Buys ms outright for $500-$1,500. Factors used to determine final payment include color art vs. b&w and number of illustrations used. Pay for separate authors and illustrators: royalty or ms payment is split. Illustrators paid by the project. Sends galleys to authors. Book catalog available for SAE and $1.25; manuscript guidelines for SAE and 1 first-class stamp.

Tips: Writers: "Visit your bookstore. Read what is out on the market, and focus on doing it better! Read your stories to children and to adults. (You'll find children are the most honest)." Illustrators: "Visit bookstores and see what illustrations are on the market. Show your illustrations to children and see if they appeal to them first before contacting a publisher." Looks for "a study guide or a very unusual story which would make us change our minds about not picking up any more children's books! It (the children's book market) is growing bigger, but at the same time the quality has been going down (quality of writing and illustrations). Lasting books are being replaced by more chapbook-flimsy paperbooks."

SHOE TREE PRESS, McDonald Publishing Company, Inc., RD 2, Box 1162 Hemlock Rd., Columbia NJ 07832. (201)496-4441. Book publisher. President: Joyce McDonald. Published 1 young reader title each in 1986 and 1987; 2 middle reader titles in 1986, 1 in 1988; 1 young adult title in 1987. 25% of books by first-time authors; 25% of books from agented writers.

Fiction: Young readers: animal, easy-to-read. Middle readers: animal, contemporary, history, problems novels, humor. Average word length: young readers—1,500-7,500; middle readers—20,000-35,000; young adults—50,000-75,000. Recently published *Best Friends, Hands Down*, by Terry Wolfe Phelan (middle readers, contemporary fiction); *Summer Captive*, by Penny Pollock (young adults, contemporary); *Aaron and the Green Mt. Boys*, by Patricia Lee Gauch (easy reader for young readers).

Nonfiction: Young readers: animal, history. Middle readers: animal, biography, history, hobbies, music/dance, nature/environment, reference. Young adults: reference. Average word length: young readers—1,500-7,500; middle readers—30,000-45,000; young adults—35,000-75,000. Recently published *Market Guide for Young Writers*, by Kathy Henderson (ages 10 and up, reference).

How to Contact/Writers: Fiction/nonfiction: Query; all unsolicited mss returned unopened. SASE (IRC) for answer to query. Reports on queries in 4 weeks; on mss in 12 weeks. Publishes a book 18-24 months after acceptance. Will consider simultaneous and photocopied submissions.

Illustration: Number of illustrations used for fiction and nonfiction: young readers—12-30; middle readers—12-30. Editorial will review ms/illustration packages submitted by authors/artists; ms/illustration packages submitted by authors with illustrations done by separate artists; and an illustrator's work for possible use in author's texts.

How to Contact/Illustrators: Ms/illustration packages: Query first. Illustrations only: Resume/tear sheets. Reports on art samples only if interested. Original artwork returned at job's completion.

Terms/Writers & Illustrators: Pays authors in royalties of 5-15% based on "sometimes retail, sometimes wholesale, it varies with author." Pay for illustrators: By the project; royalties range from 5-8% based on retail price. Sends galleys to authors; dummies to illustrators.

Tips: "Avoid getting caught up in market trends. Write about what you know, and write it from the heart." Looks for "middle years fiction and nonfiction, primarily nonfiction."

SIMON & PIERRE PUBLISHING CO. LTD., Box 39, Stn. J, Toronto Ontario, M4J 4X8 Canada. (416)463-0313. Book publisher. Director of Operations: Jean Paton. Publishes 1 young reader title/year; "occasional" middle reader/young adult titles. 80% of books by first-time authors.
Fiction: "Interested in drama and drama-related plays that have had productions (Canadian)."
Nonfiction: "Drama", dance. Average length: "64 pages." Recently published *Nature's Big Top*, by Lola Sneyd (ages 5-10, poetry); *Let's Hear It For Christmas* and *The Naciwonki Cap*, 2 plays in 1 book, by Beth McMaster (ages 5-up).
How to Contact/Writers: Nonfiction: Query; submit complete ms, "if short." SASE (IRC) for return of ms. Reports on queries in 4 weeks; on mss in 12 weeks. Publishes a book 12-16 months after acceptance. Will consider simultaneous and photocopied submissions.
Terms/Writers & Illustrators: Pays authors in royalties. Sends galleys to authors. Book catalog free on request.
Tips: "Examine publisher's books in library to ascertain which company is publishing similar books to the type you are writing. Enclose a resume with details of any previous publication and information on why you are expert on this topic (e.g., teacher or dramatist)."

SIMON & SCHUSTER (See Julian Messner.)

SKYLARK/BOOKS FOR YOUNG READERS, imprint of Bantam Books Inc., 666 Fifth Ave., New York NY 10103. Editorial Contact: Judy Gitenstein.
Fiction: Middle readers: contemporary, fantasy, historical, spy/mystery/adventure.
How to Contact/Writers: Fiction: Submit outline/synopsis and sample chapters; "You will get a form rejection if your ms is not for us. It isn't you; we don't have time to comment on them all." SASE (IRC) for answer to query and/or return of mss.
Terms/Writers & Illustrators: Pays authors in royalties of 6-8% based on retail price.

STANDARD PUBLISHING, 8121 Hamilton Ave., Cincinnati OH 45231. (513)931-4050. Book publisher. Director: Mark Plunkett. Publishes 25 picture books/year; 4 young reader titles/year; 8 middle reader titles/year; 4 young adult titles/year. 25% of books by first-time authors; 1% of books from agented writers.
Fiction: Picture books: animal. Young readers: easy-to-read. Middle readers: contemporary, sports. Young adults: contemporary, problem novels. Average word length: picture books—400; young readers—1,000; middle readers—25,000; young adults—40,000. Recently published *Happy Birthday*, by Jane Sorenson (middle readers, contemporary fiction); *Summer's Quest*, by Susanne Elliott (young adults, contemporary); *Wheeler's Big Break*, by Daniel Schantz (middle readers, contemporary).
Nonfiction: Picture books: animal, religion. Young readers, middle readers, young adults: religion. Average word length: picture books—400; young readers—1,000; middle readers—25,000; young adults—40,000. Recently published *The Little Lost Sheep*, by Marilyn Lindsay (picture book, religious); *Thank You God, for Christmas*, by Henrietta Gambill (picture book, religious); *Seven Special Days*, by Henrietta Gambill (picture book, religious).
How to Contact/Writers: Fiction/nonfiction: Query. SASE (IRC) for return of ms. Reports on queries in 3 weeks; on mss in 12 weeks. Publishes a book 18 months after acceptance. Will consider simultaneous, photocopied, computer printout and electronic submissions via disk or modem.
Illustration: Number of illustrations used for fiction: picture books—24; young readers—24; middle readers—12; young adults—12. Number of illustrations used for nonfiction: picture books—24. Editorial will review ms/illustration packages submitted by authors/artists and ms/illustration packages submitted by authors with illustrations done

by separate artists. Art Director, Frank Sutton, will review an illustrator's work for possible use in author's texts.

How to Contact/Illustrators: Ms/illustration packages: "Query." Illustrations only: "Tear sheets and resume." Reports on art samples in 3 weeks.

Terms/Writers & Illustrators: Pays authors in royalties of 5-12% based on wholesale price. Buys ms outright for $250-$1,000. Offers average advance payment of $250. Sends galleys to authors. Books catalog available for 8½×11 SAE; manuscript guidelines for letter-size SAE.

Tips: "When writing children's books, make the vocabulary level correct for the age you plan to reach. Watch spelling and sentence structure. Keep your material true to the Bible. Be accurate in quoting Scriptures and references." Looks for: "picture books."

STAR BOOKS, INC., 408 Pearson St., Wilson NC 27893. (919)237-1591. Editorial Contact: Irene Burk Harrell. "We are still a new and growing company. Although we have not yet published any children's books, it is our intention to do so as soon as the right ones come along. We have reviewed a number of manuscripts but have so far accepted only one, a legend, suitable for middle readers and up."

Fiction/Nonfiction: "Manuscripts must be somehow strongly related to the good news of Jesus Christ." Recently published *The Cat That Barked* (fiction).

How to Contact/Writers: Submit complete ms. SASE for return of ms; include Social Security number. Reports on queries in 1-2 weeks; mss in 4-8 weeks. Publishes a book 6 months after acceptance ("longer if extensive editing needed"). Will consider photocopied, computer printout submissions "if readily legible, nice dark ribbon."

Illustration: Editorial will review ms/illustration packages submitted by authors/artists; ms/illustration packages submitted by authors with illustrations done by separate artists; and illustrator's work for possible use in author's texts. "At present, we prefer informal black and white line art. As finances improve, we'll be interested in color."

How to Contact/Illustrators: Ms/illustration packages: send whole ms, 1-3 roughs of art, tear sheets. Reports on art samples within a month. Original artwork returned at job's completion.

Terms/Writers & Illustrators: Pay: "We issue contract for the whole (ms/illustration) package." Sends galleys to authors. Book catalog/guidelines available for #10 SAE and 2 first-class stamps.

Tips: "We want biblical values, conversation that sounds real, characters that come alive, stories with 'behavior modification' strengths. We want illustrations that are 'appealing.' "

STARFIRE, imprint of Bantam Books Inc., 666 Fifth Ave., New York NY 10103. (212)765-6500. Editorial Director: Beverly Horowitz. Publishes 48-60 adult titles/year.

Fiction: Young adults: contemporary, fantasy, historical novels, problem novels, romance, science fiction, spy/mystery/adventure.

How to Contact/Writers: Fiction: Query, submit outline/synopsis and sample chapters, cover letter. SASE (IRC) for answer to query and/or return of ms.

Terms/Writers & Illustrators: Pays authors in royalties of 6-8% based on retail price. Manuscript guidelines free on request.

STERLING PUBLISHING CO., INC., 2 Park Ave., New York NY 10016. (212)532-7160. Book publisher. Acquisitions Editor: Sheila Anne Barry. Publishes 2 picture books/year; 30 middle reader titles/year. 15% of books by first-time authors.

Nonfiction: Middle readers: animal, hobbies, nature/environment, sports, humor. "Since our books are highly illustrated, word length is seldom the point. Most are 96-128 pages." Recently published *World's Best Sports Riddles and Jokes*, by Joseph Rosenbloom (middle readers, humor); *World's Best True Ghost Stories*, by C.B. Colby (middle readers-young adults, very short anecdotes); *Amazing Pranks and Blunders*, by Peter Eldin (middle readers, humor).

How to Contact/Writers: SASE (IRC) for answer to query and/or return of mss. Reports on queries in 2 weeks; on mss in 6-8 weeks. Publishes a book 6-12 months after acceptance. Will consider simultaneous and photocopied submissions.

Illustration: Number of illustrations used for nonfiction: middle readers—approximately 60. Editorial will review ms/illustration packages submitted by authors/artists; ms/illustration packages submitted by authors with illustrations done by separate artists; and an illustrator's work for possible use in author's texts.

How to Contact/Illustrators: Ms/illustration packages: "Query first." Illustrations only: "Send sample photocopies of line drawings." Original artwork returned at job's completion "if desired, but usually held for future needs."

Terms/Writers & Illustrators: Pays authors in royalties of up to 10% "standard terms, no sliding scale, varies according to edition." Sends galleys to authors; dummies to illustrators. Manuscript guidelines for SAE.

Tips: Looks for: "Humor, hobbies, science books for middle-school children." Also, "mysterious occurrences, fun and games books."

THUNDER CREEK PUBLISHING CO-OP LTD. (See Coteau Books Ltd.)

TICKNOR & FIELDS (See Clarion Books.)

TOM THUMB MUSIC, Rhythms Productions, Box 34485, Los Angeles CA 90034. (213)836-4678. Audio/book packages. President: R. S. White. Publishes 3-6 picture books/year.

Fiction: "Children's educational stories—can be fantasy." Average length: "20-25 minute reading time on cassette." Recently published *Mr. Windbag in Shape Land, Mr. Windbag in Shrink Land, Mr. Windbag in The Line Country*, all by Ruth White (read-along, musical stories with songs. Educational concepts in fantasy.).

How to Contact/Writers: Fiction: Submit outline/synopsis and sample chapters. SASE (IRC) for answer to query. Reports on queries in 1 month. Will consider simultaneous and photocopied submissions.

Illustration: Number of illustrations used for fiction: picture books—12-24. Editorial will review ms/illustration packages submitted by authors/artists; ms/illustration packages submitted by authors with illustrations done by separate artists; and illustrator's work for possible use in author's texts.

How to Contact/Illustrators: Ms/illustrations: "Sample photocopy of an illustration showing artist's style." Illustrations only: "Resume and tear sheets or photocopies." Reports on art samples in 1 month.

Terms/Writers & Illustrators: Buys ms outright. Pay for separate authors and illustrators: "Writer—royalty; illustrator—outright purchase." Illustrators paid by the project. Sends galleys to authors.

Tips: Looks for: "Educationally oriented stories (we like musical stories the most) and illustrations that have appeal for preschool children. We use animators often for illustrations."

TRILLIUM PRESS, Box 209, Monroe NY 10950. (914)783-2999. Book publisher. Editorial Contact: William Neumann. Publishes 70 picture books, young readers, middle readers, young adult titles/year. 50% of books by first-time authors.

How to Contact/Writers: Fiction: Submit complete ms. Nonfiction: Query; submit complete ms. SASE (IRC) for answer to query and/or return of mss. Reports on queries in 1 week; on mss in 8 weeks. Publishes a book 6 months after acceptance. Will consider photocopied and computer printout submissions.

Illustration: Editorial will review ms/illustration packages submitted by authors/artists;

ms/illustration packages submitted by authors with illustrations done by separate artists; and illustrator's work for possible use in author's texts.

Terms/Writers & Illustrators: Pays authors in royalties. Buys ms outright. Sends galleys to authors; dummies to illustrators. Book catalog available for 9 × 12 SAE and 65¢ first-class stamp; manuscript guidelines for #10 SAE and 1 first-class stamp.

TWENTY-FIRST CENTURY BOOKS, 38 S. Market St., Frederick MD 21701. (301)698-0210. Book publisher. Editor: Gretchen Super. Publishes 5-10 young reader titles/year; 5-10 middle reader titles/year. 50% of books by first-time authors; 50% of books from agented writers.

Fiction: Recently published *Business is Looking Up*, *Friends for Life*, *Your Turn at Bat*, by Barbara Aiello and Jeffrey Shulman (middle readers, combination fiction and nonfiction; part of the Kids on the Block Book Series).

Nonfiction: Young readers, middle readers: biography, history, hobbies, nature/environment, geography, travel. Recently publishing a series on drug use and abuse, September 1989 (middle readers); a series on the civil rights movement, September 1989 (middle readers).

How to Contact/Writers: Fiction: Submit complete ms. Nonfiction: Submit outline/synopsis and sample chapters. SASE (IRC) for answer to query and/or return of ms. Reports on queries in 9-12 months; on mss in 6-9 months. Publishes a book 9-12 months after acceptance. Will consider simultaneous, photocopied, computer printout and electronic submissions via disk or modem.

Illustration: Number of illustrations used for fiction/nonfiction: young readers—12; middle readers—12. Editorial will review ms/illustration packages submitted by authors/artists; ms/illustration packages submitted by authors with illustrations done by separate artists; and illustrator's work for possible use in author's texts.

How to Contact/Illustrators: Ms/illustrators: "Outline, synopsis, sample chapters with one piece final art and roughs." Illustrators only: "Resume and tear sheets." Reports on art samples only if interested, "will keep samples on file." Original artwork returned at job's completion.

Terms/Writers & Illustrators: Pays authors in royalties of 7-15% based on retail price. Offers average advance payment of $2,000. Factors used to determine final payment include "color art vs. black-and-white, number of illustrations used, plus experience and technique used." Pay for separate authors and illustrators: "Split royalty in relation to text/illustration ratio." Sends galleys to authors; dummies to illustrators.

Tips: Writers: "Get as much experience on the small scale as possible, i.e., magazines. Find out about a publisher before submitting. We publish nonfiction and don't pay much attention to fiction. Always send SASE if you expect response. Let a variety of people, including children, read and comment on your manuscript." Illustrators: "Become knowledgeable about the printing process." Looks for: "Young and middle readers nonfiction that fits into the series format." There is an "increase in good nonfiction for all age groups. Increased interest and knowledge in children's books from parents."

UNITED METHODIST PUBLISHING HOUSE (See Abingdon Press.)

VOYAGER PAPERBACKS (See Harcourt Brace Jovanovich.)

WALKER AND CO., div. of Walker Publishing Co. Inc., 720 Fifth Ave., New York NY 10019. (212)265-3632. Book publisher. Editor-in-Chief: Amy C. Shields. Publishes 5 picture books/year; 10 young reader titles/year; 10 middle reader titles/year; 15 young adult titles/year. 15% of books by first-time authors; 65% of books from agented writers.

Fiction: Picture books: animal, contemporary, easy-to-read, fantasy, history. Young readers: animal, contemporary. Middle readers: animal, contemporary, fantasy, science fiction, sports, spy/mystery/adventure. Young adults: animal, contemporary, fantasy, history, problem novels, romance, science fiction, sports, spy/mystery/adventure. Recently published *Whale Brother*, by B. Steiner (picture book, science and nature); *The Revenge of HoTai*, by Hoobler (young adults, novel); *A Place of Silver Silence*, by Mayhar (young adults, science fiction).

Nonfiction: Picture books, young readers, middle readers, young adults: animal, biography, education, history, hobbies, music/dance, nature/environment, religion, sports. Recently published *A First Look At Horned Animals*, by Selsam/Hunt (young readers, science and nature); *From Abenaki to Zuni*, by Wolfson (young adults, American history); *Chuck Yeager, A Bio*, by Levinson (young adults, biography).

How to Contact/Writers: Fiction/nonfiction: Submit outline/synopsis and sample chapters. SASE (IRC) for return of ms. Report on queries/mss in 8-10 weeks. Publishes a book 12 months after acceptance. Will consider simultaneous, photocopied, and computer printout submissions.

Illustration: Number of illustrations used for fiction: picture books—32-48; young readers—30; middle readers—30. Number of illustrations used for nonfiction: picture books—32-48; young readers—20-30; middle readers—20-30; young adults—20-30. Editorial will review ms/illustration packages submitted by authors/artists; ms/illustration packages submitted by authors with illustrations done by separate artists; and illustrator's work for possible use in author's texts.

How to Contact/Illustrators: Ms/illustration packages: 5 chapters of ms with 1 piece of final art, remainder roughs. Illustrations only: "Tear sheets." Reports on art samples only if interested. Original artwork returned at job's completion.

Terms/Writers & Illustrators: Pays authors in royalties of 5-10% based on wholesale price "depends on contract." Offers average advance payment of $2,000-$4,000. Factors used to determine final payment include "quality, name recognition." Pay for separate authors and illustrators: "If a picture book, royalty is split 50/50. Beyond that we try to make equitable arrangements." Pay for illustrators: By the project, $500-$2,000; royalties from 10%. Sends galleys to authors; blues to illustrators. Book catalog available for 8½×11 SASE; manuscript guidelines for SASE.

Tips: Writers: "Keep writing, keep trying. Don't take rejections personally and try to consider them objectively. If 10 publishers reject a work, put it aside and look at it again after a month. Can it be improved?" Illustrators: "Have a well-rounded portfolio with different styles." Looks for: "Science and nature series for young and middle readers. Good contemporary young adult fiction."

WALKER PUBLISHING CO. INC. (See Walker & Co.)

WATERFRONT BOOKS, 98 Brookes Ave., Burlington VT 05401. (802)658-7477. Book publisher. Publisher: Sherrill N. Musty. 100% of books by first-time authors.

Fiction: Picture books, young readers, middle readers, young adults: mental health, family/parenting, health, special issues involving barriers to learning in children. Recently published *JOSH: A Boy With Dyslexia*, by Caroline Janover (ages 8-12, paperback).

Nonfiction: Picture books, young readers, middle readers, young adults: education, guidance, health, mental health, social issues. "We publish books for both children and adults on any subject that helps to lower barriers to learning in children: mental health, family/parenting, education, and social issues." Recently published *Changing Families*, by David Fassler, M.D., Michele Lash, A.T.R., Sally B. Ives, Ph.D. (ages 4-12, paper and plastic comb binding).

How to Contact/Writers: Fiction/nonfiction: Query. SASE (IRC) for answer to query. Reports on queries in 2 weeks; on mss in 6 weeks. Publishes a book 6 months after acceptance. Will consider photocopied and computer printout submissions.

Illustration: Editorial will review ms/illustration packages submitted by authors/artists and ms/illustration packages submitted by authors with illustrations done by separate artists.

How to Contact/Illustrators: Ms/illustration packages: Query first. Illustrations only: Resume, tear sheets. Reports on art samples only if interested.

Terms/Writers & Illustrators: Pays authors in royalties of 10-15% based on wholesale price. Pays illustrators by the job. Additional payment for ms/illustration packages: Negotiable. Factors used to determine final payment: Number of illustrations used. Pay for separate authors and illustrators: "amount is negotiable but it would be within industry standards." Sends galleys to authors; dummies to illustrators. Book catalog available for #10 SAE and 1 first-class stamp.

Tips: "Have your manuscript thoroughly reviewed and even copy edited, if necessary. If you are writing about a special subject, have a well-qualified professional in the field review it for accuracy and appropriateness. It always helps to get some testimonials before submitting it to a publisher. The publisher then knows she/he is dealing with something worthwhile."

FRANKLIN WATTS, INC. (See Orchard Books.)

WESTERN PRODUCER PRAIRIE BOOKS, Box 2500, Saskatoon SK S7K 2C4 Canada. (306)665-3548. Book publisher. Editorial Director: Jane McHughen. Publishes 1 middle reader title/year; 1 young adult title/year. 80% of books by first-time authors.

Fiction: Middle readers, young adults: contemporary, fantasy, history, problem novels, sports. Average word length: middle readers—40,000; young adults—50,000. Recently published *A Question of Courage*, by Irene Morck (young adults, contemporary); *The Doll*, by Cora Taylor (middle readers, fantasy/history); *Last Chance Summer*, by Diana Wieler (young adults, problem).

How to Contact/Writers: Fiction: Submit outline/synopsis and sample chapters. SASE (IRC) for return of ms. Reports on queries in 4 weeks; on mss in 8-12 weeks. Publishes a book 12 months after acceptance. Will consider simultaneous (if we are advised they are simultaneous), photocopied, and computer printout submissions (provided they are clear).

Terms/Writers & Illustrators: Pays authors in royalties of 10% based on retail price. Offers average advance payment of $1,000. Sends galleys to authors. Book catalog, manuscript guidelines free on request.

Tips: "Submit to publishers who have a strong list in the genre of your manuscripts." Looks for ms "with a Canadian connection, strong descriptions of settings, realistic dialogue, and development of the main character during the course of the story."

JANE YOLEN BOOKS (See Harcourt Brace Jovanovich.)

Magazine Publishers

Magazine publishing for the juvenile market offers good opportunities for writers and illustrators because of the diversity of styles and subject matter. Publications listed in this section comprise a vast range of needs for fiction and nonfiction, both of which use illustrations, aimed at preschool, young readers (ages 5-8), middle readers (ages 9-11), and young adults (ages 12 and up).

Some of the magazine publishers listed here include religious denominations which use their publications to provide moral guidance to readers. As you study such listings, however, keep in mind most editors' warnings not to write or illustrate "preachy" material. Most of these publications use entertaining and/or human-interest pieces to make their religious points.

A large part of the juvenile magazine market consists of educational magazines such as *Highlights for Children, 3-2-1 Contact* and *Careers* which are listed here. Each is designed for a specific age group, but all offer valuable advice and information in an entertaining, thought-provoking style. If you have a specialty in a certain field of science, sport, art or craft, a how-to article may be appropriate. Such needs will appear under the "Nonfiction" subhead of each listing.

There is also a celebrity-oriented magazine, Scotland-based *Jackie*, and nature magazines like *Ranger Rick* and National Geographic *World* that appeal to writers/illustrators interested in the subject.

Many of the magazines for children and teens are open to new writers. Religious magazines, because of limited budgets, may not always attract more established writers and are open to beginning writers. If you are new at writing or have just started drawing for the juvenile market, try submitting first to those markets which are lower paying or pay in contributor copies only. Half the battle when trying to become an established writer or illustrator is to accumulate enough published pieces to prove to more lucrative markets that you have marketable writing and/or illustration talents.

Research your markets

Each listing in this section will specify whether sample copies are available (some may not be found at the newsstand), and whether writer's and/or illustrator's guidelines can be obtained as well. You can save yourself, as well as the editor, a lot of wasted time by determining upfront if your idea is the kind that will serve the magazine's readers. Many editors will also want some input on directing the slant of an article. Read the listings to determine if illustration/text packages are considered as well. Many articles beg the use of illustrations or photography to further educate the reader or to emphasize important points. Such illustration/text packages could save the editor the time of having to find artwork that coincides with a written piece. For publications, in general, there is more emphasis on the visual because children, influenced by TV-watching, have become accustomed to more graphics and less copy.

Study each listing carefully. Also, be aware of whether the editor requires a query prior to submitting a complete manuscript (or ms as it is referred to in the listings). Refer to The Business of Children's Writing and Illustrating at the beginning of this book to learn the mechanics of writing a query letter, the proper form for submitting a manuscript, methods of tracking expenses and income, as well as information on rights commonly purchased by publications. There is also a discussion of ways to market your work in this competitive field. Knowledge of business and marketing skills, as well as understanding how a copyright can protect you, are as important to you as good research and writing and illustrating skills.

The best ways to keep abreast of any new titles that appear between editions of *Children's Writer's & Illustrator's Market* are to study your local bookstores and newsstands for new magazines as well as checking at the library.

AIM MAGAZINE, America's Intercultural Magazine, AIM Publishing Company, Box 20554, Chicago IL 60620. (312)874-6184. Articles Editor: Ruth Apilado. Fiction Editor: Mark Boone. Art Director: Bill Jackson. Quarterly magazine. Circ. 8,000. Readers are high school, college students, teachers, adults interested in helping, through the written word, to create a more equitable world. 15% of material aimed at juvenile audience.
Fiction: Young adults: history; "stories with social significance." Wants stories that teach children people are more alike than they are different. Does not want to see religious fiction. Buys 20 mss/year. Average word length: 1,000-4,000. Byline given.
Nonfiction: Young adults: interview/profile; "stuff with social significance." Does not want to see religious nonfiction. Buys 20 mss/year. Average word length: 500-2,000. Byline given.
How to Contact/Writers: Fiction: Send complete ms. Nonfiction: Query with published clips. SASE (IRC) for return of ms. Reports on queries/mss in 1 month. Will consider simultaneous and photocopied submissions.
Illustration: Buys 20 illustrations/issue. Preferred theme or style: Overcoming social injustices through nonviolent means. Will review ms/illustration packages submitted by authors/artists; ms/illustration packages submitted by authors with illustrations done by separate artists; illustrator's work for possible use with fiction/nonfiction articles.
How to Contact/Illustrators: Ms/illustration packages: Query first. Illustrations only: "Send examples of art, ask for a job." Reports on art samples in 2 months. Original art work returned at job's completion "if desired."
Terms/Writers & Illustrators: Pays on publication. Buys first North American serial rights. Publication not copyrighted. Pays $5-25 for assigned/unsolicited articles. Pays in contributor copies if copies are requested. Pays $5-25/b&w cover illustration. Sample copy $3.
Tips: "Always type, proofed. We need material of social significance, stuff that will help promote racial harmony and peace."

ANIMAL WORLD, RSPCA, Causeway, Horsham West Sussex RH12 1HG England. 0403-64181. Articles/Fiction Editor: Elizabeth Winson. Bimonthly magazine. Circ. 50,000. Magazine contains fiction/nonfiction containing some animal welfare message ages 5-17. Not anthropomorphic. 100% of material aimed at juvenile audience.
Fiction: Young readers, young adults: animal. Does not want to see anthropomorphic material. Buys 30 mss/year. Average word length: 600-1,000. Byline given.
Nonfiction: Young readers, young adults: animal. Does not want to see too technical or anthropomorphic material. Buys 30 mss/year. Average word length: 600-1,000. Byline given.
How to Contact/Writers: Fiction/nonfiction: Send complete ms. SASE (IRC) for re-

turn of ms. Reports on queries in 2 weeks; mss in 6 months. Will consider simultaneous, photocopied, and computer printout submissions.

Terms/Writers & Illustrators: Pays on publication. Buys first North American serial rights. Pays 8-18 pounds (English currency) for assigned/unsolicited articles. Pays in contributor copies "if under 16 years of age." Pays 6-36 pounds (English currency) for ms/illustration packages. Pays 20 pounds (English currency)/color cover; 6-8 pounds/ b&w inside illustration; 8-12 pounds/color inside illustration. Sample copy free with SAE and first class stamp (IRC's).

Tips: "Study the magazine and context—stay away from 'CAT' and 'DOG' stories as these are too common."

THE APPLE BLOSSOM CONNECTION, Peak Output Unlimited, Box 325, Stacyville IA 50476. (515)737-2269. Articles Editor/Art Director: Mary M. Blake. Fiction Editor: J. D. Scheneman. Monthly magazine. "The Apple Blossom Connection showcases the works of writers of all experience levels. Each issue contains poetry, fiction and nonfiction of general interest. We sometimes include one-act drama. Fresh, new, original works are preferred to reprints." 30% of material aimed at juvenile audience.

Fiction: Picture material, young readers, middle readers, young adults: animal, contemporary, fantasy, history, humorous, problem solving, religious, romance, science fiction, sports, spy/mystery/adventure. Does not want to see erotic, insensitive fiction; don't poke fun at minorities, including the overweight. Byline given.

Nonfiction: Picture material, young readers, middle readers, young adults: animal, history, how-to, humorous, interview/profile, problem solving, religious, travel. Does not want to see erotic, insensitive, prejudicial, anti-minority nonfiction. Byline given.

How to Contact/Writers: Fiction/nonfiction: Send complete ms. SASE (IRC) for answer to query and return of ms; include Social Security number with submission. Report on queries/mss in 8-12 weeks. Will consider photocopied and computer printout submissions.

Illustration: Will review ms/illustration packages by authors/artists; ms/illustration packages submitted by authors with illustrations done by separate artists; illustrator's work for possible use with fiction/nonfiction articles.

How to Contact/Illustrators: Ms/illustration packages: Query with samples. Illustrations only: Resume with samples. Reports on art samples in 2-4 weeks. Original artwork returned at job's completion.

Terms/Writers & Illustrators: Buys first North American serial rights; first rights; one-time rights; second serial (reprint rights). "Lowest payment is 1 copy and $1 and byline for The Apple Blossom Connection." Pays $10-50/b&w cover illustration; $10-75/color (cover); $1-35/b&w (inside); $1-50/color (inside). Sample copy $5. Writer's guidelines for SAE and 1 first-class stamp.

Tips: Writers: "Be patient; follow guidelines; don't rely on guidelines given in other publications unless it's a paid advertisement from the source. Use current guidelines direct from the publisher. Fiction and poetry open to freelance writers. Know your audience." Illustrators: "Submit quality samples; give some idea of the payment you require. Don't overlook the little presses. Cartoons/illustrations must be clean and camera-ready; no pencil sketches; nothing your mother would be ashamed you published."

BRILLIANT STAR, National Spiritual Assembly of the Baha' is of the U.S., 2512 Allegheny Dr., Chattanooga TN 37421. Articles/Fiction Editor: Deborah L. Bley. Art Director: Ms. Pepper Oldziey. Bimonthly magazine. Circ. 2,200. We look for "sensitivity to multi-racial, multi-cultural audience and a commitment to assisting children understand the oneness of the human family." 10% of material aimed at juvenile audience.

Fiction: Picture material: animal. Young readers, middle readers: animal, fantasy, history, humorous, problem solving, spy/mystery/adventure. Does not want to see material related to traditional Christian holidays or to secular holidays. Nothing that pontificates! Buys 20 mss/year. Average word length: 750-1,500. Byline given.

Nonfiction: Picture material: animal, history, travel. Young readers, middle readers: animal, history, how-to, humorous, interview/profile, problem solving, travel. Does not want to see crafts or activities specific to holidays. Buys 12-15 mss/year. Average word length: 500-1,000. Byline given.

How to Contact/Writers: Fiction/nonfiction: Send complete ms. SASE (IRC) for return of ms. Report on mss in 6-10 weeks. Will consider simultaneous, photocopied, and computer printout submissions.

Illustration: "Illustration assignments made after layout and type-setting done.'" Will review ms/illustration packages by authors/artists "but must understand that we finalize after layout;'" ms/illustration packages submitted by authors with illustrations done by separate artists; illustrators work for possible use with fiction/nonfiction articles. Works on assignment only.

How to Contact/Illustrators: Ms/illustration packages: Prefer samples of illustration sent to art director separate from mss. Illustrations only: Resume, tear sheets, slides, photos. Reports on art samples in 1-2 months. Original artwork returned at job's completion "only if specifically requested by artist."

Terms/Writers & Illustrators: Provides 1 complimentary copy of issue in which work appears. Sample copy with 9x12 SAE and 5 oz. worth of postage; writer's/illustrator's guidelines free with business SAE and 2 oz. worth of postage.

Tips: Writers: "'Have a story to tell! Make sure you have a conflict or problem to be resolved by the characters that give energy and life to the story. General Editorial office is open to fiction, articles, activities.'" Illustrators: "'Don't be too cute. Get past the one thing you like to draw best and be ready to expand your range. Really look at other illustrator's work for variety and use of space. Art director open to review general submissions. Need artists who can illustrate diversity of peoples without stereotyping and in a sensitive way that affirms the beauty of different racial characteristics."

CALLI'S TALES, Box 1224, Palmetto FL 34220. (813)722-2202. Articles/Fiction Editor, Art Director: Annice E. Hunt. Quarterly magazine. Circ. 100. Magazine for animal lovers of all ages. 25% of material aimed at juvenile audience.

Fiction: Young readers: animal. Does not want to see religious material. Buys 20 mss/year. Average word length: 250-800. Byline given.

Nonfiction: Young readers: animal, interview/profile. Does not want to see religious material. Buys 25 mss/year. Average word length: 250-800. Byline given.

How to Contact/Writers: Fiction/nonfiction: Send complete ms. SASE (IRC) for answer to query and return of ms. Reports on queries/mss in 3 months. Will consider simultaneous, photocopied, and computer printout submissions.

Illustration: Buys 4-6 illustrations/issue; buys 30 illustrations/year. Will review an illustrator's work for possible use with fiction/nonfiction articles and columns by other authors.

How to Contact/Illustrators: Ms/illustration packages: Send complete ms. Illustrations only: Send tear sheets. Reports on art samples in 3 months.

Terms/Writers & Illustrators: Pays on publication. Buys one-time rights. Pays in one free copy of issue. Sample copy $2; writer's/illustrator's guidelines free with SAE and first-class stamps.

Tips: "Read a sample first. Keep revising."

CAREERS, E.M. Guild, 1001 Avenue of the Americas, New York NY 10018. (212)354-8877. Editor-in-Chief: Lois Cantwell. Managing Editor: Don Rauf. Art Director: Leslie Morris. Magazine published 5 times during school year (Sept., Oct., Nov., Jan., March). Circ. 600,000. This is a magazine for high school juniors and seniors, designed to prepare students for their futures. 100% of material aimed at juvenile audience.

Fiction: Young adults: contemporary, fantasy, humorous, science fiction, sports, spy/mystery/adventure. Buys 2 mss/year. Average word length: 1,000-1,250. Byline given.

Nonfiction: Young adults: how-to, humorous, interview/profile, problem solving. Buys 30-40 mss/year. Average word length: 1,000-1,250. Byline given.

How to Contact/Writers: Fiction/nonfiction: Query. SASE (IRC) for answer to query. Reports on queries/mss in 6 weeks. Will consider photocopied, computer printout and electronic submissions via disk or modem.

Illustration: Buys 20 illustrations/issue; buys 80 illustrations/year. Will review ms/illustration packages by authors/artists; ms/illustration packages submitted by authors with illustrations done by separate artists; illustrator's work for possible use with fiction/nonfiction articles. Works on assignment "mostly."

How to Contact/Illustrators: Ms/illustration packages: Query first. Illustrations only: Send tear sheets, cards. Reports on art samples only if interested. Original artwork returned at job's completion.

Terms/Writers & Illustrators: Pays 90 days after publication. Buys first North American serial rights. Pays $250-300 assigned/unsolicited articles. Additional payment for ms/illustration packages "must be negotiated." Pays $500-1,000/color illustration; $300-700 b&w/color (inside) illustration. Sample copy $1 with SAE and $1 postage; writer's guidelines free with SAE and 1 first-class stamp.

Tips: "Know the audience of the magazine you would like to contribute to. There is as wide a scope in children's magazines as there is in adults."

CHICKADEE, for Young Children from OWL, Young Naturalist Foundation, 56 The Esplanade, Ste. 306, Toronto Ontario M5E1A7. (416)868-6001. Articles/Fiction Editor: Janis Nostbakken. Art Director: Tim Davin. Publishes 10 times/year, magazine. Circ: 160,000. CHICKADEE is a "hands-on" publication designed to interest 4-9 year olds in the world and environment around them.

Fiction: Picture material, young readers: animal, contemporary, history, humorous, sports, spy/mystery/adventure. Does not want to see religious, anthropomorphic animal, romance material. Buys 8 mss/year. Average word length: 200-800. Byline given.

Nonfiction: Picture material, young readers: animal, how-to, interview/profile, travel. Does not want to see religious material. Buys 2-5 mss/year. Average word length: 20-200. Byline given.

How to Contact/Writers: Fiction/nonfiction: Send complete ms. SAE and $1 money order for answer to query and return of ms. Report on queries/mss in 8 weeks. Will consider simultaneous, photocopied, and computer printout submissions.

Illustration: Buys 3-5 illustrations/issue; buys 40 illustrations/year. Preferred theme or style: Gentle realism/humor (but not cartoons). Will review ms/illustration packages by authors/artists; ms/illustration packages submitted by authors with illustrations done by separate artists; illustrators work for possible use with fiction/nonfiction articles. Works on assignment only.

How to Contact/Illustrators: Ms/illustration packages: Story with sample of art. Illustrations only: Tear sheets. Reports on art samples only if interested.

Terms/Writers & Illustrators: Pays on publication. Buys all rights. Pays $25-$200 for assigned/unsolicited articles. Additional payment for ms/illustration packages is $25 to $600. Pays $500 color (cover) illustration, $50-500 b&w (inside), $50-650 color (inside). Sample copy $2.50. Writer's guidelines free.

Tips: "Study the magazine carefully before submitting material. 'Read-to-me selection' most open to freelancers. Uses fiction stories. Kids should be main characters and should be treated with respect." (See listing for OWL.)

CHILDREN'S DIGEST, Children's Better Health Institute, Box 567, Indianapolis IN 46206. (317)636-8881. Articles/Fiction Editor: Elizabeth Rinck. Art Director: Lisa Nelson. Magazine published eight times/year. Circ. 125,000. For children between 8 and 11 years; approximately 33% of content is health-related.
Fiction: Middle readers: animal, contemporary, fantasy, history, humorous, problem solving, science fiction, sports, spy/mystery/adventure. Buys 25 mss/year. Average word length: 500-1,500. Byline given.
Nonfiction: Middle readers: animal, history, how-to, humorous, problem solving. Buys 16-20 mss/year. Average word length: 500-1,200. Byline given.
How to Contact/Writers: Fiction/nonfiction: Send complete ms. SASE (IRC) for return of ms; include Social Security number with submission. Reports on mss in 10 weeks. Will consider photocopied and computer printout submissions.
Illustration: Will review an illustrator's work for possible use with fiction/nonfiction articles and columns by other authors. Works on assignment only.
How to Contact/Illustrators: Ms/illustration packages: Query first. Illustrations only: Send resume and/or slides or tear sheets to illustrate work. Reports on art samples in 8-10 weeks.
Terms/Writers & Illustrators: Pays on acceptance for illustrators, publication for writers. Buys all rights. Pays 8¢/word for accepted articles. Pays $225/color (cover) illustration; $24-100/b&w (inside); $60-125/color (inside). Sample copy $.75. Writer's/illustrator's guidelines for SAE and 1 first-class stamp. (See listings for Children's Playmate, Humpty Dumpty's Magazine, Turtle Magazine.)

CHILDREN'S MINISTRIES (See Discoveries, Together Time.)

CHILDREN'S PLAYMATE, Children's Better Health Institute, Box 567, Indianapolis IN 46206. (317)636-8881. Articles/Fiction Editor: Elizabeth Rinck. Art Director: Steve Miller. Magazine published eight times/year. Circ. 135,000. For children between 5 and 7 years; approximately 33% of content is health-related.
Fiction: Young readers: animal, contemporary, fantasy, history, humorous, problem solving, science fiction, sports, spy/mystery/adventure. Buys 25 mss/year. Average word length: 200-700. Byline given.
Nonfiction: Young readers: animal, history, how-to, humorous, problem solving. Buys 16-20 mss/year. Average word length: 200-700. Byline given.
How to Contact/Writers: Fiction/nonfiction: Send complete ms. SASE (IRC) for return of ms; include Social Security number with submission. Reports on mss in 8-10 weeks. Will consider photocopied and computer printout submissions.
Illustration: Will review an illustrator's work for possible use with fiction/nonfiction articles and columns by other authors. Works on assignment only.
How to Contact/Illustrators: Ms/illustration packages: Query first. Illustrations only: "Resume and/or slides or tear sheets to illustrate work." Reports on art samples in 8-10 weeks.
Terms/Writers & Illustrators: Pays on acceptance for illustrators, publication for writers. Buys all rights. Pays 8¢/word for assigned articles. Pays $225/color (cover) illustration; $25-100/b&w (inside); $60-125/color (inside). Sample copy 75¢. Writer's/illustrator's guidelines for SAE and 1 first-class stamp. (See listings for Children's Digest, Humpty Dumpty's Magazine, Turtle Magazine.)

CHILDREN'S TELEVISION WORKSHOP (see Kid City, 3-2-1 Contact.)

CLUBHOUSE, Your Story Hour, Box 15, Berrien Springs MI 49103. (616)471-3701. Articles/Fiction Editor, Art Director: Elaine Trumbo. Bimonthly magazine. Circ. 15,000. 100% of material aimed at juvenile audience.
Fiction: Middle readers, young adults: animal, contemporary, history, humorous, prob-

lem solving, religious. Does not want to see science fiction/fantasy/Halloween or Santa-oriented fiction. Buys 50 mss/year. Average word length: 800-1,300. Byline given.

Nonfiction: Middle readers, young adults: how-to. "We do not use articles except 200-500 word items about good health: anti—drug, tobacco, alcohol; pro—nutrition." Buys 10-12 mss/year. Average word length: 200-400. Byline given.

How to Contact/Writers: Fiction/nonfiction: Send complete ms. SASE (IRC) for return of ms. Reports on queries/mss in 6 weeks. Will consider simultaneous, photocopied, and computer printout submissions.

Illustration: Buys 20-25 illustrations/issue; buys 120+ illustrations/year. Preferred theme or style: "variety." Will review an illustrator's work for possible use with fiction/nonfiction articles and columns by other authors. Works on assignment only.

How to Contact/Illustrators: Illustrations only: Send photocopies or prints of work which we can keep on file. Reports on art samples in 6 weeks. Originals usually not returned at job's completion, but they can be returned if desired.

Terms/Writers & Illustrators: Pays on acceptance. Buys first North American serial rights. Pays $25-35 for articles. "Writers and artists receive 2 copies free in addition to payment." Pays $30/b&w (cover) illustration; $7.50-25/b&w (inside). Sample copy for business SAE and 3 first-class stamps; writers/illustrator's guidelines free for business SAE and 1 first class stamp.

Tips: Writers: "Take children seriously—they're smarter than you think! Respect their sense of dignity, don't talk down to them and don't write stories about 'bad kids.'" Illustrators: "Keep it clean, vigorous, fresh-whatever your style. Send samples we can keep on file. B&w line art is best."

COBBLESTONE, The History Magazine for Young People, Cobblestone Publishing, Inc., 20 Grove St., Peterborough NH 03458. (603)924-7209. Articles/Fiction Editor: Carolyn P. Yoder. Art Director: Anne Vadeboncoeur. Monthly magazine. Circ. 47,000. "*Cobblestone* is theme related. Writers should request editorial guidelines which explain procedure and lists upcoming themes. Queries must relate to an upcoming theme. Fiction is not used often, although a good fiction piece offers welcome diversity. It is recommended that writers become familiar with the magazine (sample copies available)." 100% of material aimed at juvenile audience.

Fiction: Middle readers, young adults: history. Does not want to see pieces that do not relate to an upcoming theme. Buys 6-10 mss/year. Average word length: 750. Byline given.

Nonfiction: Middle readers, young adults: history, interview/profile, travel. Does not want to see material that does not relate to an upcoming theme. Buys 120 mss/year. Average word length: 300-1,000. Byline given.

How to Contact/Writers: Fiction/nonfiction: Query with published clips. SASE (IRC) for answer to query and return of ms. Reports on queries in 5-6 months before publication; mss in 2 months before publication. Will consider photocopied, computer printout and electronic submissions via disk or modem.

Illustration: Buys 3 illustrations/issue; buys 36 illustrations/year. Preferred theme or style: Material that is simple, clear, and accurate but not too juvenile. Sophisticated sources are a must. Will review ms/illustration packages by authors/artists; ms/illustration packages submitted by authors with illustrations done by separate artists; illustrators work for possible use with fiction/nonfiction articles. Works on assignment only.

How to Contact/Illustrators: Ms/illustration packages: Illustrations are done by assignment. Roughs required. Illustrations only: Send samples of black and white work. Illustrators should consult issues of *Cobblestone* to familiarize themselves with our needs. Reports on art samples in 1-2 months. Original artwork returned at job's completion.

Terms/Writers & Illustrators: Pays on publication. Buys all rights. Pays 10-15¢ word for assigned articles. "We will 'pay' in copies of the magazine if a writer requests." Pays

$10-125/b&w (inside) illustration. Sample copy $4.95 with 7½×10½ SAE and 5 first-class stamps; writer's/illustrator's guidelines free with SAE and 1 first-class stamp.
Tips: Writers: "Submit detailed queries which show attention to historical accuracy and which offer interesting and entertaining information. Be true to your own style. Study past issues to know what we look for. All feature articles, recipes, activities, fiction, and supplemental nonfiction are freelance contributions." Illustrators: "Submit black and white samples, not too juvenile. Study past issues to know what we look for. The illustration we use is generally for stories, recipes, and activities." (See listing for Faces, the Magazine About People.)

CRUSADER, Calvinist Cadet Corps, Box 7259, Grand Rapids MI 49510. (616)241-5616. Editor: G. Richard Broene. Art Director: Robert DeJonge. Magazine published 7 times/year. Circ. 12,000. Our magazine is for members of the Calvinist Cadet Corps—boys aged 9-14. Our purpose is to show how God is at work in their lives and in the world around them. 100% of material aimed at juvenile audience.
Fiction: Middle readers: contemporary, humorous, problem solving, religious, sports. Does not want to see fantasy, science fiction. Buys 12 mss/year. Average word length: 800-1,500.
Nonfiction: Middle readers: animal, how-to, humorous, interview/profile, problem solving, religious. Buys 6 mss/year. Average word length: 400-900.
How to Contact/Writers: Fiction/nonfiction: Send complete ms. SASE (IRC) for answer to query/return of ms. Reports on queries in 1-3 weeks; mss in 1-5 weeks. Will consider simultaneous, photocopied, and computer printout submissions.
Illustration: Buys 1 illustration/issue; buys 6 illustrations/year. Works on assignment only.
Terms/Writers & Illustrators: Pays on acceptance. Buys first rights; one-time rights; second serial (reprint rights). Pays 4-5¢/word for assigned articles; 2-5¢/word for unsolicited articles. Sample copy free with 9×12 SAE and 3 first-class stamps.
Tips: Publication is most open to fiction: write for a list of themes (available yearly in January).

DAY CARE AND EARLY EDUCATION, Human Sciences Press, 233 Spring St., New York NY 10013. (212)620-8000. Articles/Fiction Editor: Randa Nachbar. Art Director: Bill Jobson. Quarterly magazine. Circ. 2,500. Magazine uses material "involving children birth to 7." 5% of material aimed at juvenile audience.
Fiction: Picture material, young readers: contemporary, fantasy, humorous, problem solving. Average word length: 1,000-3,000. Byline given.
Nonfiction: Picture material, young readers: animal, how-to, humorous, problem solving. Average word length: 1,000-3,000. Byline given.
How to Contact/Writers: Fiction/nonfiction: Send complete ms. SASE (IRC) for answer to query and return of ms. Reports on queries in 1 month; mss in 2-3 months. Will consider photocopied submissions.
Illustration: Will review ms/illustration packages by authors/artists; ms/illustration packages submitted by authors with illustrations done by separate artists; illustrator's work for possible use with fiction/nonfiction articles.
How to Contact/Illustrators: Ms/illustration packages: Send complete ms with final art. Reports on art samples only if interested. Original artwork returned at job's completion.
Terms/Writers & Illustrators: Pays in 2 copies. Free sample copy; free writer's guidelines.

DISCOVERIES, Children's Ministries, 6401 The Paseo, Kansas City MO 64131. Editor: Molly Mitchell. Executive Editor: Robert D. Troutman. Weekly tabloid. *Discoveries* is a leisure reading piece for third through sixth graders. It is published weekly by the

Department of Children's Ministries of the Church of the Nazarene. The major purposes of *Discoveries* are to: provide a leisure reading piece which will build Christian behavior and values; provide reinforcement for Biblical concepts taught in the Sunday School curriculum. The focus of the reinforcement will be life-related, with some historical appreciation. *Discoveries'* target audience is children ages 8-12 in grades three through six. The readability goal is fourth to fifth grade." 100% of material aimed at juvenile audience.

Fiction: "Fiction—stories should vividly portray definite Christian emphasis or character-building values, without being preachy. The setting, plot, and action should be realistic." Average word length: 400-800. Byline given.

How to Contact/Writers: Fiction: Send complete ms. SASE (IRC) for return of ms. Report on mss in 4-6 weeks.

Illustration: Preferred theme or style: Cartoon—humor should be directed to children and involve children. It should not simply be child-related from an adult viewpoint. Some full color story illustrations are assigned. Samples of art may be sent for review.

Terms/Writers & Illustrators: Pays on acceptance. Buys first rights; second serial (reprint rights). Pays 3.5¢/word (first rights). Contributor receives complimentary copy of publication. Writer's guidelines free with #10 SAE.

Tips: "*Discoveries* is committed to reinforcement of the Biblical concepts taught in the Sunday School curriculum. Because of this, the themes needed are mainly as follows: faith in God, obedience to God, putting God first, choosing to please God, accepting Jesus as Savior, finding God's will, choosing to do right, trusting God in hard times, prayer; trusting God to answer, Importance of Bible memorization, appreciation of Bible as God's Word to man, Christians working together, showing kindness to others, witnessing." (See listing for Together Time.)

DOLPHIN LOG, The Cousteau Society, 8440 Santa Monica Blvd., Los Angeles CA 90069. (213)656-4422. Articles Editor: Pamela Stacey. Bimonthly magazine. Circ. 90,000. Subject matter encompasses all areas of science, history and the arts which can be related to our global water system. The philosophy of the magazine is to delight, instruct and instill an environmental ethic and understanding of the interconnectedness of living organisms, including people. Of special interest are articles on an ocean- or water-related themes which develop reading and comprehension skills. 100% of material aimed at juvenile audience.

Nonfiction: Picture material, middle readers: animal, environmental, ocean. Does not want to see talking animals. Buys 15 mss/year. Average word length: 500-1,200. Byline given.

How to Contact/Writers: Nonfiction: Query. SASE (IRC) for answer to query; include Social Security number with submission. Reports on queries in 4 weeks; mss in 8 weeks. Will consider photocopied, computer printout and electronic IBM-PC Wordstar compatible submissions via disk or modem with manuscript.

Illustration: Buys 1 illustration/issue; buys 6 illustrations/year. Preferred theme or style: Biological illustration. Will review ms/illustration packages by authors/artists; ms/illustration packages submitted by authors with illustrations done by separate artists; illustrator's work for possible use with nonfiction articles.

How to Contact/Illustrators: Ms/illustration packages: No original artwork, copies only. Illustrations only: Send tear sheets, slides. Reports on art samples in 8 weeks or only if interested. Original artwork returned at job's completion.

Terms/Writers & Illustrators: Pays on publication. Buys first North American serial rights; "translation rights." Pays $25-150 for assigned/unsolicited articles. Additional payment for ms/illustration packages the $25-150 range. Pays $25-150/b&w illustration; $25-200/color (cover); $25-200/color (inside). Sample copy $2 with SAE and 2 first-class stamps. Writer's/illustrator's guidelines free with SAE and 1 first-class stamp.

Tips: Writers: "Write simply and clearly and don't anthropomorphize." Illustrators:

"Be scientifically accurate and don't anthropomorphize. Some background in biology is helpful, as our needs range from simple line drawings to scientific illustrations which must be researched for biological and technical accuracy."

EQUILIBRIUM, Everyone's Entertainment, Eagle Publishing Productions, Box 162, Golden CO 80401. President: Gary Eagle. Quarterly magazine. Circ. 10,000. Material on or relating to balance is best. Material on antonyms (opposites) is even better but not required. 10% of material aimed at juvenile audience.

Fiction: Young readers, young adults: animal, contemporary, fantasy, history, humorous, problem solving, religious, romance, science fiction, sports, spy/mystery/adventure. Buys 40 mss/year. Average word length: 500-2,000. Byline given sometimes.

Nonfiction: Middle readers, young adults: animal, history, how-to, humorous, interview/profile, problem solving, religious, travel. Buys 60 mss/year. Average word length: 500-2,000. Byline given sometimes.

How to Contact/Writers: Fiction/nonfiction: Query. SASE (IRC) for answer to query. Reports on queries in 8 weeks; mss in 16 weeks. Will consider simultaneous, photocopied, computer printout and electronic submissions via disk (3.5 inch) or modem.

Illustration: Buys 10 illustrations/issue; buys 150 illustrations/year. Will review ms/illustration packages by authors/artists; ms/illustration packages submitted by authors with illustrations done by separate artists; illustrator's work for possible use with fiction/nonfiction articles. Works on assignment only.

How to Contact/Illustrators: Ms/illustration packages: Query first, (quick summary of ms) and final art included, captions too. Illustrations only: Send tear sheets, photographed, copied pieces. Reports on art samples in 3 months. Original artwork returned at job's completion.

Terms/Writers & Illustrators: Pays on publication. Buys second serial (reprint rights). Pays $50-100 for assigned/unsolicited articles (shorts). "Contributor copies are free with signed contract." Additional payment for ms/illustration packages within the $50-100 range; "photos help pay range." Pays $50-200/b&w (cover) illustration; $100-200/color (cover); $75/b&w (inside); $85/color (inside). Sample copy free with 9 × 14 SAE and 5 first-class stamps. Writer's/illustrator's guidelines free with #10 SAE and 2 first-class stamps.

Tips: Writers: "Be specific in your query as to why readers would enjoy your material. If on balance, state so. If on antonyms, state them. Shorter the better." Illustrators: "Glossy print would be nice. Captions are helpful."

EXPLORING, Boy Scouts of America, Box 152079, 1325 Walnut Hill Ln., Irving TX 75015-2079. (214)580-2365. Executive Editor: Scott Daniels. Art Director: Joe Connally. Magazine published "4 times a year—not quarterly." *Exploring* is a 12 page, 4-color magazine published for members of the Boy Scouts of America's Exploring program. These members are young men and women between the ages of 14-21. Interests include careers, computers, camping, hiking, canoeing. 100% of material aimed at juvenile audience.

Nonfiction: Young adults: interview/profile, problem solving, travel. Buys 12 mss/year. Average word length: 600-1,200. Byline given.

How to Contact/Writers: Nonfiction: Query with published clips. SASE (IRC) for answer to query/return of ms. Reports on queries/mss in 1 week. Will consider computer printout submissions.

Illustration: Buys 3 illustrations/issue; buys 12 illustrations/year. Will review an illustrator's work for possible use with fiction/nonfiction articles and columns by other authors. Works on assignment only.

How to Contact/Illustrators: Reports on art samples in 2 weeks. Original art work returned at job's completion.

Terms/Writers & Illustrators: Pays on acceptance. Buys first North American serial

rights. Pays $300-500 for assigned/unsolicited articles. Pays $500-800/b&w (cover) illustration; $800-1,000/color (cover); $250-500/b&w (inside); $500-800/color (inside). Sample copy with 8½×11 SAE and 5 first-class stamps. Free writer's/illustrator's guidelines.
Tips: "Read previous issues of the magazine." Looks for "short, crisp career profiles of 1,000 words with plenty of information to break out into graphics."

FACES, The Magazine About People, Cobblestone Publishing, Inc., 20 Grove St., Peterborough NH 03458. (603)924-7209. Articles/Fiction Editor: Carolyn P. Yoder. Art Director: Coni Porter. Magazine published 10 times/year (Sept.-June). Circ. 13,000. "Although *Faces* operates on a by-assignment basis, we welcome ideas/suggestions in outline form. All manuscripts are reviewed by the American Museum of Natural History in New York before being accepted. *Faces* is a theme-related magazine; writers should send for theme list before submitting ideas/queries." 100% of material aimed at juvenile audience.
Fiction: Middle readers, young adults: contemporary, history, religious, anthropology. Does not want to see material that does not relate to a specific upcoming theme. Buys 10 mss/year. Average word length: 750. Byline given.
Nonfiction: Middle readers, young adults: history, interview/profile, religious, travel, anthropology. Does not want to see material not related to a specific upcoming theme. Buys 70 mss/year. Average word length: 300-1,000. Byline given.
How to Contact/Writers: Fiction/nonfiction: Query with published clips. SASE (IRC) for answer to query and return of ms. Reports on queries in 5-6 months before publication; mss 2 months before publication. Will consider photocopied, computer printout and electronic submissions via disk or modem.
Illustration: Buys 3 illustrations/issue; buys 30 illustrations/year. Preferred theme or style: Material that is meticulously researched (most articles are written by professional anthropologists); simple, direct style preferred but not too juvenile. Will review ms/ illustration packages by authors/artists; ms/illustration packages submitted by authors with illustrations done by separate artists; illustrator's work for possible use with fiction/ nonfiction articles. Works on assignment only.
How to Contact/Illustrators: Ms/illustration packages: Illustration is done by assignment. Roughs required. Illustrations only: Send samples of black and white work. Illustrators should consult issues of *Faces* to familiarize themselves with our needs. Reports on art samples in 1-2 months. Original artwork returned at job's completion.
Terms/Writers & Illustrators: Pays on publication. Buys all rights. Pays 10-15¢/word for assigned articles. "On occasion, a writer requests copies of the issue in lieu of cash payment." Pays $10-125/b&w (inside) illustration. Sample copy $3.95 with 7½×10½ SAE and 5 first-class stamps. Writer's/illustrator's guidelines free with SAE and 1 first-class stamp.
Tips: "Writers are encouraged to study past issues of the magazine and become familiar with our style and content. Writers with anthropological and/or travel experience are particularly encouraged; *Faces* is about world cultures. All feature articles, recipes, and activities are freelance contributions." Illustrators: "Submit black and white samples, not too juvenile. Study past issues to know what we look for. The illustration we use is generally for retold legends, recipes, and activities." (See listing for Cobblestone, the History Magazine for Young People.)

THE FRIEND MAGAZINE, The Church of Jesus Christ of Latter-day Saints, 50 E. North Temple, Salt Lake City UT 84150. (801)240-2210. Managing Editor: Vivian Paulsen. Art Director: Dick Brown. Monthly magazine. Circ. 210,000. Magazine for 3-11 year olds. 100% of material aimed at juvenile audience.
Fiction: Uses history, humorous, religious, ethnic, mainstream, nature, adventure pieces. Does not want to see controversial issues, political, horror, fantasy. Buys 200 mss/year. Average word length: 400-1,000. Byline given.

Nonfiction: Uses animal, how-to, religious. Does not want to see controversial issues, political, horror, fantasy. Buys 200 mss/year. Average word length: 400-1,000. Byline given.
How to Contact/Writers: Fiction/nonfiction: Send complete ms. Reports on mss in 2 months. Will consider computer printout submissions.
Terms/Writers & Illustrators: Pays on acceptance. Buys all rights. Pays 8-11¢/word for unsolicited articles. Free sample copy. Free writer's guidelines.
Tips: "The *Friend* is published by the Church of Jesus Christ of Latter-day Saints for boys and girls up to twelve years of age. All submissions are carefully read by the *Friend* staff, and those not accepted are returned within two months when a self-addressed stamped envelope is enclosed. Submit seasonal material at least eight months in advance. Query letters are not encouraged. Authors may request rights to have their work reprinted after their manuscript is published."

HIGH ADVENTURE, Assemblies of God, 1445 Boonville Ave., Springfield MO 65802. (417)862-2781, Ext. 4181. Articles Editor: Johnnie Barnes. Quarterly magazine. Circ. 85,000. Magazine is designed to provide boys with worthwhile, enjoyable, leisure reading; to challenge them in narrative form to higher ideals and greater spiritual dedication; and to perpetuate the spirit of Royal Rangers through stories, ideas, and illustrations. 75% of material aimed at juvenile audience.
Fiction: Buys 100 mss/year. Average word length: 1,200. Byline given.
Nonfiction: Articles: Christian living, devotional, Holy Spirit, salvation, self-help; biography; missionary stories; news items; testimonies.
How to Contact/Writers: Fiction/nonfiction: Send complete ms. SASE (IRC) for return of ms; include Social Security number with submission. Reports on queries in 6-8 weeks. Will consider simultaneous and photocopied submissions. Will review ms/illustration packages by authors/artists; ms/illustration packages submitted by authors with illustrations done by separate artists; illustrator's work for possible use with fiction/nonfiction articles.
How to Contact/Illustrators: Ms/illustration packages: Send complete ms with final art. Illustrations only: Most of our artwork is done inside building.
Terms/Writers & Illustrators: Pays on acceptance. Buys first rights. Pays 2¢/word for unsolicited articles. Sample copy free with 8½×11 SASE. Free writer's/illustrator's guidelines.

HIGHLIGHTS FOR CHILDREN, 803 Church St., Honesdale PA 18431. (717)253-1080. Articles/Fiction Editor: Leah White. Art Director: John R. Crane. Monthly (July-August issue combined) magazine. Circ. 2.5 million. Our motto is "Fun With a Purpose.'" We are looking for quality fiction and nonfiction that appeals to children, will encourage them to read, and reinforces positive values. All art is done on assignment. 100% of material aimed at juvenile audience.
Fiction: Picture material: animal, contemporary, fantasy, history, humorous, problem solving. Young readers, middle readers: animal, contemporary, fantasy, history, humorous, problem solving, science fiction, sports, mystery/adventure. Does not want to see: war, crime, violence. Buys 150 + mss/year. Average word length: 600-900. Byline given.
Nonfiction: Picture material: animal, history, how-to, humorous, problem solving. Young readers, middle readers: animal, history, how-to, humorous, interview/profile, problem solving, foreign, science, nature, arts, sports. Does not want to see: trendy topics, fads, personalities who would not be good role models for children, guns, war, crime, violence. Buys 75 + mss/year. Average word length: 900. Byline given.
How to Contact/Writers: Fiction: Send complete ms. Nonfiction: Query. SASE (IRC) for return of ms; include Social Security number with submission. Reports on queries in 1-3 weeks; mss in 4-8 weeks. Will consider photocopied and computer printout submissions (good quality—would rather not see dot matrix).

All rights to this pen and ink piece by Kit Wray were purchased for use in the "Hidden Pictures" section of an issue of Highlights for Children. Editor-in-Chief, Dr. Walter B. Barbe feels this scene is interesting, active, easily identifiable, and pleasing to the eye. "Some of the hidden objects are placed in negative space for added interest," he concludes.

© Highlights for Children 1988

Illustration: Preferred theme or style: Realistic, some stylization, cartoon style acceptable. Works on assignment only.

How to Contact/Illustrators: Ms/illustration packages: Art is done on assignment only. Illustrations only: Photocopies, tear sheets, or slides. Resume optional. Reports on art samples in 4-6 weeks.

Terms/Writers & Illustrators: Pays on acceptance. Buys all rights. Pays 14¢/word for unsolicited articles. Pays $400-$550 color (cover) illustration; $200-$350 color (inside) illustration. Writer's/illustrator's guidelines for 9x12 SAE and $1.05 postage.

Tips: Writers: "Study the market. Analyze several issues of the magazines you want to write for. Send for writer's guidelines. Send in professional-looking work." Illustrators: "Know the market. Demonstrate by your portfolio that you can produce the kind of art the magazine needs. Be flexible, willing to work with art director's requests. Illustrations should be colorful not monochromatic. We would like to avoid hard outline drawings that would give the impression of cartooning. More illustration-like. Children should be happy and enjoying activities as *Highlights'* slogan is "Fun with a Purpose." This does not mean that children should be doubled up with laughter. Cover subjects that have been used or will be used are: picnic scene, kite flying, pet parade, building a snowman, trick or treating, children blowing bubbles, clowns at a circus, carnival scene, sledding down-hill, cookie baking, playing in leaves, tree house, St. Bernard puppies, beach sandcastle, leprechaun's home, elephants at zoo, making Valentines, magic show, horseback riding, winter feeding birds, library scenes, playing in attic, George Washington, dinosaurs, ocean fishing, vegetable garden, 4th of July, bathing dog, mice in pumpkin house, Thanksgiving/Grandma's, cutting Xmas tree, ice skating, art class, city scene, bears camping, baseball game, at the beach.'" Looks for: crafts, party plans, puzzles.

HOB-NOB, 994 Nissley Rd., Lancaster PA 17601. (717)898-7807. Articles/Fiction/Poetry Editor, Art Director: M. K. Henderson. Semiannual magazine. Circ. 350. *Hob-Nob* began as a "family" publication, and prefers to avoid any material that could or should not be read by younger readers. Occasional stories by or for children/teenagers are used,

depending on submissions. 20% of prose in current issue aimed at juvenile audience.
Fiction: Young readers: animal, humorous. Middle readers: animal, contemporary, fantasy, humorous. Young adults: contemporary, fantasy, humorous, problem solving, religious, romance, science fiction, sports, spy/mystery/adventure. Does not want to see religious proselytizing material geared to specific denominations or categories of denominations (i.e., "fundamentalist"); "clean" only, no bathroom language. Buys 60 mss/year, (all age levels — 7 juveniles in current issue). Average word length: 2,000. Byline given.
Nonfiction: Young readers: animal, humorous. Middle readers: humorous, interview/profile. Young adults: humorous, interview/profile, problem solving. Buys 10 mss/year, (all ages); juvenile — none in current issue. Average word length: 1,000. Byline given.
How to Contact/Writers: Fiction/nonfiction: Send complete ms. SASE (IRC) for answer to query/return of ms. Reports on queries/mss in 2 months or less. Will consider photocopied and computer printout submissions.
Illustration: "I don't have space for large illustrations so I use cuts, suitable drawings from miscellaneous small ones sent by certain readers." Preferred theme or style: black and white only, no intermediate values. Will review ms/illustration packages submitted by authors/artists. Small picture(s) appropriate to a submitted ms.
How to Contact/Illustrators: Ms/illustration packages: Send complete ms and final b&w drawing, small size (or I'll reduce it). Reports on art samples in 2 months or less. Original artwork returned at job's completion if requested and SASE supplied.
Terms/Writers & Illustrators: Pays on publication. Buys first North American serial rights. Pays in contributor copies. Sample copy for $3. Writer's guidelines free or sent with sample if requested.
Tips: Will consider short poetry (up to 16 lines) by and for juveniles. "Write what children will enjoy — test out on your own children if possible." Looks for: "Shorter fiction, especially humor or whimsy. First time contributors may submit only in January and February. (Established contributors may submit September through February only)." Publication most open to "cartoons." Current minimum of two years before new contributors' work can appear.

THE HOME ALTAR, Meditations for Families with Children, Augsburg Fortress, 426 S. Fifth St., Box 1209, Minneapolis MN 55440. Articles/Fiction Editor: M. Elaine Dunham, Box 590179, San Francisco CA 94159-0179. Quarterly magazine. Circ. approx. 60,000. This is a booklet of daily devotions, used primarily by Lutheran families. Each day's reading focuses on a specific Bible passage. 98% of material aimed at juvenile audience.
Fiction: Young readers, middle readers: religious. Buys 360 mss/year. Average word length: 125-170. Byline given.
Nonfiction: Young readers, middle readers: religious. Average word length: 125-170. Byline given.
How to Contact/Writers: Fiction/nonfiction: Query with published clips.
Illustration: Buys 100 illustrations/year. Works on assignment only.
How to Contact/Illustrators: Reports on art samples only if interested. Original art work sometimes returned at job's completion.
Terms/Writers & Illustrators: Pays on acceptance. "Rights purchased vary." Pays $10 for assigned articles. Free writer's guidelines for 6x9 SAE and 85¢ in first-class stamps.
Tips: "Read the magazine to which you'd like to contribute. Reread it. Think carefully about whether your style is compatible with the style of the magazine, or whether you can make your style compatible with the magazine's."

HUMPTY DUMPTY'S MAGAZINE, Children's Better Health Institute (div. Benjamin Franklin Literary & Medical Soc.), 1100 Waterway Blvd., Box 567, Indianapolis IN 46206. (317)636-8881. Articles/Fiction Editor: Christine French Clark. Art Director: Larry Simmons. Magazine published 8 times/year — Jan., Feb/Mar, April/May, June/

\

July, Aug/Sept., Oct., Nov., Dec. HDM is edited for kindergarten children, approximately ages 4-6. It includes fiction stories (easy-to-reads; read alouds; rhyming stories; rebus stories), nonfiction articles (some with photo illustrations), poems, crafts, recipes, and puzzles. Much of the content encourages development of better health habits. "All but 2 pages aimed at the juvenile market. The remainder may be seasonal and/or more general."

Fiction: Picture material: animal, contemporary, fantasy, humorous, sports, health-related. Young readers: animal, contemporary, fantasy, humorous, science fiction, sports, spy/mystery/adventure, health-related. Does not want to see bunny-rabbits-with-carrot-pies stories! Also, talking inanimate objects are very difficult to do well. Beginners (and maybe everyone) should avoid these. Buys 35-50 mss/year. Average word length: 700. Byline given.

Nonfiction: Picture material, young readers: animal, how-to, humorous, interview/profile, health-related. Does not want to see long, boring, encyclopedia rehashes. "We're open to almost any subject (although most of our nonfiction has a health angle), but it must be presented creatively. Don't just string together some facts." Buys 6-10 mss/year. Average word length: 700. Byline given.

How to Contact/Writers: Send complete ms. Nonfiction: Send complete ms with bibliography if applicable. SASE (IRC) for return of ms; include Social Security number with submission. "No queries, please!" Reports on mss in 8-10 weeks. Will consider photocopied and computer printout (letter quality) submissions.

Illustration: Buys 13-16 illustrations/issue; buys 90-120 illustrations/year. Preferred theme or style: Realistic or cartoon. Will review ms/illustration packages by authors/artists; ms/illustration packages submitted by authors with illustrations done by separate artists; illustrator's work for possible use with fiction/nonfiction articles. Works on assignment only.

How to Contact/Illustrators: Ms/illustration packages: Send slides, printed pieces, or photocopies. Illustrations only: Send slides, printed pieces or photocopies. Reports on art samples only if interested.

Terms/Writers & Illustrators: Writers: Pays on publication. Artists: Pays within 6-8 weeks. Buys all rights. "One-time book rights may be returned if author can provide name of interested book publisher and tentative date of publication." Pays about 8¢/word for unsolicited stories/articles; payment varies for poems and activities. Up to 10 complimentary issues are provided to author with check. Pays $225/color cover illustration; $35-65 per page b&w (inside); $40-125/color (inside). Sample copy for 75¢. Writer's/illustrator's guidelines free with SASE.

Tips: Writers: "Study current issues and guidelines. Observe, especially, word lengths and adhere to requirements. It's sometimes easier to break in with recipe or craft ideas, but submit what you do best. Don't send your first, second, or even third drafts. Polish your piece until it's as perfect as you can make it." Illustrators: "Please study the magazine before contacting us. Your art must have appeal to three- to seven-year-olds." (See listings for Children's Digest, Children's Playmate, Turtle Magazine.)

IN-BETWEEN, Art and Entertainment Between the Lakes, Six Lakes Arts Communications Inc., 43 Chapel St., Seneca Falls NY 13148. (315)568-4265. Articles/Fiction Editor: Stephen Beals. Art Director: Wayne Lohr. Bimonthly magazine. Estab. 1987. Circ. 1,500. Magazine includes "arts and entertainment, music, theatre, exhibitions, history, short stories and poetry." 10% of material aimed at juvenile audience.

Fiction: Young readers, middle readers, young adults: history, spy/mystery/adventure. Does not want to see religious, romance, sports, science fiction material. Publishes 1-2 mss/year. Byline given.

Nonfiction: Young readers, middle readers, young adults: history, how-to, interview/profile. Does not want to see religious material. Publishes 1-2 mss/year. Average word length: 500-2,500. Byline given.

How to Contact/Writers: Fiction/nonfiction: Send complete ms. SASE (IRC) for answer to query and return of ms. Reports on queries in 2 months; mss in 3 months. Will consider simultaneous, photocopied, computer printout and electronic submissions via disk or modem (Apple MacIntosh).

Illustration: Publishes 1 illustration/issue; Publishes 3-4 illustrations/year. Preferred theme or style: Pen and ink. Will review ms/illustration packages by authors/artists; ms/illustration packages submitted by authors with illustrations done by separate artists; illustrator's work for possible use with fiction/nonfiction articles.

How to Contact/Illustrators: Ms/illustration packages: Send complete ms with final art or samples. Illustrations only: Send samples — copies ok. Reports on art samples in 2 months. Original art work returned at job's completion.

Terms/Writers & Illustrators: Pays in copies. "We hope to begin paying writers and illustrators in the future." Free sample copy and writer's guidelines.

Tips: "We have a 'Kids Corner' section and an annual contest."

INSIGHTS, NRA News for Young Shooters, National Rifle Assoc. of America, 1600 Rhode Island Ave. NW, Washington DC 20036. (202)828-6290. Articles Editor: Brenda Dalessandro. Monthly magazine. Circ. 45,000. "Insights promotes the shooting sports. We teach the safe and responsible use of firearms for competition shooting, hunting or recreational shooting. Our articles are instructional yet entertaining. We teach but don't preach. We emphasize safety." 100% of material aimed at juvenile audience.

Fiction: Young adults: animal, history, humorous, sports. "Fiction that does not relate to the shooting sports or positively promote the safe and ethical use of firearms will not be considered." Buys 12 mss/year. Average word length: 600-1,500. Byline given.

Nonfiction: Young adults: animal, history, how-to, humorous, interview/profile, "all these categories must involve the shooting sport." Buys 40 mss/year. Average word length: 600-1,500. Byline given.

How to Contact/Writers: Fiction/nonfiction: Query, send complete ms. SASE (IRC) for answer to query; include Social Security number with submission. Reports on queries/mss in 2 months. Will consider photocopied and computer printout submissions.

Illustration: Buys 1 illustration/issue; buys 7 illustrations/year. Will review ms/illustration packages submitted by authors with illustrations done by separate artists. Works on assignment only.

How to Contact/Illustrators: Ms/illustration packages: Query first. Illustrations only: Tear sheets or slides would be great! Illustrator should have technical knowledge of firearms and shooting.

Terms/Writers & Illustrators: Pays on acceptance. Buys first North American serial rights, second serial (reprint rights). Pays $200 for assigned/unsolicited articles. Additional payment for ms/illustration packages: $350. Pays $150-$200 b&w (inside) illustration. Sample copy free with 10x12 SAE and 3 first class stamps; writer's/illustrator's guidelines free with business SAE and 1 first-class stamp.

Tips: Writers: "You have to know your subject. Kids are smart and quickly pick up on inaccuracies. As an authority, your credibility is then zilch. Material should instruct without sounding preachy. We do not buy material that shows shooting in a bad light. We show our readers the correct, safe and ethical way to use a firearm." Illustrators: "When illustrating a story, stick to the description in the plot. We find young readers don't like illustrations when they differ from the story. Forego creative license this time. Wildlife art must be anatomically and environmentally correct. Shooting scenes must be safe and instructionally correct."

JACKIE, D.C. Thomson and Co. Ltd., Albert Square, Dundee DD1 9QJ Scotland. (0382)23131 Ext. 4146. Fiction Editor: Judey Paris. Weekly magazine. 100% of material aimed at teenage audience.

Fiction: Young adults: contemporary, humorous, problem solving, romance. Buys 100 mss/year. Average word length: 1,200-1,500. Byline given.

Nonfiction: Young adults: interview/profile, problem solving. Buys "very few" mss/year. Average word length: 1,200-1,500.

How to Contact/Writers: Fiction/nonfiction: send complete ms. SASE (IRC) for answer to query and return of ms. Reports on queries in 1 week; mss in 2 weeks. Will consider simultaneous submissions.

Illustration: Will review an illustrator's work for possible use with fiction/nonfiction articles and columns by other authors. Works on assignment only.

How to Contact/Illustrators: Ms/illustration packages: Query first, but packages not usually accepted. Illustrations only: Send tear sheets. Reports on art samples in 1 week. Original artwork returned at job's completion (depending on contract).

Terms/Writers & Illustrators: Pays on acceptance. Buys all rights. Pays 50-70 pounds (English currency) for assigned/unsolicited articles. Pays 60-80 pounds (English currency)/color (inside) illustration. Writer's/illustrator's guidelines free with SAE.

Tips: "Study the magazine and market before contributing." Looks for "fiction which is aimed at teenage girls with some emphasis on romance."

This work was designed "to illustrate a whimsical story about children having a garage sale," says William Eastlake, director of publications for Gospel Publishing House. Steve Lopez, Springfield, Missouri, illustrated this piece using watercolor dyes. All rights to this piece were purchased by the publishing house; it was used as a cover illustration for Junior Trails. "Steve is able to capture childlike enthusiasm in the faces of the characters he draws. He uses available space well and draws a reader into the story," explains Eastlake.

© General Council of the Assemblies of God 1988

JUNIOR TRAILS, Gospel Publishing House, 1445 Boonville Ave., Springfield MO 65802. (417)862-2781. Articles/Fiction Editor: Cathy Ketcher. Quarterly magazine. Circ. 70,000. Junior Trails is a 4-page take-home paper for fifth and sixth graders. Its articles consist of fiction stories of a contemporary or historical nature. The stories have a moral slant to them to show how modern day people can work out problems in acceptable ways, or give examples in history from which we can learn.

Fiction: Middle readers: contemporary, history, humorous, problem solving, religious, sports, spy/mystery/adventure. Does not want to see science fiction, mythology, ghosts and witchcraft. Buys 80 mss/year. Average word length: 800-1,800. Byline given.

Nonfiction: Middle readers: animal, history, how-to, humorous, problem solving, religious, travel. Buys 30 mss/year. Average word length: 300-1,000. Byline given.

How to Contact/Writers: Fiction/nonfiction: Send complete ms. SASE (IRC) for answer to query; return of ms; include Social Security number with submission. Reports on queries in 2 weeks; mss in 6-8 weeks. Will consider simultaneous, photocopied, and computer printout submissions.

Terms/Writers & Illustrators: Pays on acceptance. Buys first rights; one-time rights; second serial (reprint rights); simultaneous rights. Pays 2-3¢/word for unsolicited articles. Sample copy free with 9 × 12 SASE.

Tips: "Submit stories with which children can identify. Avoid trite, overused plots and themes. Make children be children — not babies or super, adult-like people. Let your characters weave the story. Don't fill up space with unnecessary details. We are always in need of good fiction stories. We tend to get a lot of very long stories that will not fit in our available space. Short fiction stories seem hard to find at times." Looks for: "fiction that presents believable characters working out their problems according to Bible principles, in other words, present Christianity in action, without being preachy; articles with reader appeal, emphasizing some phase of Christian living, presented in a down-to-earth manner; biography or missionary material using fiction technique; historical, scientific or nature material with a spiritual lesson; fillers that are brief, purposeful, usually containing an anecdote, and always with a strong evangelical emphasis."

KEYNOTER, Key Club International, 3636 Woodview Trace, Indianapolis IN 46268. (317)875-8755. Articles Editor: Jack Brockley. Art Director: James Patterson. Monthly magazine. Circ. 125,000. As the official magazine of the world's largest high school service organization, we publish nonfiction articles that interest teen-agers and will help our readers become better students, better citizens, better leaders.

Nonfiction: Young adults: how-to, humorous, problem solving. Does not want to see first-person accounts; short stories. Buys 15 mss/year. Average word length: 1,800-2,500. Byline given.

How to Contact/Writers: Nonfiction: Query. SASE (IRC) for answer to query and return of ms; include Social Security number with submission. Reports on queries/mss in 1 month. Will consider simultaneous, photocopied, and computer printout submissions.

Illustration: Buys 2-3 illustrations/issue; buys 15 illustrations/year. Will review ms/illustration packages by authors/artists; ms/illustration packages submitted by authors with illustrations done by separate artists; illustrator's work for possible use with nonfiction articles. Works on assignment only.

How to Contact/Illustrators: Ms/illustration packages: Because of our publishing schedule, we prefer to work with illustrators/photographers within Indianapolis market. Illustrators only: Send resume; tear sheets; slides; samples; or photos. Reports on art samples only if interested. Original artwork returned at job's completion if requested.

Terms/Writers & Illustrators: Pays on acceptance. Buys first North American serial rights. Pays $75-300 for assigned/unsolicited articles. Sample copy free with 8½ × 11 SAE and 65¢ first-class stamp. Writer's guidelines free with SAE and 1 first-class stamp.

Tips: "Read the publications for which you will be writing. We are most interested in teen-age issues. Be prepared to interview experts; consider sources outside your hometown."

KID CITY, (A new name for the Electric Company Magazine), Children's Television Workshop, 1 Lincoln Plaza, New York NY 10023. (212)595-3456. Editor: Maureen Hunter-Bone. Magazine published 10 times a year. Circ. 260,000.

Fiction: Young readers: animal, contemporary, history, humorous, science fiction, sports, spy/mystery/adventure. Buys 3 mss/year. Average word length: 500-750. Byline given.

Nonfiction: Young readers: animal, history, how-to, interview/profile. Does not want to see religious material. Buys 10 mss/year. Average word lenth: 200-300. Byline given.

How to Contact/Writers: Fiction: Send complete ms. Nonfiction: Query. SASE (IRC)

for answer to query and return of ms. Reports on queries/mss in 4 weeks. Will consider photocopied, and computer printout submissions.
Illustration: Buys 5 illustrations/issue. Works on assignment only.
Terms/Writers & Illustrators: Pays on acceptance. Buys all rights. Pays $25-250 for assigned articles. Writer's guidelines free with SASE. Sample copy with SASE and $1.50.
Tips: Writers: "Be deft, original, not cutesy or moralistic. Avoid cliches but be real, too—don't go off the deep end into fantasy, either." Illustrators: "Send lots of sample cards to art directors. Write or call to bring in portfolios." Looks for: "fiction, photo-essays." (See listing for 3-2-1 Contact.)

LIGHTHOUSE, Lighthouse Publications, Box 1377, Auburn WA 98071-1377. Fiction Editor: Lynne Trindl. Bimonthly magazine. Circ. 500. Magazine contains timeless stories and poetry for family reading. 15-20% of material aimed at juvenile audience.
Fiction: Young readers, middle readers: animal, contemporary, humorous, sports, spy/mystery/adventure. Young adults: animal, contemporary, humorous, problem solving, romance, sports, spy/mystery/adventure. Does not want to see anything not "G-rated", any story with a message that is not subtly handled. Buys 15 mss/year. Average word length: 2,000. Byline given.
How to Contact/Writers: Fiction: Send complete ms. SASE (IRC) for return of ms and/or response; include Social Security number with submission. Reports on mss in 1 month. Will consider photocopied and computer printout submissions.
Terms/Writers: Pays on publication. Buys first North American serial rights; first rights. Sample copy for $2. Writer's guidelines free with regular SAE and 1 first-class stamp.
Tips: "All sections are open to freelance writers—just follow the guidelines and stay in the categories listed above."

LISTEN, Celebrating Positive Choices, Narcotics Education, Inc., 6830 Laurel St. NW, Washington DC 20012. (202)722-6726. Articles/Fiction Editor: Gary B. Swanson. Art Director: Paul Hey. Monthly magazine. Circ. 100,000. *Listen* offers positive alternatives to drug use for its teenage readers. 100% of material aimed at juvenile audience.
Fiction: Young adults: contemporary, humorous, problem solving. Buys 12 mss/year. Average word length: 1,000-1,500. Byline given.
Nonfiction: Young adults: how-to, interview/profile, problem solving. Buys 50 mss/year. Average word length: 1,000-1,200. Byline given.
How to Contact/Writers: Fiction/nonfiction: Send complete ms. SASE (IRC) for answer to query and return of ms. Reports on queries/mss in 2 months. Will consider photocopied and computer printout submissions.
Illustration: Buys 2 illustrations/issue. Will review ms/illustration packages submitted by authors/artists. Works on assignment only.
How to Contact/Illustrators: Illustrations only: Resume and tear sheets should be sent to art director, Pacific Press Publishing Assoc., Box 7000, Boise ID 83707.
Terms/Writers & Illustrators: Pays on acceptance. Buys first North American serial rights. Pays $150 for assigned articles; $100 for unsolicited articles. Sample copy for $1.50 and SASE. Writer's guidelines free with SASE.
Tips: *Listen* is a magazine for teenagers. It encourages development of good habits and high ideals of physical, social, and mental health. It bases its editorial philosophy of primary drug prevention on total abstinence from alcohol and other drugs. Because it is used extensively in public high-school classes, it does not accept articles and stories with overt religious emphasis. Four specific purposes guide the editors in selecting materials for *Listen*: 1) To portray a positive lifestyle and to foster skills and values that will help teenagers deal with contemporary problems, including smoking, drinking, and using drugs. This is *Listen*'s primary purpose. 2) To offer positive alternatives to a lifestyle of drug use of any kind. 3) To present scientifically accurate information about

the nature and effects of tobacco, alcohol, and other drugs. 4) To report medical research, community programs, and educational efforts which are solving problems connected with smoking, alcohol, and other drugs. *Positive Alternatives*. These articles should offer their readers activities that increase one's sense of self-worth through achievement and/or involvement in helping others. They are often categorized by three kinds of focus: 1) Hobbies—Recent subjects have been model railroading, autograph collecting, remote-control aircraft, amateur radio, photography, genealogy. 2) Recreation—*Listen* has recently featured articles on canoeing, orienteering, amateur golf, horseback riding, ice-boating. 3) Community Service—Recent subjects have been caring for injured raptor birds, working at summer camps for children with cancer, serving as teenage police cadets, volunteering for rescue work. Cartoons: May be slanted against using tobacco, alcohol, and other drugs; or may be of general interest to teenagers. Pays $15 each.

MY FRIEND, A Magazine for Children, Daughters of St. Paul/St. Paul Books and Media, 50 St. Paul's Ave., Jamaica Plain, Boston MA 02130. (617)522-8911. Articles/Fiction Editor: Sister Anne Joan, fsp. Art Director: Sister Annette Margaret, fsp. Magazine published 10 times/year. Circ. 14,500. *My Friend* is a magazine of inspiration and entertainment for a predominantly Catholic audience. Our readers are from 6-12 years of age.

Fiction: Picture material: animal, contemporary, religious. Young readers: contemporary, fantasy, history, humorous, problem solving, religious, sports, adventure. Middle readers: contemporary, history, humorous, problem solving, religious, sports, adventure. Young adults: religious. Does not want to see poetry, animals as main characters in religious story, stories whose basic thrust would be incompatible with Catholic values. Buys 50 mss/year. Average word length: 450-750. Byline given.

Nonfiction: Picture material: animal, religious. Young readers: history, how-to, humorous, interview/profile, religious. Middle readers: history, interview/profile, problem solving, religious. Does not want to see material that is not compatible with Catholic values; "new age" material. Buys 10 mss/year. Average word length: 450-750. Byline given.

How to Contact/Writers: Fiction/nonfiction: Send complete ms. SASE (IRC) for answer to query and return of ms. Reports on queries in 3 weeks; mss in 3-4 weeks. Will consider simultaneous, photocopied, and computer printout submissions.

Illustration: Buys 2 illustrations/issue; buys 15-20 illustrations/year. Preferred theme or style: Realistic depictions of children, but open to variety! Looking for a "Bible stories" artist, too. Will review ms/illustration packages by authors/artists; ms/illustration packages submitted by authors with illustrations done by separate artists; illustrator's work for possible use with fiction/nonfiction articles.

How to Contact/Illustrators: Ms/illustration packages: Send complete ms with copy of final art. Reports on art samples in 2 weeks. Original artwork not returned at job's completion "unless previously requested and arranged."

Terms/Writers & Illustrators: Pays on publication. Buys one-time rights. Pays in contributor copies, "it is our usual compensation." Additional payment for ms/illustration packages: "I suppose this would be negotiable. Rarely happens." Sample copy free with 9 × 12 SAE and 4 first-class stamps. Writer's/illustrator's guidelines free with SAE and 1 first-class stamp.

Tips: Writers: "One thing I would like to suggest (and it's really more about writing than about contacting publishers) is: Make sure that your story really reflects a child's point of view and way of thinking. We use a lot of fiction stories (contemporary and historical) involving children. Right now, we're especially looking for stories that would appeal to boys. We are not looking for poetry, unless it is humorous." Illustrators: "Please contact us! For the most part, we need illustrations for fiction stories; usually one 'main' illustration and a second supporting picture."

NATIONAL GEOGRAPHIC WORLD, National Geographic Society, 17th and M Streets NW, Washington DC 20036. (202)857-7000. Editor: Pat Robbins. Submissions Editor: Eleanor Shannahan. Photo Editor: Larry Nighswander. Art Director: Ursula Vosseler. Monthly magazine. Circ. 1.1 million. "National Geographic *World* features factual stories on outdoor adventure, natural history, sports, science, and history for children ages 8 through 12. Full-color photographs are used to attract young readers and the text easily guides them through the story." 100% of material aimed at juvenile audience. "*World* does not publish fiction.
Nonfiction: "*World* does not publish manuscripts from outside writers. Story ideas that lend themselves to photo stories will be considered, and, if accepted, a finder's fee will be paid for an original idea. All writing is done by staff or on assignment." Picture material: animal, history, how-to, travel. Middle readers: animal, history, how-to, travel. Average word length: 90-600.
How to Contact/Writers: Nonfiction: Query only—no ms please. SASE (IRC) for answer to query. Reports on queries in 6-8 weeks.
Illustration: Assignment only.
How to Contact/Illustrators: Ms/illustration packages: Query story idea first. Illustrations only: Submit samples in slide form or tear sheets. Reports on art samples only if interested. Original artwork returned at job's completion; NGS retains copyright.
Terms/Writers & Illustrators: Pays on publication. Buys one-time rights. Pays $75-350 for assigned articles. Free sample copy; contributors guidelines available free.
Tips: "All *World* stories are written by staff or contract writers.For *World*, the story proposal is the way to break in. Think through the focus of the story and outline what action photos are available. Keep in mind that *World* is a visual magazine. A story will work best if it has a very tight focus and if the photos show children interacting with their surroundings as well as with each other."

NOAH'S ARK, A Newspaper for Jewish Children, 8323 Southwest Freeway, #250, Houston TX 77074. (713)771-7143. Articles/Fiction Editor: Debbie Israel Dubin. Art Director: Nachman. Monthly tabloid. Circ. 450,000. All submissions must have Jewish content and positive Jewish values. The newspaper is sent to more than 400 religious schools and submissions must be appropriate for educational use as well. 100% of material aimed at juvenile.
Fiction: Young readers, middle readers: contemporary, history, religious, sports. Does not want to see Christian and secular material. Buys 3 mss/year. Average word length: 650. Byline given.
Nonfiction: Young readers, middle readers: history, how-to, humorous, interview/profile, problem solving, religious, travel. Does not want to see secular, Christian nonfiction. Buys 1 ms/year, "only because more not submitted." Average word length: 500. Byline given.
How to Contact/Writers: Fiction/nonfiction: Send complete ms. SASE (IRC) for answer to query and return of ms. Report on mss 6-8 weeks. Will consider photocopied and computer printout submissions.
Terms/Writers & Illustrators: Pays on acceptance. Buys first North American serial rights. Pays 5¢/word for unsolicited articles. Sample copy free with #10 SAE and 1 first-class stamp. Writer's guidelines free with SAE and 1 first-class stamp.
Tips: "Send appropriate material. We receive mostly inappropriate submissions; very few submissions have Jewish values as required."

ODYSSEY, Kalmbach Publishing Co., 1027 N. 7th St., Milwaukee WI 53233. (414)272-2060. Articles Editor: Nancy Mack. Art Director: Jane Borth-Lucius. Monthly magazine. Circ. 100,743. Magazine covers astronomy and space exploration for children ages 8-14. 100% of material aimed at juvenile audience.
Nonfiction: Middle readers, young adults: how-to, humorous, astronomy, space sci-

ence. Does not want to see very general or overview articles. Buys 20-30 mss/year. Average word length: 600-2,000. Byline given.

How to Contact/Writers: Nonfiction: Query. SASE (IRC) for answer to query and return of ms. Reports on queries/mss in 10 weeks. Will consider simultaneous, photo-copied, and computer printout submissions.

Illustration: Buys 10-12 illustrations/year. Will review ms/illustration packages by authors/artists; ms/illustration packages submitted by authors with illustrations done by separate artists; illustrator's work for possible use with fiction/nonfiction articles. Works on assignment only.

How to Contact/Illustrators: Ms/illustration packages: Query first. Illustrations only: Send tear sheets and/or slides. Reports on art samples in 10 weeks. Original artwork returned at job's completion.

Terms/Writers & Illustrators: Pays on publication. Buys one-time rights. Pays $100-350 for assigned/unsolicited articles. Additional payment for ms/illustration packages is $350-1,000. Pays $100-350/color (cover/inside) illustration; $100-300/b&w (cover/inside). Sample copy free with 9 × 11 SAE and 4 first-class stamps. Writer's guidelines free with SAE and 1 first-class stamp.

Tips: "At Odyssey, short, offbeat articles have the best chance of acceptance. Major articles usually are handled by staff or contributing editors." Looks for "short humorous articles and experiments. Keep the writing very simple (usually the topic will be technical)."

ON THE LINE, Mennonite Publishing House, 616 Walnut Ave., Scottdale PA 15683. (412)887-8500. Editor: Virginia Hostetler. "Monthly in weekly parts" magazine. Circ. 10,000. 100% of material aimed at juvenile audience.

Fiction: Buys 52 mss/year. Average word length: 900-1,200. Byline given.

Nonfiction: Middle readers: animal, history, how-to, humorous, interview/profile, problem solving, religious. Does not want to see articles written from an adult perspective. Average word length: 200-900. Byline given.

How to Contact/Writers: Fiction/nonfiction: Send complete ms. SASE for return of ms. Reports on queries/mss in 1 month. Will consider simultaneous, photocopied, and computer printout submissions "if print is good quality."

Illustration: Buys 1-2 illustrations/issue; buys 52 illustrations/year. "Illustrations are done on assignment only, to accompany our stories and articles—our need for new artists is very limited." Will review ms/illustration packages submitted by authors/artists. Works on assignment only.

How to Contact/Illustrators: Illustrations only: Prefer samples they do not want returned; these stay in our files. Reports on art samples only if interested. Original art work returned at job's completion.

Terms/Writers & Illustrators: Pays on acceptance. Buys one-time rights; second serial (reprint rights). Pays 2-4¢/word for assigned/unsolicited articles. Pays $12-50/color (inside) illustration. Sample copy free with 7 × 10 SAE. Free writer's guidelines.

OWL MAGAZINE, The Discovery Magazine for Children, Young Naturalist Foundation, Ste. 306, 56 The Esplanade, Toronto Ontario M5E 1A7 Canada. (416)868-6001. Editor: Sylvia Funston. Managing Editor: Elizabeth MacLeod. Art Director: Tim Davin. Magazine published 10 times/year. Circ. 160,000. *Owl* helps children over eight discover and enjoy the world of science and nature. We look for articles that are fun to read, that inform from a child's perspective and that motivate hands-on interaction. *Owl* explores the reader's many interests in the natural world in a scientific, but always entertaining, way.

Fiction: Middle readers, young adults: animal, contemporary, fantasy, humorous, science fiction, sports, spy/mystery/adventure. Does not want to see romance, religion, anthropomorphizing. Average word length: 500-1,000. Byline given. "We publish only

3-4 pieces of fiction per year and they are usually only excerpts from books."
Nonfiction: Middle readers, young adults: animal, biology, high-tech, how-to, humor, interview/profile, travel. Does not want to see religious topics, anthropomorphizing. Buys 20 mss/year. Average word length: 200-1,500. Byline given.
How to Contact/Writers: Fiction/nonfiction: Query with published clips. SASE (IRC) for return of ms. Report on queries in 4-6 weeks; mss in 6-8 weeks. Will consider photocopied and computer printout submissions.
Illustration: Buys 3-5 illustrations/issue; buys 40-50 illustrations/year. Preferred theme or style: lively, involving, fun, with emotional impact and appeal. Works on assignment only.
How to Contact/Illustrators: Illustrations only: Send tear sheets and slides. Reports on art samples only if interested. Original artwork returned at job's completion.
Terms/Writers & Illustrators: Pays on acceptance. Buys all rights. Pays $35-600 for assigned/unsolicited articles. Pays $600-700/color (inside) illustration. Sample copy $2.50. Free writer's guidelines.
Tips: Writers: "Talk to kids and find out what they're interested in; read kid's magazines; make sure your research is thorough and find good consultants who are doing up-to-the-minute research. Be sure to read the magazine carefully to become familiar with *Owl*'s style." Illustrators: "Talk to kids and find out what work appeals to them; look at kid's magazines and books. Look through *Owl* to see what styles we prefer." (See listing for Chickadee.)

PENNYWHISTLE PRESS, Gannett, Box 500-P, Washington DC 20044. (703)276-3796. Articles/Fiction Editor: Anita Sama. Art Director: Eileen Kelly. Weekly tabloid. Circ. 2.5 million. "We are an educational supplement for kids from 4 to 14 years old. We generally buy fiction from freelancers about kids in real life situations." 100% of material aimed at juvenile audience.
Fiction: Picture material, young readers, middle readers, young adults: animal, contemporary, history, humorous, problem solving, science fiction, sports, spy/mystery/adventure. Does not want to see stories that include talking animals. Buys 30 mss/year. Average word length: 200-600. Byline given.
How to Contact/Writers: Fiction: Send complete ms. Large SASE for return of ms. Reports on mss in 2 months. Will consider photocopied and computer printout submissions.
Illustration: Buys 2 illustrations/issue; buys 4 illustrations/year. Will review ms/illustration packages by authors/artists; ms/illustration packages submitted by authors with illustrations done by separate artists; illustrator's work for possible use with fiction/nonfiction articles.
How to Contact/Illustrators: Illustrations only: Send tear sheets. Reports on art samples only if interested. Original artwork returned at job's completion.
Terms/Writers & Illustrators: Pays on acceptance. Buys all rights. Pays $125 for unsolicited articles. Additional payment for ms/illustration package is $250-300. Sample copy 75¢.

PIONEER, Brotherhood Commission, SBC, 1548 Poplar Ave., Memphis TN 38134. (901)272-2461. Articles Editor: Tim Bearden. Monthly magazine. Circ. 30,000. Magazine contains boy interests, sports, crafts, sports personalities, religious.
Nonfiction: Young adults: animal, how-to, humorous, interview/profile, problem solving, religious, travel. Buys 15 mss/year. Average word length: 600-800. Byline given.
How to Contact/Writers: Nonfiction: Send complete ms. SASE (IRC) for return of ms; include Social Security number with submission. Reports on queries in 1 month; mss in 2 months. Will consider simultaneous, photocopied, and computer printout submissions.
Illustration: Buys 1-2 illustrations/issue; buys 12 illustrations/year. Will review ms/illus-

tration packages by authors/artists; ms/illustration packages submitted by authors with illustrations done by separate artists; illustrator's work for possible use with fiction/nonfiction articles.

How to Contact/Illustrators: Ms/illustration packages: Send complete ms with final art.

Terms/Writers & Illustrators: Pays on acceptance. Buys one-time rights, simultaneous rights. Pays $25-35 for unsolicited articles. Sample copy free with #10 SAE and 2 first-class stamps. Writer's/illustrator's guidelines free with SAE and 1 first-class stamp.

POCKETS, Devotional Magazine for Children, The Upper Room, 1908 Grand, Box 189, Nashville TN 37202. (615)340-7333. Articles/Fiction Editor: Janet M. Bugg. Art Director: Chris Schechner, Ste. 206, 3100 Carlisle Plaza, Dallas TX 75204. Magazine published 11 times/year. Circ. 60,000. Stories should help children 6 to 12 experience a Christian lifestyle that is not always a neatly wrapped moral package, but is open to the continuing revelation of God's will.

Fiction: Young readers, middle readers: contemporary, fantasy, history, religious, "Retold Bible stories." Does not want to see violence. Buys 26-30 mss/year. Average word length: 800-2,000. Byline given.

Nonfiction: Young readers, middle readers: history, interview/profile, religious, "communication activities." Does not want to see how-to articles. Our nonfiction reads like a story. History is in form of role-model stories as is profile. Buys 10 mss/year. Average word length: 800-2,000. Byline given.

How to Contact/Writers: Fiction/nonfiction: Send complete ms. SASE (IRC) for return of ms. Report on mss in 4 weeks. Will consider simultaneous, photocopied, and computer printout submissions.

Illustration: Buys 30 illustrations/issue. Preferred theme or style: varied; both 4-color and 2-color. Will review ms/illustration packages by authors/artists; ms/illustration packages submitted by authors with illustrations done by separate artists; illustrator's work for possible use with fiction/nonfiction articles. Works on assignment only.

How to Contact/Illustrators: Ms/illustration packages: No final art. Illustrations only: Send resume, tear sheets, slides to Chris Schechner, Ste. 206, 3100 Carlisle Plaza, Dallas TX 75204. Reports on art samples only if interested. Original artwork returned at job's completion.

Terms/Writers & Illustrators: Pays on acceptance. Buys first North American rights. Pays $250 for assigned articles; 7-10¢/word for unsolicited articles. Pays $500/color (cover) illustration; $50-500/color (inside). Sample copy free with 7×9 SAE and 4 first-class stamps. Writer's/illustrator's guidelines free with SAE and 1 first-class stamp.

Tips: "Ask for our themes first. They are set yearly in the fall."

PRIMARY FRIEND, Wesleyan Publishing House, 6060 Castleway W. Dr., Box 50434, Indianapolis IN 46250. (317)842-0444, ext. 193. Articles/Fiction Editor/Art Director: Diane Duvall. Quarterly magazine. Circ. 31,000. "*Primary Friend* is a Sunday School take-home paper for children ages 6-8 years old. All contributors need to keep in mind the ages of the children this publication is for." 100% of material aimed at juvenile audience.

Fiction: Young readers: animal, contemporary, history, humorous, problem solving, sports, spy/mystery/adventure. Does not want to see animals praying, romance, science fiction, fantasy. Buys 4 mss/year. Average word length: 450-600. Byline given.

Nonfiction: Young readers: animal, history, humorous, problem solving, religious, travel. Does not want to see animals praying, science fiction, fantasy. Buys 4 mss/year. Average word length: 450-600. Byline given.

How to Contact/Writers: Fiction/nonfiction: Send complete ms. SASE (IRC) for answer to query and return of ms; include Social Security number with submission. Report on mss in 1-2 months. Will consider computer printout submissions.

Illustration: Will review ms/illustration packages by authors/artists; ms/illustration packages submitted by authors with illustrations done by separate artists; illustrators work for possible use with fiction/nonfiction articles.
How to Contact/Illustrators: Ms/illustration packages: Send complete ms and final art. Illustrations only: Send color slides. Reports on art samples in 1-2 months.
Terms/Writers & Illustrators: Pays on publication. Buys first rights. Publication not copyrighted. Sample copy free with #10 SAE and 1 first-class stamp. Writer's/illustrator's guidelines free with #10 SAE and 1 first-class stamp.
Tips: "The following are turn-offs: a letter of recommendation from a teacher, a letter of recommendation from a pastor, tear sheets. The ability of the writer will be apparent. A resume might be a way for the editor to become acquainted with the writer without the use of a letter of recommendation." Advice to new writers: "Be yourself. Don't copy someone else's writing technique. Use a technique that is you—not your teacher's or your friend's. Remember your childhood and how it was for you to be a child. Have the children in your stories act in a developmentally appropriate manner." Advice to new artists: "Use bright, clear colors which captivate the action and attract reader interest. Draw children (not little adults)."

R-A-D-A-R, Standard Publishing, 8121 Hamilton Ave., Cincinnati OH 45231. (513)931-4050. Articles/Fiction Editor: Margaret Williams. Art Director: Frank Sutton. Weekly magazine. Circ. 105,000. R-A-D-A-R is a weekly take-home paper for boys and girls who are in grades 3-6. Our goal is to reach these children with the truth of God'sWord, and to help them make it the guide of their lives. Many of our features, including our stories, now correlate with the Sunday-school lesson themes. Send for a quarterly theme list and sample copies of R-A-D-A-R. Keep in mind that others will be submitting stories for the same themes—this is not an assignment.
Fiction: Middle readers: animal, contemporary, history, humorous, problem solving, religious, sports, spy/mystery/adventure. Does not want to see fantasy or science fiction. Buys 150 mss/year. Average word length: 400-1,000. Byline given.
Nonfiction: Middle readers: animal, history, how-to, humorous, interview/profile, problem solving, religious, travel. Buys 50 mss/year. Average word length: 400-1,000. Byline given.
How to Contact/Writers: Fiction/nonfiction: Send complete ms. SASE (IRC) for answer to query and return of ms; include Social Security number with submission. Reports on queries/mss 6-8 weeks. Will consider simultaneous (but prefer not to), photocopied (must be clean copies), and computer printout submissions. Reprint submissions must be retyped.
Illustration: Will review ms/illustration packages by authors/artists; ms/illustration packages submitted by authors with illustrations done by separate artists; illustrator's work for possible use with fiction/nonfiction articles. Works on assignment only; there have been a few exceptions to this.
How to Contact/Illustrators: Illustrations only: Send resume, tear sheets; samples of art can be photocopied. Reports on art samples only if interested.
Terms/Writers & Illustrators: Pays on acceptance. Buys first rights, one-time rights, second serial; all rights to art. Pays 3¢/word for unsolicited articles, few are assigned. Contributor copies given "not as payment, but all contributors receive copies of their art/articles." Pays $60/b&w (cover) illustration; $40/b&w (inside) "line art only—color is added by our art department." Sample copy free with 9⅜ × 4¼ SAE and 1 first-class stamp. Writer's/illustrator's guidelines free with 9⅜ × 4¼ SAE and 1 first-class stamp. (See listing for Straight.)

RANGER RICK, National Wildlife Federation, 8925 Leesburg Pike, Vienna VA 22184. (703)790-4000. Editor: Gerald Bishop. Art Director: Donna Miller. Monthly magazine. Circ. 950,000. "Our audience ranges from ages six to twelve, though we aim the reading

Jean Pidgeon, Baltimore, Maryland, sold one-time rights to this piece for use in an article on turkeys that appeared in **Ranger Rick** *magazine. The piece was rendered in pencil and airbrush using Dr. Martin's Dyes. Donna Miller, design director for the National Wildlife Federation, feels this art is successful because of its "great action and color. Jean has a great sense of humor,"* *she adds.*

level of most material at nine-year-olds or fourth graders." 100% of material aimed at juvenile audience.

Fiction: Animal, fantasy, humorous, science fiction. Buys 4 mss/year. Average word length: 900. Byline given.

Nonfiction: Animal, humorous. Buys 20-30 mss/year. Average word length: 900. Byline given.

How to Contact/Writers: Fiction: Query with published clips; send complete ms. Nonfiction: Query with published clips. SASE (IRC) for answer to query and return of ms; include Social Security number with submission. Reports on queries/mss in 6 weeks. Will consider computer printout submissions.

Illustration: Buys 6-8 illustrations/issue; buys 75-100 illustrations/year. Preferred theme or style: Nature, wildlife. Will review an illustrator's work for possible use with fiction/nonfiction articles and columns by other authors. Works on assignment only.

How to Contact/Illustrators: Illustrations only: Send resume, tear sheets. Reports on art samples in 6 weeks. Original artwork returned at job's completion.

Terms/Writers & Illustrators: Pays on acceptance. Forms, buys all rights (first N.A. serial rights negotiable). Pays up to $550 for full-length of best quality. For illustrations, buys one-time rights. Pays $250-1,000 for color (inside, per page) illustration. Sample copy $2. Writer's guidelines free with SAE.

Tips: "Fiction and nonfiction articles may be written on any aspect of wildlife, nature, outdoor adventure and discovery, domestic animals with a 'wild' connection (such as domestic pigs and wild boars), science, conservation, or related subjects. To find out what subjects have been covered recently, consult our annual indexes and the *Children's Magazine Guide*. These are available in many libraries. The National Wildlife Federation (NWF) discourages the keeping of wildlife as pets, so the keeping of such pets should not be featured in your copy. Avoid stereotyping of any group. For instance, girls can enjoy nature and the outdoors as much as boys can, and mothers can be just as knowledgeable as fathers. The only way you can write successfully for *Ranger Rick* is to know the kinds of subjects and approaches we like. And the only way you can do that is to read the magazine. Recent issues can be found in most libraries or are available from our office for $2 a copy." Illustrators: "Start small, with less demanding magazines."

SCHOOL MAGAZINE, BLAST OFF!, COUNTDOWN, ORBIT, TOUCHDOWN, New South Wales Dept. of Education, Box A242, Sydney NSW 2000 Australia. (02)261-7231. Editor: Anna Fienberg. 4 monthly magazines. Circ. 305,000. *School Magazine* is a literary magazine that is issued free to all N.S.W. public schools. Private schools and individuals subscribe for a small fee. We include stories, articles, plays, poems, crosswords. The 4 magazines issued each month are graded according to age level, 8-12 years. 100% of material aimed at juvenile audience.
Fiction: Young readers: animal, contemporary, fantasy, humorous. Middle readers: animal, contemporary, fantasy, history, humorous, problem solving, romance, science fiction, spy/mystery/adventure. Buys 30 mss/year. Average word length: 500-2,500. By-line given.
Nonfiction: Young readers: animal, humorous, interview/profile. Middle readers: animal, history, humorous, interview/profile, problem solving, travel. Does not want to see political topics. Buys 30 mss/year. Average word length: 500-2,000. Byline given.
How to Contact/Writers: Fiction/nonfiction: Send complete ms. SASE (IRC) for return of ms. Reports on queries in 2 months. Will consider photocopies and computer printout submissions "as long as it is clear and legible."
Terms/Writers & Illustrators: "Payment when accounts done, usually 2 weeks after acceptance." Buys one-time rights. "Pays $112 per thousand words." Free sample copy.
Tips: "Subscribe to *School Magazine*—read as much children's literature as possible." Looks for: "Both fiction and articles. Fantasy, real-life both acceptable for fiction. Good quality is the main criteria."

SHOFAR, Sr. Publications Ltd., 43 Northcote Dr., Melville NY 11747. (516)643-4598. Articles Editor: Gerald H. Grayson. Magazine published monthly Oct. through May—double issues Dec./Jan. and April/May. Circ. 10,000. For Jewish children 8-13. 100% of material aimed at juvenile audience.
Fiction: Middle readers: contemporary, humorous, religious, sports. Buys 10-20 mss/year. Average word length: 500-1,000. Byline given.
Nonfiction: Middle readers: history, humorous, interview/profile, religious. Buys 10-20 mss/year. Average word length: 500-1,000. Byline given.
How to Contact/Writers: Fiction/nonfiction: Send complete ms. Will consider simultaneous, photocopied, computer printout, and electronic submissions via disk or modem (only MacIntosh).
Illustration: Buys 3-4 illustrations/issue; buys 15-20 illustrations/year. Works on assignment only.
How to Contact/Illustrators: Ms/illustration packages: Query first. Illustrations only: Send tear sheets. Reports on art samples only if interested. Original artwork returned at job's completion.
Terms/Writers & Illustrators: Buys one-time rights. Pays $25-125 for assigned articles. Additional payment for ms/illustration packages $50-250. Pays $25-100/b&w cover illustration; $50-150/color (cover). Sample copy free with 9 × 12 SAE and 3 first-class stamps. Free writer's/illustrator's guidelines.

THE SINGLE PARENT, Journal of Parents Without Partners, Inc., Parents Without Partners, Inc., 8807 Colesville Rd., Silver Spring MD 20910. (301)588-9354. Articles/Fiction Editor/Art Director: Allan Glennon. Bimonthly magazine. Circ. 140,000. Members of PWP are single parents who are divorced, widowed, or never married. All our material is related to this basic fact. We look at the positive side of our situation, and are interested in all aspects of parenting, and in the particular situation of single parenting. 10% of material aimed at juvenile audience.

Fiction: Young readers, middle readers, young adults: contemporary, fantasy, humorous, problem solving, science fiction, spy/mystery/adventure. Does not want to see anthropomorphic material. Buys 12 mss/year. Average word length: 800-1,500. Byline given.

Nonfiction: Young readers, middle readers, young adults: humorous, problem solving. "We do not ordinarily use nonfiction aimed at children, but could be persuaded by a particularly good piece." Does not want to see material unrelated to single-parent children and families. Average word length: 800-1,800. Byline given.

How to Contact/Writers: Fiction/nonfiction: Send complete ms. SASE (IRC) for answer to query and return of ms; include Social Security number with submission. Reports on queries/mss in 3 weeks. Will consider simultaneous, photocopied, and computer printout submissions.

Illustration: Buys 4-6 illustrations/issue. Preferred theme or style: Line art, sometimes with mechanicals. No special preference for style, but lean toward realistic. Will review ms/illustration packages by authors/artists; ms/illustration packages submitted by authors with illustrations done by separate artists; illustrator's work for possible use with fiction/nonfiction articles. Works on assignment only.

How to Contact/Illustrators: Ms/illustration packages: Send complete ms with final art with prepaid return envelope. Illustrations only: Send nonreturnable samples in whatever form the artist prefers. Reports on art samples only if interested. Original artwork returned at job's completion.

Terms/Writers & Illustrators: Pays on publication. Buys one-time rights. Pays $50-175 for assigned articles; $35-175 for unsolicited articles. Additional payment for ms/illustration packages: $50-75. Pay $100-150/color (cover) illustration; $50-75/b&w (inside); $50-75/color (inside). Sample copy $1. Writer's/illustrator's guidelines free with SASE.

Tips: Writers: "Study your target; do not submit material if you've never seen the magazine. In stories where the protagonist undergoes a behavior change, build up a credible reason for it. 'Comes to realize' is not a credible reason. We are overstocked at the moment with children's stories, but still buy one occasionally that we're unable to resist. Our greatest need is for articles for adults, in particular, articles on parenting from the single father's perspective." Illustrators: "Get examples of your work to as many editors as possible, but remember, there are hundreds of others doing the same thing. I review all samples that are submitted, and put those that appeal to me in a separate file as potential illustrators for the magazine. To get into the 'may call on' file, provide me with nonreturnable samples that illustrate the broadest range of your work—I may not appreciate your cartoon style, but think your realistic style is super or vice versa."

SKYLARK, 2233 171st St., Hammond IN 46323. (219)989-2262. Articles Editor: Shelia Binkley. Fiction Editor: Eunice Madison. Art Director: Cathy Kadow. Annual magazine. Circ. 500-750. 30% of material aimed at juvenile audience.

Fiction: Picture material, young readers, middle readers, young adults: animal, contemporary, fantasy, history, humorous, problem solving, religious, romance, science fiction, sports, spy/mystery/adventure. Does not want to see material about Satan worship, graphic sex. Byline given.

Nonfiction: Picture material, young readers, middle readers, young adults: animal, history, how-to, humorous, interview/profile, problem solving, religious, travel. Does not want to see material about Satan worship, graphic sex. Byline given.

How to Contact/Writers: Fiction/nonfiction: Send complete ms. SASE (IRC) for return of ms. Reports on queries/mss in 2 months. Will consider simultaneous, photocopied, and computer printout submissions.

Illustration: Will review ms/illustration packages by authors/artists; ms/illustration packages submitted by authors with illustrations done by separate artists; illustrators work for possible use with fiction/nonfiction articles.

How to Contact/Illustrators: Illustrations only: Artwork. Reports on art samples in 2 months. Original artwork returned at job's completion "if a SASE included with artwork."
Terms/Writers & Illustrators: Pays in contributor's copies. Sample copy $3 with SAE. Writer's/illustrator's guidelines free with SASE.
Tips: Writers: "Do not send handwritten material, typed double-spaced only." Illustrators: "Use ink, pencil does not reproduce well, also send black and white only."

STANDARD PUBLISHING (See R-A-D-A-R, Straight.)

STONE SOUP, The Magazine by Children, Children's Art Foundation, Box 83, Santa Cruz CA 95063. (408)426-5557. Articles/Fiction Editor, Art Director: Ms. Gerry Mandel. Magazine published 5 times a year. Circ. 10,000. "We publish fiction, poetry, book reviews, and artwork by children ages 6-13." 100% of material aimed at juvenile audience.
Fiction: Picture material, young readers, middle readers, young adults: animal, contemporary, fantasy, history, humorous, problem solving, science fiction, sports, spy/mystery/ adventure. Does not want to see: school assignments, formula writing of any kind. Buys 30 mss/year. Byline given.
Nonfiction: Picture material, young readers, middle readers, young adults: interview/ profile, problem solving. Does not want to see: School assignments. Buys 10 mss/year. Byline given.
How to Contact/Writers: Fiction/nonfiction: Send complete ms. SASE (IRC) for return of ms. Reports on queries in 2 weeks; mss in 6 weeks. Will consider photocopied and computer printout submissions.
Illustration: Buys 5 illustrations/issue; buys 25 illustrations/year. Will review ms/illustration packages by authors/artists; ms/illustration packages submitted by authors with illustrations done by separate artists; illustrators work for possible use with fiction/ nonfiction articles.
How to Contact/Illustrators: Ms/illustration packages: Send final art. Illustrations only: Send samples of artwork. Reports on art samples in 6 weeks.
Terms/Writers & Illustrators: Pays on acceptance. Buys all rights. Pays $8-50 for assigned articles. "We pay for unsolicited work in copies." Pays range for illustrations is $8-50. Sample copy $2. Free writer's/illustrator's guidelines.

STRAIGHT, Standard Publishing, 8121 Hamilton Ave., Cincinnati OH 45231. (513)931-4050. Articles/Fiction Editor: Carla J. Crane. Art Director: Frank Sutton. "Quarterly in weekly parts" magazine. Circ. 60,000. *Straight* is a magazine designed for today's Christian teenagers.
Fiction: Young adults: Contemporary, humorous, problem solving, religious, sports. Does not want to see science fiction, fantasy, historical. Buys 100-115 mss/year. Average word length: 1,100-1,500. Byline given.
Nonfiction: Young adults: how-to, humorous, interview/profile, problem solving, religious. Does not want to see devotionals. Buys 24-30 mss/year. Average word length: 500-1,000. Byline given.
How to Contact/Writers: Fiction/nonfiction: Query or send complete ms. SASE (IRC) for answer to query and return of ms; include Social Security number with submission. Report on queries in 1-2 weeks; mss in 4-6 weeks. Will consider simultaneous, photocopied, and computer printout submissions.
Illustration: Buys 40-45 illustrations/year. Preferred theme or style: Realistic, cartoon. Will review ms/illustration packages submitted by authors/artists "on occasion." Works on assignment only.
How to Contact/Illustrators: Ms/illustration packages: Query first. Illustrations only: Art done on assignment only. Artists must work through the art director.

Terms/Writers & Illustrators: Pays on acceptance. Buys first rights; one-time rights; second serial (reprint rights). Sample copy free with business SAE. Writer's/illustrator's guidelines free with business SAE.

Tips: "Study the copies and guidelines and get to know teenagers: how they talk, act, and feel. Write fiction from the teenager's point of view. Fiction must appeal to teenagers and have an interesting, well-constructed plot. The main characters should be contemporary teens who cope with modern-day problems using Christian principles. Stories should be uplifting, positive and character-building, but not preachy. Conflicts must be resolved realistically, with thought-provoking and honest endings. Accepted length is 1,100 to 1,500 words. Nonfiction is accepted. We use devotional pieces, articles on current issues from a Christian point of view, and humor. Nonfiction pieces should concern topics of interest to teens, including school, family life, recreation, friends, part-time jobs, dating and music." (See listing for R-A-D-A-R.)

3-2-1 CONTACT, Children's Television Workshop, One Lincoln Plaza, New York NY 10023. (212)595-3456. Articles Editor: Jonathan Rosenbloom. Fiction Editor: Eric Weiner. Art Director: Al Nagy. Magazine published 10 times/year. Circ. 440,000. This is a science and technology magazine for 8-14 year olds. Features cover all areas of science and nature. 100% of material aimed at juvenile audience.

Fiction: Middle readers: science fiction, spy/mystery/adventure. Young adults: science fiction, spy/mystery/adventure. "All of our stories must have a science slant. No fantasy, history, religion, romance." Buys 10 mss/year. Average word length: 750-1,000. Byline given.

Nonfiction: Middle readers: animal, how-to, interview/profile. Young adults: animal, how-to, interview/profile. Does not want to see religion, travel or history. Buys 20 mss/year. Average word length: 750-1,000. Byline given.

How to Contact/Writers: Fiction/nonfiction: Query with published clips. SASE (IRC) for answer to query. Reports on queries in 3 weeks. Will consider photocopied submissions.

Illustration: Buys 15 illustrations/issue; buys 150 illustrations/year. Works on assignment only.

How to Contact/Illustrators: Illustrations only: Send tear sheets. Reports on art samples only if interested. Original artwork returned at job's completion.

Terms/Writers & Illustrators: Pays on acceptance. Pays $100-400 for assigned/unsolicited articles. Pays $500-1,000/color (cover) illustration; $150-300/b&w (inside); $175-350/color (inside). Sample copy for $1.50 and 8 × 14 SASE; writer's/illustrator's guidelines free with 8½ × 11 SASE.

Tips: Looks for "features. We do not want articles based on library research. We want on-the-spot interviews about what's happening in science now." (see listing for Kid City)

TOGETHER TIME, Children's Ministries, 6401 The Paseo, Kansas City MO 64131. Editor: Lynda T. Boardman. Executive Editor: Robert D. Troutman. Weekly tabloid. "*Together Time* is a take home reading piece for 2 and 3 year-olds and their parents. It correlates with ADLDERSGATE GRADED CURRICULUM for twos and threes. The major purposes of *Together Time* are to: provide a home reading piece to help parents build Christian behavior and values in their children, provide life-related home reinforcement for Biblical concepts taught in the S.S. curriculum. *Together Time's* target audience is children ages 2 and 3." 100% of material aimed at juvenile audience.

Fiction: Picture material: religious. "Fiction stories should have definite Christian emphasis or character-building values, without being preachy. The setting, plot, and action should be realistic." Average word length: 150-200. Byline given.

How to Contact/Writers: Fiction: Send complete ms. SASE (IRC) for return of ms. Reports on mss in 10-12 weeks.

Terms/Writers: Pays on acceptance. Buys first rights. Pays 3.5¢/word for unsolicited articles. Complimentary copy mailed to contributor. Writer's guidelines free with #10 SAE.

Tips: *"Together Time* is planned to reinforce the Biblical concepts taught in the S.S. curriculum. Because of this, the basic themes needed are as follows: security in knowing there is a God, God is creator and giver of good gifts, Jesus is God's son, Jesus is a friend and helper, the Bible is God's special book, introduction to God's love and forgiveness, asking forgiveness (from parents, teacher, friends, and God), expressing simple prayers, church is a special place where we learn about God, each person is special and loved by God, accept failure without losing self-confidence, desire to be like Jesus, desire to be helpful, appreciate God's world, appreciate community helpers." (See listing for Discoveries.)

TOUCH, Calvinettes, Box 7259, Grand Rapids MI 49510. (616)241-5616. Editor: Joanne Ilbrink. Managing Editor: Carol Smith. Art Director: Chris Cook. Monthly (with combined issues May/June, July/Aug.) magazine. Circ. 14,300. *"Touch* is designed to help girls ages 9-14 see how God is at work in their lives and in the world around them." 100% of material aimed at juvenile audience.

Fiction: Middle readers: animal, contemporary, history, humorous, problem solving, religious, romance. Does not want to see unrealistic stories and those with trite, easy endings. Buys 40 mss/year. Average word length: 400-1,000. Byline given.

Nonfiction: Middle readers: how-to, humorous, interview/profile, problem solving, religious. Buys 5 mss/year. Average word length: 200-800. Byline given.

How to Contact/Writers: Fiction/nonfiction: Send complete ms. SASE (IRC) for return of ms. Report on mss in 2 months. Will consider simultaneous, photocopied, and computer printout submissions.

Illustration: Buys 1-2 illustrations/issue; buys 10-15 illustrations/year. Prefers illustrations to go with stories. Will review ms/illustration packages by authors/artists; ms/illustration packages submitted by authors with illustrations done by separate artists. Works on assignment only.

How to Contact/Illustrators: Ms/illustration packages: "We would prefer to consider finished art with a ms." Illustrations only: "A sample of their work could be submitted in tear sheets or rough drafts." Reports on art samples only if interested.

Terms/Writers & Illustrators: Pays on publication. Buys first North American serial rights; first rights; second serial (reprint rights); simultaneous rights. Pays $20-50 for assigned articles; $5-30 for unsolicited articles. "We send complimentary copies in addition to pay." Additional payment for ms/illustration packages: $5-20. Pays $25-50/b&w (cover) illustration; $15-25/b&w (inside) illustration. Writer's guidelines free with SAE and first class stamps.

Tips: Writers: "The stories should be current, deal with children's problems and joys, and help girls see God at work in their lives through humor as well as problem solving." Illustrators: "Keep trying! Write for guidelines and our biannual update. It is difficult working with artists who are not local."

TQ, Teen Quest, Good News Broadcasting Assoc., Box 82808, Lincoln NE 68501. (402)474-4567. Articles/Fiction Editor: Barbara Comito. Art Director: Victoria Valentine. Monthly (combined July/August issue) magazine. Circ. 72,000. Ours is a magazine for Christian teenagers. Articles and fiction purchased from freelancers must have a Christian basis, be relevant to contemporary teen culture, and be written in a style understandable and attractive to teenagers. Artwork must be likewise appropriate. 100% of material aimed at juvenile audience.

Fiction: Young adults: contemporary, fantasy, humorous, problem solving, religious, romance, science fiction, sports, spy/mystery/adventure. Does not want to see historical material. Buys 40 mss/year. Average word length: 1,500-3,000. Byline given.

Nonfiction: Young adults: how-to, humorous, interview/profile, problem solving, religious, travel. Buys 30 mss/year. Average word length: 500-2,000. Byline given.

How to Contact/Writers: Fiction/nonfiction: Query. SASE (IRC) for answer to query and return of ms. Reports on queries in 6 weeks; mss in 6-8 weeks. Will consider simultaneous, photocopied, and computer printout submissions.

Illustration: Buys 5 illustrations/issue; buys 50 illustrations/year. Preferred theme or style: Realistic, somewhat contemporary, but not too far out of the mainstream. Works on assignment only.

How to Contact/Illustrators: Ms/illustration packages: Query only. Illustrations only: Send tear sheets. Reports on art samples only if interested. Original art work returned at job's completion.

Terms/Writers & Illustrators: Pays on completion of assignment. Buys one-time rights. Pays 8-10¢/word for assigned articles; 4-7¢/word for unsolicited articles. Sample copy for 10×12 SAE and 5 first-class stamps; writer's/illustrator's guidelines for business-size envelope and 1 first-class stamp.

Tips: Writers: "Just familiarize yourself with the magazine to which you're submitting. Get to know what we like, our style. Fiction: be current; Christian message without being 'preachy.' Most stories we buy will center on the lives and problems of 14 to 17 year-old characters. The problems involved should be common to teens (dating, family, alcohol and drugs, peer pressure, school, sex, talking about one's faith to non- believers, standing up for convictions, etc.) in which the resolution (or lack of it) is true to our reader's experiences. In other words, no happily-ever-after endings, last-page spiritual conversions or pat answers to complex problems. We're interested in the everyday (though still profound) experiences of teen life — stay away from sensationalism." Illustrators: "Fiction: assignment only; send samples of work."

TURTLE MAGAZINE, For Preschool Kids, Ben Franklin Literary & Medical Society, Children's Better Health Institute, Box 567, Indianapolis IN 46206. (317)636-8881. Articles/Fiction Editor: Beth Wood Thomas. Art Director: Ricardo Gonzalez. Monthly/bimonthly magazine, Feb/Mar., April/May, June/July and August/September. Circ. approx. 650,000. *Turtle* uses bedtime or naptime stories that can be read to the child. Also used are health-related articles. 100% of material aimed at juvenile audience.

Fiction: Picture material: animal, health. Does not want to see stories about monsters or scary things. Stories in which the characters indulge in unhealthy activity like eating junk food — unless a moral is taught. Buys 50 mss/year. Average word length: 200-600. Byline given.

Nonfiction: Picture material: animal, health. Buys 20 mss/year. Average word length: 200-600. Byline given.

How to Contact/Writers: Fiction/nonfiction: Send complete ms. SASE (IRC) for return of ms; include Social Security number with submission. Reports on mss in 8-10 weeks. Will consider computer printout submissions.

Terms/Writers & Illustrators: Sample copy for 75¢. Writer's/illustrator's guidelines free with SAE and 1 first-class stamp.

Tips: "We need more stories that reflect these changing times but at the same time communicate good, wholesome values. We are especially in need of holiday material — stories, articles, and activities. Characters in realistic stories should be up-to-date. Many of our readers have working mothers and/or come from single-parent homes." (See listings for Children's Digest, Children's Playmate, Humpty Dumpty's Magazine.)

TYRO MAGAZINE, TYRO Publishing, 194 Carlbert St., Sault Ste. Marie ON P6A 5E1 Canada. (705)253-6402. Articles Editor: George Hemingway. Fiction Editor: Stan Gordon. Art Director: Lorelee. Bimonthly magazine. Circ. 1,000. "TYRO is a practice medium for developing writers and accepts almost anything worthy." 15% of material aimed at juvenile audience.

Fiction: "We have published material and will consider submissions in any area and

level." Buys 80 mss/year. Average word length: 5,000. Byline given.
Nonfiction: "We will consider any of these: animal, history, how-to, humorous, interview/profile, problem solving, religious, travel." Buys 6 mss/year. Average word length: 5,000. Byline given.
How to Contact/Writers: Fiction: Send complete ms. Nonfiction: Query. SASE (IRC) for answer to query and return of ms. Reports on queries/mss in 1 month. Will consider photocopied and computer printout submissions.
Illustration: "We use only camera-ready, b&w art." Buys "up to 5" illustrations/issue; buys "up to 30" illustrations/year. Will review ms/illustration packages by authors/artists; ms/illustration packages submitted by authors with illustrations done by separate artists; illustrator's work for possible use with fiction/nonfiction articles.
How to Contact/Illustrators: Ms/illustration packages: Send complete ms with final art. Reports on art samples in 1 month. Original artwork returned at job's completion.
Terms/Writers & Illustrators: "Since we are a practice vehicle, no fees paid." Pays in contributor copies. Sample copy $5. Writer's guidelines free with SAE.
Tips: "Many believe that because children's literature is often simple it is easy to write. That's not so. It's a discipline that requires as much, if not more, skill as any writing."

VENTURE, Christian Service Brigade, Box 150, Wheaton IL 60189. (312)665-0630. Articles/Fiction Editor: Steven Neideck. Art Director: Robert Fine. Bimonthly magazine. Circ. 23,000. The magazine is designed "to speak to the concerns of boys from a biblical perspective. To provide wholesome, entertaining reading for boys." 100% of material aimed at juvenile audience.
Fiction: Middle readers, young adults: animal, contemporary, history, humorous, problem solving, religious, sports, spy/mystery/adventure. Does not want to see fantasy, romance, science fiction. Buys 12 mss/year. Average word length: 1,000-1,500. Byline given.
Nonfiction: Middle readers, young adults: animal, history, how-to, humorous, interview/profile, problem solving, religious, travel. Buys 3 mss/year. Average word length: 1,000-1,500. Byline given.
How to Contact/Writers: Fiction/nonfiction: Query; send complete ms. SASE (IRC) for answer to query and return of ms. Reports on queries in 1 week; mss in 2 weeks. Will consider simultaneous, photocopied, and computer printout submissions.
Illustration: Buys 1 illustration/issue; buys 6 illustrations/year. Will review ms/illustration packages by authors/artists; ms/illustration packages submitted by authors with illustrations done by separate artists; illustrator's work for possible use with fiction/nonfiction articles.
How to Contact/Illustrators: Ms/illustration packages: query first. Illustrations only: Send tear sheets, slides. Reports on art samples in 2 weeks. Original art work returned at job's completion.
Terms/Writers & Illustrators: Pays on publication. Buys first North American serial rights; first rights; one-time rights; second serial (reprint rights). Pays $75-150 for assigned articles; $30-100 for unsolicited articles. Additional payment for ms/illustration packages: $100-200. Pays $35-125/b&w (cover) illustration; $35-50/b&w (inside) illustration. Sample copy $1.50 with 9 × 12 SAE and 85¢ postage. Writer's/illustrator's guidelines free with SAE and 1 first-class stamp.
Tips: "Write about children's interests, not your own interests."

WEE WISDOM MAGAZINE, A Children's Magazine, Unity School of Christianity, Unity Village MO 64025. (816)524-3550, ext. 329. Editor: Judy Gehrlein. Published 10 times/year, magazine. 100% of material aimed at juvenile audience.
Fiction: Picture material, young readers, middle readers, young adults: animal, contemporary, fantasy, history, humorous, problem solving, religious, science fiction, sports, spy/mystery/adventure. Does not want to see anything on war, crime; avoid negative perspective. Buys 60 mss/year. Average word length: 800. Byline given.

Judy Gehrlein, editor of Wee Wisdom *magazine purchased first rights to this piece by Carolyn Bowser, Kansas City, Missouri. "Carolyn is a pro. Her work reflects years of hard work developing her skills as an illustrator," Gehrlein explains, "It is good art. It has humor, great color, the children love it!" This art, done in watercolor, was used on the cover of* Wee Wisdom *for its 95th anniversary-birthday issue.*

How to Contact/Writers: Fiction: Send complete ms. SASE (IRC) for return of ms. Report on mss in 8 weeks. Will consider computer printout submissions.

Illustration: Buys 25 illustrations/issue; buys 250 illustrations/year. Preferred theme or style: We assign according to literature. Will review ms/illustration packages by authors/artists; ms/illustration packages submitted by authors with illustrations done by separate artists; illustrators work for possible use with fiction articles. Works on assignment only.

How to Contact/Illustrators: Ms/illustration packages: no queries, full manuscript, sample illustration package. Illustrations only: Samples of their choice. We are interested in freelancers in children's art. We are most interested in seeing their work—perhaps their range in work. Reports on art samples in 6 weeks. "Originals returned one year after publication."

Terms/Writers & Illustrators: Pays on acceptance. Buys first North American serial rights. Pays 5-9¢/word for stories. "We pay the same rate for assigned work and unsolicited. We rarely assign stories. Contributor copies are sent at no charge." Pays $80 full page (2-color) illustration, $30-60 fraction (2-color) illustration; $100 full page (4-color) illustration, $30-60 fraction (4-color) illustration; $200 double cover illustration; $200 calendar (always 4-color, always a package). Free sample copy. Writer's/illustrator's guidelines free with SASE.

Tips: Writers: "Use dialogue in stories taken from real life rather than imagination. Develop characters that express real feelings and explore human relationships through behavior and dialogue. Do not over describe with adjectives. Send us fresh, free creations. We need to read your fresh, individual approach to children's stories, mainly fiction of no more than 800 words. We're looking for up-to-date kids with basic values. We must have positive yet plausible solutions to real situations. We select very few poems within a year. We are open to puzzles and riddles for 4-12 year olds." Illustrators: "We are always looking for illustrators who project humor, beauty and fun for children."

WITH, Faith & Life Press, Mennonite Publishing House, Box 347, 722 Main, Newton KS 67114. (316)283-5100. Articles/Fiction Editor, Art Director: Susan Janzen. Monthly magazine. Circ. 6,500. Magazine published for teenagers in Mennonite congregations. We deal with issues affecting teens and try to help them make choices reflecting an Anabaptist-Mennonite faith. 100% of material aimed at juvenile audience.
Fiction: Teenagers: contemporary, humorous, problem solving, religious, sports. Buys 30 mss/year. Average word length: 1,200-2,000. Byline given.
Nonfiction: Young adults: how-to, humorous, interview/profile, problem solving, religious. Buys 5-6 mss/year. Average word length: 1,000-1,750. Byline given.
How to Contact/Writers: Fiction: Send complete ms. Nonfiction: Query. SASE (IRC) for answer to query and return of ms. Reports on queries in 1 month; mss in 3 months. Will consider simultaneous, photocopied, and computer printout submissions.
Illustration: Buys 6-8 illustrations/issue; buys 70-75 illustrations/year. Preferred theme or style: Candids/interracial. Will review ms/illustration packages by authors/artists; ms/illustration packages submitted by authors with illustrations done by separate artists; illustrator's work for possible use with fiction/nonfiction articles.
How to Contact/Illustrators: Ms/illustration packages: Query first. Illustrations only: Send slides 8×10 b&w prints preferred. Reports on art samples in 1 month. Original art work returned at job's completion.
Terms/Writers & Illustrators: Pays on acceptance. Buys one-time rights; second serial (reprint rights). Pays $40-80 for assigned articles; $20-80 for unsolicited articles. Additional payment for ms/illustration packages: $30-100. Pays $25-50/b&w (cover) illustration; $25-35/b&w (inside) illustration. Sample copy $1.25 with 9×12 SAE and 85¢ postage. Writer's/illustrator's guidelines free.
Tips: Writers: "Fiction and poetry are most open to freelancers." Illustrators: "We use almost exclusively illustrations from freelancers. Since we can't use color photos, I appreciate submissions that are b&w. Art can be 2-color."

YOUNG AMERICAN, America's Newspaper for Kids, Young American Publishing Co., Inc., Box 12409, Portland OR 97212. (503)230-1895. Articles/Fiction Editor: Kristina Linden. Art Director: Richard Ferguson. Monthly (national) tabloid. Circ. 4,000,000+.
Fiction: Young readers, middle readers, young adults: animal, contemporary, fantasy, history, humorous, problem solving, science fiction, sports, spy/mystery/adventure. Does not want to see religious themes. Buys 12-15 mss/year. Average word length: 500-1,000. Byline given.
Nonfiction: Young readers, middle readers, young adults: animal, history, how-to, humorous, interview/profile, problem solving. Does not want to see preachy, moralistic themes. Buys 75 mss/year. Average word length: 350. Byline given sometimes.
How to Contact/Writers: Fiction/nonfiction: Send complete ms. SASE (IRC) for answer to query/return of ms; include Social Security number with submission. Reports on queries/mss in 4 months. Will consider photocopied and computer printout submissions.
Illustration: "Future plans are to increase freelance illustrations." Will review ms/illustration packages by authors/artists; ms/illustration packages submitted by authors with illustrations done by separate artists; illustrator's work for possible use with fiction/nonfiction articles.
How to Contact/Illustrators: Ms/illustration packages: Submit complete ms. Illustrations only: Send examples of style. Reports on art samples in 4 months. Original art work returned at job's completion.
Terms/Writers & Illustrators: Pays on publication. Buys first North American serial rights; may buy reprint rights. Pay is "negotiable" for assigned articles. Pay for illustrations is "negotiable." Sample copy for $1.50. Writer's/illustrator's guidelines free with SASE.
Tips: "Know today's kids—quote them when possible. Fiction—don't be condescending."

THE YOUNG CRUSADER, National WCTU, 1730 Chicago Ave., Evanston IL 60201. (312)864-1396. Managing Editor: Michael C. Vitucci. Monthly magazine. Circ. 3,500. The magazine is geared to the 8-12 year old child. It stresses high morals and good character. Nature and informational stories are also used. Above all, the stories should not be preachy or religious as the magazine is used in public schools. 100% of material aimed at juvenile audience.

Fiction: Middle readers: contemporary, problem solving, positive character building. Does not want to see preachy, religious-type stories. Buys 4 mss/year. Average word length: 550-650. Byline given.

Nonfiction: Middle readers: animal, history, interview/profile, problem solving, travel. Buys 10 mss/year. Average word length: 550-650. Byline given.

How to Contact/Writers: Fiction/nonfiction: Send complete ms. Will consider simultaneous, photocopied, and computer printout submissions. "I require submissions to be copies. If used, I will publish, if not used, the manuscript will be destroyed."

Terms/Writers & Illustrators: Pays on publication. Buys second serial (reprint rights); simultaneous rights. Pays ½¢/word for assigned/unsolicited articles. Free sample copy.

Tips: "Don't write down to the child. Writers often underestimate their audience." Looks for: "nonfiction stories stressing good character and high morals."

YOUNG NATURALIST FOUNDATION (See listings for Chickadee, Owl.)

YOUTH UPDATE, St. Anthony Messenger Press, 1615 Republic St., Cincinnati OH 45210. (513)241-5615. Articles Editor: Carol Ann Morrow. Art Director: Julie Lonneman. Monthly newsletter. Circ. 42,000. Each issue focuses on one topic only. *Youth Update* addresses the faith and Christian life questions of young people and is designed to attract, instruct, guide and challenge its audience by applying the gospel to modern problems and situations. The students who read *Youth Update* vary in their religious education and reading ability. Write for the average high school student. This student is 15-years-old with a C+ average. Assume that they have paid attention to religious instruction and remember a little of what "sister" said. When writing avoid glib phrases and cliches. Aim more toward "table talk than teacher talk."

Nonfiction: Young adults: religious. Does not want to see travel material. Buys 12 mss/year. Average word length: 2,300-2,400. Byline given.

How to Contact/Writers: Nonfiction: Query. SASE (IRC) for answer to query; include Social Security number with submission. Reports on queries/mss in 6 weeks. Will consider photocopied, computer printout and electronic submissions via disk or modem.

Terms/Writers & Illustrators: Pays on acceptance. Buys first North American serial rights. Pays $325-400 for assigned/unsolicited articles. Sample copy free with #10 SAE and 1 first-class stamp.

Tips: "Read the newsletter yourself—3 issues at least. In the past, our publication has dealt with a variety of topics including: dating, lent, teenage pregnancy, baptism, loneliness, rock and roll, confirmation and the Bible. When writing, use the *New American Bible* as translation."

Young Writer's/
Illustrator's Markets

Students—this is your section. You have probably noticed that many of your favorite magazines are either wholly or partly devoted to publishing writing, artwork and photos created by you. In this section you can find each publication's special writing or art needs, as well as the method of submitting work each prefers. Granted, many of these markets are low paying or pay in copies only (like some adult markets), but the satisfaction of seeing your first work published will be worth the effort you have made in its creation.

Just as in the adult market, the more you write, draw or photograph, the more skill you develop at your chosen craft. Also, like the fledgling adult writer or illustrator, the more published clips you have to show, the more you will be taken seriously by other markets as a writer who produced salable material and who met deadlines.

You may not have successes at first—the publishing field is competitive—but the experience of producing a written piece or illustration that is your very best work can be satisfying in itself. If one publication doesn't accept your work, keep submitting to others. Sometimes the subject matter you have created isn't appropriate for the type of magazine you submitted to. The next magazine or book publisher you query could be your winning sale!

Study each listing carefully to determine what the subject needs are, who to send your query or manuscript (ms in the listing) to, and how they want work submitted. You can do a little research beforehand and ask for a sample copy and writer's/illustrator's guidelines if they are available. Study this material so you can get a better feel for the type of material most published by each publication. A contact person is given in the listing, so you can send material to that person's attention. Remember, don't give up. It sometimes takes writers and artists a long time to get published but once you have, you're on your way to building up your reputation as a "professional" writer or artist. Good luck!

AGORA: THE MAGAZINE FOR GIFTED STUDENTS, AG Publications, Inc., Box 10975, Raleigh NC 27605. (919)787-6832. Magazine. Published "quarterly during academic year." Audience consists of "academically advanced high school and middle school students." Purpose in publishing works by children: to publicize student accomplishments; give students a chance to network. Requirements to be met before work is published: subscribe to _Agora_; a teacher's signature. Instructions for annual _Agora_ Writing Competitions available—deadline April 25.
Magazines: Uses short stories (fiction-2,000 words); travel, public issues and scientific articles, literary essays, book reviews (1,500-2,000 words); short lyric poetry (25-100 lines), one-act plays, art and photos. Pays $10-25 prizes for contest winners. "We hope to increase amount as subscription base increases." Submit mss to Sally Humble, _Agora_ editor.

BITTERROOT, Box 489, Spring Glen NY 12483. Magazine. Published 3 times/year. Purpose in publishing works by children: we inspire all poets who seek their own identity through original poetry, realistic or fantastic. We discourage stereotyped forms in poetry that imitate fixed patterns and leave no individual mark. Requirements to be met before work is published: contributors are "usually high school level."

Poetry: 1% of magazine written by children. Uses poetry, poetry book reviews. "Short poems preferred." Pays in copies. Submit mss to Menke Katz, editor-in-chief. Send 3 or 4 poems with SASE. Will accept typewritten mss. Include SASE. Reports in 6 weeks.

Artwork: Looks for only black and white line drawings. Pays in copies. Submit artwork to Rivke Katz, art editor. SASE. Reports in 6 weeks.

CHILDREN'S DIGEST, Box 567, Indianapolis IN 46206. (317)636-8881. Magazine. Published 8 times/year. Audience consists of children between 8 and 12. Purpose in publishing works by children: to encourage children to express themselves through writing. Requirements to be met before work is published: require proof of originality before publishing stories. Writer's guidelines available on request.

Magazines: 10% of magazine written by children. Uses 1 fiction story (about 200 words), 6-7 poems, 15-20 riddles, 7-10 letters/issue. "There is no payment for manuscripts submitted by readers." Submit mss to *Children's Digest* (Elizabeth A. Rinck, editor). Submit complete ms. Will accept typewritten, legibly handwritten, computer printout mss. Reports in 8-10 weeks.

CHILDREN'S PLAYMATE, Box 567, Indianapolis IN 46206. (317)636-8881. Magazine. Audience consists of children between 5 and 7 years of age. Purpose in publishing works by children: to encourage children to write. Writer's guidelines available on request.

Magazines: 10% of magazine written by children. Uses 6-7 poems, 8-10 jokes, 8-10 riddles/issue. "There is no payment for manuscripts submitted by children." Submit mss to *Children's Playmate* (Elizabeth A. Rinck, editor). Submit complete ms. Will accept typewritten, legibly handwritten, computer printout mss. Reports in 8-10 weeks. "No material may be returned."

Artwork: Publishes artwork by children. "Prefers dark-colored line drawings on white paper. No payment for children's artwork published." Submit artwork to *Children's Playmate.*

CLUBHOUSE, Box 15, Berrien Springs MI 49103. (616)471-9009. Magazine. Publishes 1 section by kids in each issue, bimonthly. "Audience consists of kids 9-14; philosophy is God loves kids, kids are neat people." Purpose in publishing works by children: encouragement; demonstration of talent. Requirements to be met before work is published: age 9-14; parent's note verifying originality.

Magazines: 1/16th of magazine written by children. Uses adventure, historical, everyday life experience (fiction/nonfiction-1,200 words); health-related short articles; poetry (4-24 lines of "mostly mood pieces and humor." Payment for ms: prizes for children, money for adult authors. Query. Will accept typewritten, legibly handwritten, computer printout mss. SASE – "will not be returned without SASE." Reports in 6 weeks.

Artwork: Publishes artwork by children. Looks for all types of artwork-white paper, black pen. Pays in prizes for kids. Send black pen on white paper to Elaine Trumbo, editor. SASE – "won't be returned without SASE."

Tips: "All items submitted by kids are held in a file and used when possible. We normally suggest they do not ask for return of the item. We will not be accepting manuscripts or unassigned artwork until April of 1990."

CREATIVE KIDS, Box 6448, Mobile AL 36660. (205)478-4700. Magazine. Published 8 times/year (Oct.-May). "All of our material is by children, for children." Purpose in publishing works by children: to create a product that is good enough for publication and to offer an opportunity to see their work in print. Requirements to be met before work is published: age 5-18 – must have statement by teacher or parent verifying originality. Writer's guidelines available on request.

Magazines: Uses "about 6" fiction stories (200-750 words); "about 6" nonfiction stories (200-750 words); poetry, plays, ideas to share (200-750 words)/issue. Pays in "free magazine"/ms. Submit mss to Fay L. Gold, editor. Will accept typewritten, legibly handwritten mss. SASE. Reports in 4 weeks.

Artwork: Publishes artwork by children. Looks for "any kind of drawing, cartoon, or painting." Pays in "free magazine." Send original or a photo of the work to Fay L. Gold, editor. No photocopies. SASE. Reports in 4 weeks.

Tips: "*Creative Kids* is a magazine by kids, for kids. The work represents children's ideas, questions, fears, concerns, and pleasures. The material never contains racist, sexist, or violent expression. The purpose is to encourage youngsters to create a product that is good enough for publication. A person may submit one or more pieces of work. Each piece must be labeled with the student's name, birth date, grade, school, home address, and school address. Include a photograph, if possible. Recent school pictures are best. Material submitted to *Creative Kids* must not be under consideration by any other publisher. Items should be carefully prepared, proofread, and double checked. All activities requiring solutions must be accompanied by the correct answers."

CREATIVE WITH WORDS PUBLICATIONS, Box 223226, Carmel CA 93940. (408)649-1862. Books. Published 1 time/year. Audience consists of children, schools, libraries, adults, reading programs. Purpose in publishing works by children: to offer them an opportunity to get started in publishing. "Work must be original, unedited, and not published before; age must be given (up to 19 years old)." Writer's guidelines available on request.

Books: Uses fiction fairy tales, folklore items (1,000 words); poetry "language art work" (not to exceed 30 lines). Pays: 20% off each copy of publication in which fiction or poetry by children appears. Submit mss to Editor: Brigitta Geltrich. Send query; submit complete ms; teacher must submit. Will accept typewritten and/or legibly handwritten mss. SASE. Reports in 2-8 weeks.

Artwork: Publishes artwork by children (language art work). Pay: 20% off every copy of publication in which work by children appears. Submit artwork to Editor: Brigitta Geltrich.

DRAGONFLY: EAST/WEST HAIKU QUARTERLY, Box 11236, Salt Lake City UT 84118. Magazine. Published quarterly. "We publish for an audience interested in haiku (a Japanese form of poetry written in many different languages). Children can write this form of poetry as well as adults can, often with a refreshing perspective. We like to encourage children to try this kind of writing." Requirements to be met before work is published: submissions with name, address, age and/or grade. Writer's guidelines available on request. "They are, however, the same as for adults."

Magazines: 1-3% of magazine written by children. Uses 1-6 haiku by younger writers. We will publish more if we receive more good haiku from them. Young writers receive a free copy of the issue in which their poem appears. Submit mss to Editor: Richard Tice. Submit complete ms. Will accept typewritten, legibly handwritten, computer printout mss. SASE.

Tips: The teacher or parent should study our guidelines and a sample copy, then help the child or teen understand the form.

THE FLYING PENCIL PRESS, Box 7667, Elgin IL 60121. Books. Publishes 1 book by children/year. "Audience is general (family, schools, libraries). Philosophy is freedom of expression and creativity." Purpose in publishing works by children: to encourage and support young writers. Requirements to be met before work is published: age 8-14, following current guidelines. Writer's guidelines available on request.

Books: Uses fiction stories (200-2,000 words); nonfiction (200-2,000 words); poems (4-32 lines). Pays in author's copy, awards/ms. Submit ms to Charlotte Towner Graeber, editor. "We prefer fiction, nonfiction and poems to be typewritten, but will accept hand written material if it is clear and readable. Material must be the original work of the submitting author. Enclose a self addressed stamped envelope (SASE) if you wish material we do not accept for publication to be returned. Remember to keep a copy of your writing in case the original is lost in handling or mailing. You will be notified by mail in 4-6 weeks if your work is accepted for Flying Pencil publication."

Artwork: Publishes artwork by children. Artwork—black and white line art, size limit 8 × 10; cartoons—1 to 8 frames, black and white, size limit 8 × 10. Pays in copies. Artwork, illustrations and cartoons should be on unlined white paper. SASE. "Keep a copy of artwork in case original is lost in the mail." Submit to Charlotte Towner Graeber, editor. Reports in 4-6 weeks.

FUTURIFIC, the Foundation for Optimism, Futurific Inc., 280 Madison Ave., New York NY 10016. (212)684-4913. Magazine. Published monthly. Audience consists of people interested in an accurate report of what is ahead. "We do not discriminate by age. We look for the visionary in all people. They must say what will be. No advice or 'may-be.' " Writer's guidelines available on request.

Magazines: Submit mss to B. Szent-Miklosy, publisher. Will accept typewritten, legibly handwritten, computer printout mss. SASE.

Artwork: Publishes artwork by children. Looks for "what the future will look like." Pay is negotiable. Send b&w drawings or photos. Submit artwork to B. Szent-Miklosy, publisher. SASE.

GIFTED CHILDREN MONTHLY, Box 115, Sewell NJ 08080. (609)582-0277. Newsletter. Audience is parents of gifted children. There is a 4-page insert for kids; compliments adult section. Requirements to be met before work is published: 4-14 years old. Writer's guidelines available on request.

Magazines: 18% of magazine written by children. Uses 5 fiction stories (50 words average); 10 nonfiction articles. Pays $3 or a product from our catalog. Submit ms to Robert Baum, managing editor. Will accept typewritten, legibly handwritten, computer printout mss. "Only responds if material used—sometimes many months. Contributor copies sent."

Artwork: Publishes artwork by children. Interested in poster contest, editorial cartoons. Pays $3 or a product from our catalog. Submit artwork to Robert Baum, managing editor.

HIGHLIGHTS FOR CHILDREN, 803 Church St., Honesdale PA 18431. (717)253-1080. Magazine. Published monthly (July-August issue combined). "We strive to provide wholesome, stimulating, entertaining material which will encourage children to read. Our audience is children 2-12." Purpose in publishing works by children: to encourage children's creative expression. Requirements to be met before work is published: age limit 15.

Magazines: 15-20% of magazine written by children. Uses 9-15 pieces of prose and poetry: "Our Own Pages"; 15-20 jokes and riddles; 3-5 letters to the editor. Submit mss to the Editor. Submit complete ms. Will accept typewritten, legibly handwritten, computer printout mss. Responds in 3-6 weeks.

Artwork: Publishes artwork by children. No cartoon or comic book characters. No commercial products. Submit black-and-white artwork for "Our Own Pages." Color for others. Responds in 3-6 weeks.

LIFEPRINTS, Blindskills, Box 5181, Salem OR 97304. (503)581-4224. Magazine. Published 5 times/year. Magazine includes blind and visually impaired successes, teenagers. **Magazines:** Uses nonfiction anecdotal material. We do not pay; nonprofit. Editor: Carol M. McCarl. Will accept manuscripts in typed, brailled, or in cassette formats. A

Highlights for Children *Editor-in-Chief,* **Dr. Walter B. Barbe, purchased rights to use Melissa Hawthorne's (Bettendorf, Iowa) illustration as a child's contribution in the "Our Own Pages" section. Barbe felt that the piece, drawn in pen, was original and imaginative.**

Trip to the Park

© Highlights for Children 1988

small honorarium is awarded to students whose articles are published in *Lifeprints*.

MERLYN'S PEN, The National Magazine of Student Writing, Box 1058, East Greenwich RI 02818. (401)885-5175. Magazine. Published every 2 months during the school year, September to May. "We publish over 200 manuscripts annually by students in grades 7-10. The entire magazine is dedicated to young adult's writing. Our audience is classrooms, libraries, and students from grades 7-10." Requirements to be met before work is published: writers must be in grades 7-10, and must follow submission guidelines for preparing their manuscripts. When a student is accepted, he/she, a parent and a teacher must sign a statement of originality.

Magazines: 100% of magazine written by children. Uses 6-8 short stories, plays (fiction); 2-3 nonfiction essays; poetry; letters to the editor; editorials; reviews of previously published works; reviews of books, music, movies. No word limit on any material. Pays for ms in three copies of the issue and a paperback copy of *The Elements of Style* (a writer's handbook). Also, a discount is offered for additional copies of the issue. Submit mss to R. Jim Stahl, editor. Submit complete ms. Will only accept typewritten mss. SASE. "All rejected manuscripts have an editor's constructive critical comment in the margin." Reports in 11 weeks.

Artwork: Publishes artwork by children. Looks for black and white line drawings, cartoons, color art for cover. Pays in 3 copies of the issue to the artist, and a discount is offered for additional copies. Send unmatted original artwork. Submit artwork to R. Jim Stahl, editor. SASE. Reports in 11 weeks.

Tips: "All manuscripts and artwork must be submitted with a cover sheet listing: name, age and grade, home address, home phone number, school name, school phone number, school address, teacher's name. SASE must be large enough and carry enough postage for return."

MY FRIEND, 50 St. Paul's Ave., Jamaica Plain, Boston MA 02130. (617)522-8911. Magazine. Published 10 times/year. Audience consists of children ages 6-12, primarily Roman Catholics. Purpose in publishing works by children: to stimulate reader participation and to encourage young Catholic writers. Requirements to be met before work is published: we accept work from children ages 6-16. Requirements regarding originality included in guidelines. Writer's guidelines available for SASE.

Magazines: Uses an occasional fiction story 3-4 times/year (300 words); we would like to include something in nonfiction every other issue (400-500 words). Pays in 3 copies of the issue in which the child's work appears. Submit mss to Sister Anne Joan, fsp, editor. Query for nonfiction. Will accept typewritten, legibly handwritten, computer printout mss. SASE. Reports in 2-4 weeks.

Artwork: Publishes artwork by children. Looks for anything "happy." Maximum size 11×17. Pays in 3 copies of the issue in which child's work appears. Artwork cannot be returned. Submit artwork to Sister Anne Joan, fsp, editor. Reports in 2-4 weeks.

Tips: "We are initiating a 'Junior Reporter' feature which will give young writers the chance to do active research on a variety of topics. Children may ask for an 'assignment' or suggest topics they'd be willing to research and write on. This would be mainly where our interest in children's writing would lie."

THE MYTHIC CIRCLE, Mythopoeic Society, Box 6707, Altadena CA 91001. Editor: Lynn Maudlin and Christine Lowentrout. Art Director: Lynn Maudlin. Quarterly magazine. Estab. 1987. Circ. 150. We are a fantasy writer's workshop in print featuring reader comments in each issue. 5% of publication aimed at juvenile market.

Nonfiction: How-to, interview/profile. "We are just starting with nonfiction – dedicated to how to write and publish. Buys "maximum of 4" mss/year. Average word length: 250-2,000. Byline given.

How to Contact/Writers: Fiction: send complete ms. Nonfiction: query. SASE (IRC) for answer to query and return of ms. Reports on queries/mss in 1 month. Will consider photocopied, computer printout (dark dot matrix) and electronic submissions via disk (query for details).

Illustration: Buys 10 illustrations/issue; buys 40 illustrations/year. Preferred theme or style: fantasy, soft science fiction. Will review ms/illustration packages submitted by authors/artists; ms/illustration packages submitted by authors with illustrations done by separate artists; illustrator's work for possible use with fiction/nonfiction articles and columns by other authors.

How to Contact/Illustrators: Ms/illustration packages: complete with art. Illustrations only: Send tear sheets. Reports on art samples in 3-6 weeks. Original artwork returned at job's completion (only if postage paid).

Terms/Writers and Illustrators: Pays on publication. Buys one-time rights. Pays in contributor copies. Sample copy $3.50. Writer's guidelines free with SAE and 1 first-class stamp.

Tips: "We are a good outlet for a story that hasn't sold but 'should' have – good feedback and tips on improvement. We do have a 'Mythopoeic Youth' section with stories and art by those under 18 years."

NOAH'S ARK, A NEWSPAPER FOR JEWISH CHILDREN, #250, 8323 Southwest Fwy., Houston TX 77074. (713)771-7143. Newspaper. Published monthly. "All submissions must have Jewish content and positive Jewish values. Readers are aged 6-12 on six continents. Therefore, content should not be just for American audience. Purpose in publishing works by children is to enhance newspaper, therefore, only quality material accepted – work must be good enough that other children would enjoy it." Requirements to be met before work is published: must be age 6-12. Percentage of publication written by children "varies." Uses fiction/nonfiction rarely – but would consider. Does not pay for children's contributions. Submit mss to Debbie Israel Dubin, managing editor. Submit complete ms. Will accept typewritten, legibly handwritten, computer printout mss. SASE. Reports in 1 month.

Artwork: Publishes artwork by children. Looks for submissions with Jewish content and positive Jewish values. Submit artwork to Debbie Israel Dubin, managing editor. SASE.

PRISM MAGAZINE, Lauderdale Publishing, Box 7375, Ft. Lauderdale FL 33338. (305)563-8805. Newspaper. Bimonthly. "While many people realize the need to develop young talent, there has been little opportunity for gifted young people to see their creations published and to create a network of communication with other gifted young people. We see *Prism* as a vehicle not only for the publication of work, but also as the beginning of that vital network. For the first issue, we have gathered contributions from as many geographic areas and age groups as possible. We found that some young people were shy about creating materials, because they were unsure of the format, but we are sure once you have seen *Prism* you will understand the wide latitude we have built into the concept." Writer's guidelines available on request.

Magazines: "Math, science, philosophy, history, literature, the future, your personal experiences, humor, current events, all are topics we would like to see discussed in *Prism*." Pays in copies. Submit ms to Sherry Friedlander, publisher or T. Constance Coyne, editor.

Artwork: Publishes artwork by children. Artwork, photos and cartoons are the expressions and feelings of young people all over the United States and in many foreign countries. Pays in copies. Submit artwork to Sherry Friedlander, publisher or T. Constance Coyne, editor.

REFLECTIONS, Box 368, Duncan Falls OH 43734. (614)674-5209. Magazine. Published January and June. Purpose in publishing works by children: to encourage writing. Requirements to be met before work is published: statement of originality and signed by teacher or parent. Writer's guidelines available on request (with SASE).

Melissa Pinson, Savannah, Georgia sold rights to this illustration to accompany a story she wrote titled "Linda's Lesson." The pencil drawing was included to convey "an exchange of emotions between two friends," she explains. Dean Harper, editor of Reflections, *published the story/illustration package because the story "is very tightly written" and "the drawing is very impressive."*

Magazines: 100% of magazine written by children. Uses 1-3 fiction stories (1,000-2,000 words); 1-3 nonfiction articles (1,000-2,000 words); poetry. Pays in contributor's copy. Editor: Dean Harper. Submit complete ms. Will accept typewritten, legibly handwritten, computer printout mss. "Please include your name, age, school, address, and your teacher's name. Be certain to include a self-addressed stamped envelope with your manuscripts. Make the statement that this is your own original work, then date it and sign your name. Your teacher or parent should also sign it." Reports in 2 weeks.
Artwork: Publishes artwork by children. Pays in contributor's copy. Editor: Dean Harper. SASE. Reports in 2 weeks.
Tips: "We hope we are encouraging young people to read and write."

RHYME TIME POETRY NEWSLETTER, Hutton Publications, Box 1870, Hayden ID 83835. (208)772-6184. Newsletter. Bimonthly. We prefer traditional rhymed poetry by any age group. Purpose in publishing works by children: to encourage young writers. Writer's guidelines available on request.
Magazines: 5% of magazine written by children. Uses short rhymed poems. Pays in copies. Submit mss to Linda Hutton, editor. Submit complete ms. Will accept typewritten and computer printout mss. SASE. Reports in 4 weeks.
Artwork: Publishes artwork by children. Looks for black and white drawings up to 3 × 5 on seasonal subjects. Pays in copies. Submit artwork to Linda Hutton, editor. SASE. Reports in 4 weeks.

SHOE TREE, National Association for Young Writers, 215 Valle del Sol Dr., Santa Fe NM 87501. (505)982-8596. Magazine. Published 3 times/year. "We encourage young writers to use writing as a serious form of communication to raise their performance standards and improve skills. We accept only the finest work. The goal of the NAYW is the encouragement of children's writing." We publish work by young writers, ages 6-14. Writer's guidelines available on request.
Magazines: 95% of magazine written by children; one adult author-to-author column.

"We asked Adam to work with this story because we knew his work, having watched it grow," begins Sheila Cowing, editor-in-chief of Shoe Tree, a publication of the National Association for Young Writers (NAYW). "We understood that his experience might be similar to that in the story. We knew he had fine drawing skills as well as sensitivity." This pencil sketch, drawn in halftones, was created by Adam Pesapane, Chatham, New Jersey. Cowing feels this piece is so successful "because it is illustrative of the mood of the story—the threat of junior high boys is really evident in the drawing."

Uses 5-10 fiction stories; 2-6 nonfiction articles; and personal narratives, humor, book reviews, 6-10 poems. Pays with 2 complimentary copies. Sheila Cowing, editor-in-chief. Submit complete ms. Will accept typewritten, legibly handwritten, computer printout mss. Reports in 2 months.
Artwork: Publishes artwork by children. "We use art mostly for illustration so we solicit. Send, or have teacher send, samples of artwork and then we solicit. Also use pictures for full-color or b&w cover." Pays with 2 complimentary copies. Submit artwork by student or teacher, either photocopy or original. Sheila Cowing, editor-in-chief. Reports in 2 months.

STONE SOUP, The Magazine by Children, Children's Art Foundation, Box 83, Santa Cruz CA 95063. (408)426-5557. Articles/Fiction Editor, Art Director: Ms. Gerry Mandel. Magazine. Bimonthly. Circ. 10,000. "We publish fiction, poetry, and artwork by children through age 13. Our preference is for work based on personal experiences and close observation of the world."
Magazines: 100% of magazine written by children. Uses animal, contemporary, fantasy, problem-solving, science fiction, spy/mystery/adventure fiction stories. Does not want to see classroom assignments and formula writing. Buys 50 mss/year. Byline given. Uses animal, interviews/profile, problem solving, travel nonfiction articles. "We don't publish straight nonfiction, but we do publish stories based on real events and experiences." Buys 10 mss/year. Byline given. Send complete ms. SASE. Reports in 6 weeks. Will accept computer printout submissions.
Artwork: Buys 6 illustrations/issue; 30/year. Send samples of artwork. Reports in 6 weeks. Original artwork returned at job's completion.
Terms/Writers and Illustrators: Pays on acceptance. Buys all rights. Pays $5-15/solicited article. Pays $5-15/b&w inside illustration. All other contributors paid in copies. Sample copy $2. Free writer's/illustrator's guidelines.
Tips: "Look closely at the magazine to get an idea of the kind of work we publish."

STRAIGHT MAGAZINE, Standard Publishing, 8121 Hamilton Ave., Cincinnati OH 45231. (513)931-4050. Magazine. Weekly. Magazine includes fiction pieces and articles for Christian teens 13-19 years old to inform, encourage and uplift them. Purpose in publishing works by children: give them an opportunity to express themselves. Requirements to be met before work is published: must submit their birth date and SS# (if they have one). Writer's guidelines available on request, "included in regular guidelines."
Magazines: 15% of magazine written by children. Uses fiction (500-1,000 words); personal experience pieces (500-700 words); poetry (approx. 1 per issue). Pays flat fee for poetry; per word for stories/articles. Submit mss to Carla J. Crane, editor. Submit complete ms. Will accept typewritten and computer printout mss. SASE. Reports in 4-6 weeks.
Artwork: Publishes artwork by children. Looks for "anything that will fit our format." Pays flat rate. Submit artwork to Carla Crane, editor. SASE. Reports in 4-6 weeks.

THUMBPRINTS, 215 Ellington St., Caro MI 48723. (517)673-4902. Newsletter. Monthly. "Our newsletter is designed to be of interest to writers and allow writers a place to obtain a byline." Purpose in publishing works by children: to encourage them to seek publication of their work. Writer's guidelines available on request, "same guidelines as for adults."
Newsletter: Percentage of newsletter written by children "varies from month to month." Pays in copies. Submit ms to Joan Sayers, editor. Submit complete ms or have teacher submit. Will accept typewritten and computer printout mss. SASE. Reports in 6-8 weeks.
Artwork: Publishes artwork by children. Looks for art that expresses our monthly

theme. Pays in copies. Send pencil or ink drawing no larger than 3×4. Submit artwork to Joan Sayers, editor.

Tips: "We look forward to well written articles and poems by children. It's encouraging to all writers when children write and are published."

TURTLE, Ben Franklin Literary & Medical Society, Children's Better Health Institute, 1100 Waterway Blvd., Box 567, Indianapolis IN 46206. (317)636-8881. Magazine. *"Turtle* is generally a health related magazine geared toward children from ages 2-5. Purpose in publishing works by children: we enjoy giving children the opportunity to exercise their creativity." Requirements to be met before work is published: for ages 2-5, publishes artwork or pictures that you have drawn or colored all by yourself. Writer's guidelines available on request.

Artwork: Publishes artwork by children. There is no payment for children's artwork. All artwork must have the child's name, age, and complete address on it. Submit artwork to *Turtle* Magazine Executive Editorial Director: Beth Wood Thomas. "No artwork can be returned."

WOMBAT: A JOURNAL OF YOUNG PEOPLE'S WRITING AND ART, WOMBAT, Inc., Box 8088, Athens GA 30603. (404)549-4875. Newspaper. Published 6 times a year. "Illiteracy in a free society is an unnecessary danger which can and must be remedied. *Wombat*, by being available to young people and their parents and teachers, is one small incentive for young people to put forth the effort to learn to read and write (and draw) better … to communicate better … to comprehend better and—hopefully—consequently, to someday possess greater discernment, judgement, and wisdom as a result." Purpose in publishing works by children: to serve as an incentive …, to encourage them to work hard at their reading, writing, and—yes—drawing/art skills …, to reward their efforts. Requirements to be met before work is published: ages 6-16; all geographic regions, statement that work is original is sufficient.

Magazines: 95% of magazine written by children. Have one 2-4 page "Guest Adult Article" in most issues/when available (submitted). Uses any kind of fiction (3,000 words max.) but avoid extreme violence, religion or sex (approaching pornography); uses any kind of nonfiction of interest to 6-16 year olds (3,000-4,000 words); cartoons, puzzles, jokes, games and solutions. Pays in copies and frameable certificates. Submit mss to Publisher: Jacquelin Howe. Submit complete ms; teacher can submit; parents, librarians, students can submit. Will accept typewritten, legibly handwritten, computer printout mss. Responds in 1-2 weeks with SASE; up to 12 months with seasonal or holiday works (past season or holiday). Written work is not returned. SASE permits *Wombat* to notify sender of receipt of work.

Artwork: Publishes artwork by children. Looks for: works on paper, not canvas. Photocopies OK if clear and/or reworked for clarity and strong line definition by the artist. Pays in copies and frameable certificates. Submit artwork to Publisher: Jacquelin Howe. "Artwork, only, will be returned if requested and accompanied by appropriate sized envelope, stamped with sufficient postage."

WRITERS NEWSLETTER, 1530 7th St., Rock Island IL 61201. (309)798-3980. Newsletter. Audience consists of adults and children, to present good creative writing to others. Purpose in publishing works by children: giving children a chance to have their work read and published.

Newsletter: 25% of newsletter written by children. Uses 1-2 fiction stories (500 words); 1-2 nonfiction articles; poetry (1 page any kind—no more than 25 lines). Pays in 1 copy. Submit mss to Betty Mowery, editor. Submit complete ms. Will accept typewritten, legibly handwritten, computer printout mss. SASE. Reports in 1 week.

Artwork: Publishes artwork by children. Looks for "any kind" of artwork. Pays in 1 copy. Send drawing with black ink submitted flat. Submit artwork to Betty Mowery, editor. SASE. Report in 1 week.

Tips: "Sample copies can be obtained for $1." Will not return rejected mss unless SASE is sent with mss.

WRITING!, General Learning Corp., 60 Revere Dr., Northbrook IL 60062-1563. (312)564-4070. Magazine. Monthly, September-May. Editorial philosophy is to encourage students in grades 7-12 to write and to write well. Purpose in publishing works by children: to encourage similar efforts by our readers. Requirements to be met before work is published: "most student writers are within the age range of our readers, who are students in grades 7-12. We do require proof of original work."

Magazines: 10% of magazine written by children. "We print at least 1 student-written submission per issue. Student writing department accepts all kinds of writing — poetry, fiction, nonfiction (200-400 words). Pay: reward for selection is publication. Submit ms to Alan Lenhoff, editor. Submit complete ms. Will accept typewritten, legibly handwritten, computer printout mss. "Submissions cannot be returned. Students whose submissions have been chosen for publication will be notified by mail."

Contests
and Awards

Winning a contest can be a great boon to your career in terms of prizes and reputation. Especially satisfying is the recognition by peers of your work as the best in the profession.

There are many types of contests listed here. Read carefully—some are for children and teens; others are open only to those residing in specific geographic locations; others are open only to a certain level of writer or illustrator (i.e., beginning or professional). Send away for entry/information forms to determine the exact deadline, the entry fee (many are listed here), and prizes. Some contests also stipulate that entries only cover a certain topic, cause or issue. Be sure you're clear about such subject needs prior to investing time in creating the work.

For beginners, contests sponsored by book publishers can provide an opportunity to get your foot in the door. Many times this is the only time a publisher will consider the work of an unpublished writer or illustrator.

Some contests aren't open to you directly, that is, you can't apply but you must be nominated by your publisher or professional organization. If you are interested in being nominated for an award, and you're not sure if the editor at your publishing house is aware of it, do bring it to his attention. Such a nomination is a good publicity tool for the publisher as well as for you.

JANE ADDAMS CHILDREN'S BOOK AWARD, 980 Lincoln Place, Boulder CO 80302. Contact: Jean Gore, chairperson. Annual contest/award. Estab. 1953. Purpose of the contest/award: to honor a book that most effectively promotes the cause of peace, social justice, and world community. Previously published submissions only (the year before the award is given). Deadline for entries: April 1. Entries not returned. No entry fee. Awards a hand-illuminated scroll and silver seals for the book jackets. Judging by a committee composed mainly of children's librarians. Works will be displayed at the award ceremony.

ALBERTA WRITING FOR YOUTH COMPETITION, Alberta Culture & Multiculturalism, 12th Fl., CN Tower, 10004-104 Ave., Edmonton Alberta T5J 0K5 Canada. (403)427-2554. Contact: Judy Hoyman, consultant. Contest/award held every two years. Estab. 1980. Purpose of the contest/award: to encourage and develop writers in the juvenile market in Alberta. Unpublished submissions only. Deadline for entries: December 31 (even years). SASE for contest/award rules and entry forms. No entry fee. Awards for best book manuscript, $2,000 cash award from Alberta Culture and Multiculturalism, $1,000 cash advance against royalties from publisher, $1,500 12-month option for film/television from Allarcom Limited, book publishing from Doubleday Canada Ltd. Judging by independent panel of qualified judges. "Should publishing co-sponsor choose to publish winning manuscript, rights are purchased." Requirements for entrants: only those Canadian citizens or landed immigrants resident in Alberta at the time of submission and for a period of 12 out of the preceding 18 months. "Book to be published by Doubleday Canada Ltd., usually within 18 months of winning the competition."

AMERICA & ME ESSAY CONTEST, Farm Bureau Insurance, 7373 W. Saginaw, Box 30400, Lansing MI 48909. (517)323-7000. Communications/Advertising Technician: Blythe Redman. Annual contest/award. Estab. 1968. Purpose of the contest/award: to give Michigan 8th graders the opportunity to express their thoughts/feelings on America and their roles in America. Unpublished submissions only. Deadline for entries: mid-November. SASE for contest/award rules and entry forms. "We have a school mailing list. Any school is eligible to participate located in Michigan." Entries not returned. No entry fee. Awards savings bonds and plaques for state top ten ($500-1,000), certificates and plaques for top 3 winners from each school. Judging by home office employee volunteers. Requirements for entrants: "participants must work through their schools or our agents sponsoring schools. No individual submissions will be accepted. Top ten essays and excerpts from other essays are published in booklet form following the contest. State capital/schools receive copies."

THE AMERICAN ASSOCIATION OF UNIVERSITY WOMEN AWARD IN JUVENILE LITERATURE, North Carolina Literary and Historical Assoc., 109 E. Jones St., Raleigh NC 27611. (919)733-7442. Annual contest/award. Previously published submissions only; must be published "during the 12 months ending June 30 of the year for which the award is given." Deadline for entries: July 15. SASE for contest/award rules and entry forms. Judging by North Carolina division of American Assoc. of University Women. Requirements for entrants: entry's author or authors must have maintained either legal or physical residence, or a combination of both in North Carolina for the three years preceding the close of the contest period; three copies of each entry must be submitted to the secretary of the North Carolina Literary and Historical Association.
Tips: "In reaching a decision, members of each Board of Award will consider creative and imaginative quality, excellence of style, universality of appeal, and relevance to North Carolina and her people. All works will be judged without regard to length."

AMHA MORGAN ART CONTEST, American Morgan Horse Assoc., Box 960, Shelburne VT 05482. (802)985-4944. PR Coordinator: Stacey Thibaud. Annual contest/award. The art contest consists of three categories: Morgan art (pencil sketches, oils, water colors, paintbrush), Morgan cartoons, Morgan speciality pieces (sculptures, carvings). Unpublished submissions only. Deadline for entries: January 15. SASE for contest/award rules and entry forms. Entries not returned. Entry fee is $1. Awards $50 first prize and AMHA ribbons to top 5 places. "All work submitted becomes property of The American Morgan Horse Association. Selected works may be used for promotional purposes by the AMHA." Requirements for entrants: "we consider all work submitted." Works displayed at convention in Florida.
Tips: This year the Morgan Horse Association, Inc. will be sponsoring two judgings. The first will be divided into three age groups: 13 years and under, 14-21 years and adult. The second judging will be divided into three categories and open to all ages. The top 5 places will receive official 1988 Art Contest Ribbons. Each art piece must be matted, have its own application form, have its own entry fee.

ANNUAL CONTEST, Creative With Words Publications, Box 223226, Carmel CA 93922. (408)649-1862. Contest/Award Director: Brigitta Geltrich. Annual contest/award. Unpublished submissions only. Deadline for entries: December 31. SASE for contest/award rules and entry forms. SASE for return of entries "if not winning poem." Entry fee is $1/poem. Awards: $15; $10; $5, $1; honorable mention. Judging by selected guest editors. Contest open to any writer.
Tips: Writer must request contest rules.

AVON FLARE YOUNG ADULT NOVEL COMPETITION, Avon Books, 105 Madison Ave., New York NY 10016. (212)481-5609. Contest/award held every two years. Estab. 1983. Purpose of the contest/award: to find and encourage teenage writers. Unpublished submissions only. Deadline for entries: August 31 of odd numbered years. SASE for contest/award rules and entry forms. SASE for return of entries. No entry fee. Awards a $2,500 advance. Judging by the editors of Avon Books. Rights to winning material purchased. Requirements for entrants: "you are eligible to submit a manuscript if you will be no younger than 13 and not older than 18 years of age as of December 31. The book will be published one year after selection."

Tips: "Each manuscript should be approximately 125 to 200 pages, or about 30,000 to 50,000 words. All manuscripts must be typed, double-spaced, on a single side of the page only. Be sure to keep a copy of your manuscript; we cannot be responsible for the manuscripts. With your manuscript, please enclose a letter that includes your name, address, telephone number, age, and a short description of your novel." For information contact Gwen Montgomery, associate editor.

MARGARET BARTLE ANNUAL PLAYWRITING AWARD, Community Childrens Theatre of Kansas City, 8021 E. 129th Terrace, Grandview MO 64030. (816)761-5775. Chairman: E. Blanche Sellens. Annual contest/award. Estab. 1950. Unpublished submissions only. Deadline for entries: January. SASE for contest/award rules and entry forms. SASE for return of entries. No entry fee. Awards $500. Judging by a committee of five.

THE BIG APPLE AWARDS, Peak Output/The Apple Blossom Connection, Box 325, Stacyville IA 50476. Editor: Jacquelyn D. Scheneman. Contest is now offered monthly. Original, unpublished works only. Three different categories in each of three divisions: fiction, nonfiction and poetry. Cash prizes guaranteed; publication of winning entries and some honorable mentions in "The Apple Blossom Connection." SASE for current guidelines on categories, length requirements, entry fees, deadlines and awards.

BOOK OF THE YEAR FOR CHILDREN, Canadian Library Association, Ste. 602, 200 Elgin St., Ottawa ON K2P 1L5 Canada. (613)232-9625. Chairperson, Canadian Association of Children's Librarians. Annual contest/award. Estab. 1947. "The main purpose of the award is to encourage writing and publishing in Canada of good books for children up to and including age 14. If, in any year, no book is deemed to be of Award calibre, the award shall not be made that year. To merit consideration, the book must have been published in Canada and its' author must be a Canadian citizen or a permanent resident of Canada." Previously published submissions only; must be published between January 1 and December 1. Deadline for entries: January 1. SASE for contest/award rules and entry forms. Entries not returned. No entry fee. Awards a medal. Judging by committee of members of the Canadian Association of Childrens Librarians. Requirements for entrants: contest open only to Canadian authors or residents of Canada. "Winning books are on display at CLA headquarters."

THE BOSTON GLOBE-HORN BOOK AWARDS, The Boston Globe & The Horn Book, Inc., The Horn Book, 31 St. James Ave., Boston MA 02116. (617)482-5198. Contest/Award Directors: Stephanie Loer and Anita Silvey. Writing Contact: Stephanie Loer, children's book editor for *The Boston Globe*, 298 North St., Medfield MA 02052. Annual contest/award. "Awards are for picture books, nonfiction and fiction. Three honor books are also chosen for each category." Books must be published between July 1, 1988 through June 30, 1989. Deadline for entries: May 1, 1989. "Publishers usually nominate books." Award winners receive $500 and silver engraved bowl, honor book winners receive a silver plate." Judging by three judges involved in children's book field who are chosen by Anita Silvey, editor-in-chief for *The Horn Book* and Stephanie Loer, children's book editor for *The Boston Globe*. "*The Horn Book* publishes speeches given at awards ceremonies. The book must be available/distributed in the U.S. The awards are given at the fall conference of the New England Round Table of Children's Librarians."

CALDECOTT AWARD, Association for Library Service to Children, division of the American Library Association, 50 E. Huron, Chicago IL 60611. (312)944-6780. Executive Director ALSC: Susan Roman. Annual contest/award. Estab. 1938. Purpose of the contest/award: to honor the artist of the most distinguished picture book for children published in the U.S. Must be published year preceding award. Deadline for entries: December. SASE for contest/award rules and entry forms. Entries not returned. No entry fee. "Medal given at ALA Annual Conference during the Newbery/Caldecott Banquet."

CANADIAN AUTHOR & BOOKMAN CREATIVE WRITING CONTEST, CA&B/Canadian Authors Association, Ste. 104, 121 Avenue Rd., Toronto ON M5R 2G3 Canada. (416)926-8084. Contest/Award Director: Editor. Publisher: Diane Kerner. Annual contest/award. Estab. 1983. Categories: fiction, nonfiction, poetry. Unpublished submissions only (except in school paper). Deadline for entries: mid-February. "Form must come from magazine. Teacher nominates." Entries not returned. No entry fee. Awards $100 for each fiction, poetry and nonfiction—teachers get matching award; $500 scholarship. Judging by CA&B staff-selected judges. Contest open to high school, private school, college and university students. Works published in summer issue of magazine.

CHILDREN'S BOOK AWARD, Institute for Reading Research-IRA, 800 Barksdale Rd., Newark DE 19714-8139. (302)731-1600. Public Information Associate: Patricia C. Dubois. Annual contest/award. Categories: young readers—4-10, older readers—10-16. Must be published between January 1989 and December 1989. Deadline for entries: December 1 of each year. SASE for contest/award rules and entry forms. Awards a $1,000 stipend. Requirements for entrants: Must be a writer's first or second book.
Tips: "Award is presented each year at our annual convention."

CHILDREN'S READING ROUND TABLE AWARD, Children's Reading Roundtable of Chicago, 3930 North Pine Grove, #1507, Chicago IL 60613. (312)477-2271. "Entries are made by nomination by CRRT Members only." Annual award. Estab. 1953. Purpose of the award: longtime commitment to children's books. Award recipients have been authors, editors, educators, and illustrators.

THE CHRISTOPHER AWARD, The Christophers, 12 E. 48 St., New York NY 10017. (212)759-4050. Christopher Awards Coordinator: Peggy Flanagan. Annual contest/award. Estab. 1969 (for young people; books for adults honored since 1949). Previously published submissions only; must be published between January 1 and December 31. Deadline for entries: "books should be submitted all year." Entries not returned. No entry fee. Awards a bronze medallion. Books are judged by both reading specialists and young people. Requirements for entrants: "only published works are eligible and must be submitted during the calendar year in which they are first published."
Tips: "The award is given to works, published in the calendar year for which the award is given, that 'have achieved artistic excellence . . . affirming the highest values of the human spirit.' They must also enjoy a reasonable degree of popular acceptance."

DELACORTE JUVENILE, 666 Fifth Ave., New York NY 10103. (212)765-6500. Contact: Ellen Johnson. Delacorte sponsors a First Young Adult Novel by First Novelist contest. Submit contemporary fiction. Write for more information. Include SASE.

FICTION CONTEST, *Highlights for Children*, 803 Church St., Honesdale PA 18431. (717)253-1080. "Mss should be addressed to Fiction Contest. Editor: Kent L. Brown Jr." Annual contest/award. Estab. 1980. Purpose of the contest/award: to stimulate interest in writing for children and reward and recognize excellence. Unpublished submissions only. Deadline for entries: March 31; entries accepted after January 1 only. SASE for contest/award rules and entry forms. SASE for return of entries. No entry fee. Awards 3 prizes of $750 each in cash, (or, at the winner's election, attendance at the Highlights Foundation Writers Workshop at Chautauqua). Judging by *Highlights*

editors. Winning pieces are purchased for the cash prize of $750. Requirements for entrants: contest open to any writer. Winners announced in June.
Tips: "This year's contest is for action/adventure stories up to 900 words. Stories should be consistent with *Highlights* editorial requirements."

DOROTHY CANFIELD FISHER CHILDREN'S BOOK AWARD, Vermont Department of Libraries, Vermont State PTA and Vermont Congress of Parents and Teachers, 138 Main St., Montpelier VT 05602. Chairman (currently): Betty Lallier. Annual contest/award. Estab. 1957. Purpose of the contest/award: to encourage Vermont children to become enthusiastic and discriminating readers by providing them with books of good quality by living American authors published in the current year. Previously published entries are not eligible. Deadline for entries: "January of the following year." SASE for contest/award rules and entry forms. No entry fee. Awards a scroll presented to the winning author at an award ceremony. Judging is by the children grades 4-8. They vote for their favorite book. Requirements for entrants: "the book must be copyrighted in the current year. It must be written by an American author living in the U.S."

FOSTER CITY ANNUAL WRITERS CONTEST, Foster City Committee for the Arts, 650 Shell Blvd., Foster City CA 94404. Contest Chairman: Ted Lance. Annual contest/award. Estab. 1974. Categories: fiction, humor, children's story, poetry. Unpublished submissions only. Contest is kicked off in April each year (dates may vary) and ends August 31. SASE for contest/award rules and entry forms. SASE for return of entries. Entry fee is $5 for each entry. Awards $300 first prize for the best fiction work of not more than 3,000 words; $300 first prize for the best entry in the category of prose humor; $300 first prize for the best children's story of not more than 2,000 words; $300 first prize for the best work in poetry. Poetry work not to exceed two double-spaced pages in length. Only one poetic work judged per entry fee. Rosettes will be awarded also in all four categories for first prize and honorable mention. Judging by members of the Peninsula Press Club. Requirements for entrants: entries must be original, previously unpublished and in English.

DON FREEMAN MEMORIAL AWARDS, Society of Children's Bookwriters, Box 296, Mar Vista, Los Angeles CA 90066. (818)347-2849. President: Steve Mooser. Annual contest/award. Estab. 1974. Purpose of the contest/award: to encourage artists to pursue their craft. Unpublished submissions only. Deadline for entries: October 15. SASE for contest/award rules and entry forms. SASE for return of entries. No entry fee. Awards a grant of $1,000. Judging by a "panel of people in the field." Requirements for entrants: must be a member of the SCBW.

AMELIA FRANCES HOWARD-GIBBON MEDAL, Canadian Library Association, Ste. 602, 200 Elgin St., Ottawa ON K2P 1L5 Canada. (613)232-9625. Chairperson, Canadian Association of Children's Librarians. Annual contest/award. Estab. 1971. Purpose of the contest/award: "the main purpose of the award is to honor excellence in the illustration of children's book(s) in Canada. To merit consideration the book must have been published in Canada and its illustrator must be a Canadian citizen or a permanent resident of Canada." Previously published submissions only; must be published between January 1 and December 31. Deadline for entries: February 1, 1989. SASE for contest/award rules and entry forms. Entries not returned. No entry fee. Awards a medal. Judging by selection committee of members of Canadian Association of Children's Librarians. Requirements for entrants: illustrator must be Canadian or Canadian resident. Winning books on display at CLA Headquarters.

JEFFERSON CUP AWARD, Virginia Library Association, Children and Young Adult and Round Table, 80 S. Early St., Alexandria VA 22304. (703)823-6966. 1989 Chairperson: Lindsay Ideson. Annual contest/award. Estab. 1982. "The award is given for the best book published for children in the fields of American history, biography or historical fiction." Must be published between January 1 - December 31 "of the year under consideration." Deadline for entries: February 1. "Books are nominated by publishers and by children's librarians. A writer could submit a book which meets our criteria by sending it to the current chair of the committee, but the best way would be to have his publisher send copy (or copies) of it to the members of the committee." Entries not returned. No entry fee. The author appears at VLA's annual meeting and receives a Jefferson Cup! Judging by a committee made up of librarians (mostly children's) and others interested in children's literature. "The author appears at the annual meeting of VLA to give a speech, receive the award and to have an autographing session. We arrange for copies of the book to be there for purchase."

ELIAS LIEBERMAN STUDENT POETRY AWARD, Poetry Society of America, 15 Gramercy Park, New York NY 10003. (212)254-9628. Contest/Award Director: Elise Paschen. Annual contest/award. Purpose of the contest/award: award is for the best unpublished poem by a high or preparatory school student (grades 9-12) from the U.S. and its territories. Unpublished submissions only. Deadline for entries: December 31. SASE for contest/award rules and entry forms. Entries not returned. No entry fee. Award: $100. Judging by a professional poet. Requirements for entrants: contest open to all high school and preparatory students from the U.S. and its territories. School attended, as well as name and address, should be noted. Line limit: none. "The award-winning poem will be included in a sheaf of poems that will be part of the program at the award ceremony, and sent to all PSA members."

VICKY METCALF AWARDS (BODY OF WORK), Canadian Authors Association, Ste. 104, 121 Avenue Rd., Toronto ON M5R 2G3 Canada. (416)926-8084. Contest/Award Director: Awards Chairman. Annual contest/award. Estab. 1963. Purpose of the contest/award: to honor writing inspirational to Canadian youth. Previously published submissions only. Deadline for entries: December 31. SASE for contest/award rules and entry forms. Entries not returned. No entry fee. Awards $2,000. Judging by panel of CAA-appointed judges including past winner.
Tips: "The prizes are given solely to stimulate writing for children by Canadian writers," said Mrs. Metcalf when she established the award. "We must encourage the writing of material for Canadian children without setting any restricting formulas."

VICKY METCALF SHORT STORY AWARD, Canadian Authors Association, Ste. 104, 121 Avenue Rd., Toronto ON M5R 2G3 Canada. (416)926-8084. Contest/Award Director: Awards Chairman. Annual contest/award. Estab. 1982. Purpose of the contest/award: to honor writing by a Canadian inspirational to Canadian youth. Previously published submissions only; must be published between January 1 and December 31. Deadline for entries: December 31. SASE for contest/award rules and entry forms. Entries not returned. No entry fee. Awards $1,000 and $1,000 to Canadian editor of winning story. Judging by CAA-selected panel including past winners.

NATIONAL JEWISH BOOK AWARD FOR CHILDREN'S LITERATURE, (Shapolsky Award), JWB Jewish Book Council, 15 E. 26th St., New York NY 10010. (212)532-4949. Awards Coordinator: Dr. Marcia W. Posner. Annual contest/award. Estab. 1950. Previously published submissions only; must be published in 1988 for June 1989 award, 1989 for 1990 award, etc. Deadline for entries: November 30. SASE for contest/award rules and entry forms. Entries not returned. No entry fee. Awards $750. Judging by 3 authorities in the field. Requirements for entrants: contest for best Jewish children's books, published only for ages 8-14. Books will be displayed at the awards ceremony in NYC in June.

NATIONAL JEWISH BOOK AWARD—PICTURE BOOKS, (Marcia & Louis Posner Award), JWB Jewish Book Council, 15 E 26th St., New York NY 10010. (212)532-4949. Awards Coordinator: Dr. Marcia W. Posner. Annual contest/award. Estab. 1980. Previously published submissions only; must be published the year prior to the awards ceremony—1988 for 1989, 1989 for 1990. Deadline for entries: November 30. SASE for contest/award rules and entry forms. Entries not returned. No entry fee. Awards $750. Judging by 3 authorities in the field. Requirements for entrants: subject must be of Jewish content, published. Works displayed at the awards ceremony.

NEW JERSEY POETRY CONTEST, NJIT Alumni Association, 323 Martin Luther King Blvd., Newark NJ 07102. (201)596-3441. Contest Director: Dr. Herman A. Estrin. Annual contest/award. Estab. 1977. Purpose of the contest/award: to encourage young poets to write poetry and to have it eventually published. Unpublished submissions only. Deadline for entries: February 10. SASE for contest rules and entry forms. Entries not returned. No entry fee. Awards a citation with the poet's name and the name of the poem. Also, the poem will be published in an anthology. Judging by teachers of English. Requirements for entrants: poet must be a NJ resident. "The published anthology can be obtained through NJIT Alumni office."

NEWBERY MEDAL AWARD, Association for Library Service to Children division of the American Library Association, 50 E Huron, Chicago IL 60611. (312)944-6780. Executive Director, ALSC: Susan Roman. Annual contest/award. Estab. 1922. Purpose of the contest/award: for the most distinguished contribution to American children's literature published in the U.S. Previously published submissions only; must be published prior to year award is given. Deadline for entries: December. SASE for contest/award rules and entry forms. Entries not returned. No entry fee. Medal awarded at banquet during annual conference. Judging by Newbery Committee. Works displayed at ALA Midwinter Meeting where announcement of winner is made.

1989 MANNINGHAM POETRY TRUST STUDENT CONTESTS, National Federation of State Poetry Societies, Inc., Box 607, Green Cove Springs FL 32043. Chairman: Robert E. Dewitt. Purpose of the contest/award: "two separate contests: grades 6-8; grades 9-12. Poems can have been printed and can have won previous awards. All winning poems will be published. Each winner will receive a copy of the chapbook." Deadline for entries: April 15, 1989. "Submit one poem neatly typed on standard typewriter paper. Submit one original and one copy. On copy only, type: (1) name (2) complete home mailing address (3) school (4) grade. On copy only, put simple certification: 'This poem is my original work,' and signature." Awards $50 first; $30 second; $20 third; and five honorable mentions of $5 each.
Tips: Winners will be announced at the 1989 NFSPS convention, and checks will be mailed shortly thereafter. Send SASE if you wish to receive a winner's list.

THE 1989 NATIONAL WRITTEN & ILLUSTRATED BY . . . AWARDS CONTEST FOR STUDENTS, Landmark Editions, Inc., Box 4469, Kansas City MO 64127. (816)241-4919. Contest/Award Director: Alida Braden. Annual awards contest with 3 published winners. Estab. 1986. Purpose of the contest/award: to encourage and celebrate the creative efforts of students. There are three age categories (6-9 years of age; 10-13; and 14-19). Unpublished submissions only. Deadline for entries: May 1, 1989. Contest rules available for self-addressed, stamped, business-sized envelope. "Need to send a self-addressed, sufficiently stamped book mailer with book entry" for its return. No entry fee. Prize: "book is published." Judging by national panel of educators, editors, illustrators and authors. "Each student winner receives a publishing contract allowing Landmark to publish the book. Copyright is in student's name and student receives royalties on sale of book.Author/illustrators may enter who are of ages from 6-19. Books must be in proper contest format and submitted with entry form signed by a teacher or librarian. Students may develop their illustrations in any medium of their choice, as long as the illustrations remain two-dimensional and flat to the surface of the paper." Works will be published in 1990, Kansas City, MO for distribution nationally and internationally.

OGS ESSAY CONTEST, Ohio Genealogical Society, Box 2625, Mansfield OH 44906. (419)522-9077. Director of Education: Jana Sloan Broglin. Annual contest/award. Estab. 1986. Purpose of the contest/award: to develop an interest in genealogy. Deadline for entries: April 1, 1989, "one month before State Convention." SASE for contest/ award rules and entry forms. Entries not returned. No entry fee. Awards 1st place Senior division $400; 1st place Junior division $200. Judging by Education Committee of OGS. Requirements for entrants: students ages 9-18 in Ohio, or child or grandchild of OGS member if outside of Ohio, same ages though. Works will be published in Ohio Genealogical Society "Report."

PUBLISH-A-BOOK CONTEST, Raintree Publishers, 310 W. Wisconsin Ave., Milwaukee WI 53203. (414)273-0873. Marketing Manager: Dr. Denise A. Wenger. Send written entries: PAB Contest. Annual contest/award. Estab. 1984. Purpose of the contest/award: to stimulate 4th, 5th, and 6th graders to write outstanding stories for children. Unpublished submissions only. Contest theme for 1989: magic, mystery, and monsters. Deadline for entries: January 31. SASE for contest/award rules and entry forms. "Entries must be sponsored by a teacher or librarian." Entries not returned. No entry fee. Grand prizes: Raintree will publish four winning entries in the fall of 1989. Each winner will receive a $500 author's fee and ten free copies of the published book. The sponsor named on each of these entries will receive twenty free books from the Raintree catalog. Honorable mentions: each of the twenty honorable mention writers will receive $25. The sponsor named on each of these entries will receive ten free books from the Raintree catalog. Judging by an editorial team. Contract issued for Grand Prize winners. Payment and royalties paid. Requirements for entrants: contest is open only to 4th, 5th, and 6th graders enrolled in a school program in the United States or other countries. Books will be displayed and sold in the United States and foreign markets. Displays at educational association meetings, book fairs.

RHYME TIME CREATIVE WRITING CONTEST, Hutton Publications, Box 1870, Hayden ID 83835. (208)772-6184. Editor: Linda Hutton. Monthly contest/award. Estab. 1981. Contest for poetry and fiction of various types; rules for #10 SASE. Contests are for *Rhyme Time, Mystery Time, Writer's Info, Christian Outlook*. Contests for both published and unpublished entries. Deadline for entries: 1st or 15th of each month. SASE for contest/award rules and entry forms. Entries not returned. Entry fee is $1-2 maximum; some contests with no fee. Awards $7.50-$50 prizes as well as subscriptions. Judging by Hutton Publications staff. Rights acquired only if winning work is published; otherwise no. Requirements for entrants: contest open to all. Restrictions of mediums for illustrators: India ink up to 3×5; we use very little artwork. Work will be published in *Christian Outlook, Mystery Time, Rhyme Time* or *Writer's Info*.

CARL SANDBURG LITERARY ARTS AWARDS, Friends of the Chicago Public Library, 78 E. Washington St., Chicago IL 60602. (312)269-2922. Annual contest/award. Categories: fiction, nonfiction, poetry, children's literature. Previously published submissions only; must be published between June 1 and May 31 (the following year). Deadline for entries: September 1. SASE for contest/award rules and entry forms. Entries not returned. No entry fee. Awards trophy and $500. Judging by authors, reviewers, book buyers, librarians. Requirements for entrants: native or resident of the six county metropolitan area, two copies submitted by September 1. All entries become the property of the Friends.

SCIENCE WRITING AWARD IN PHYSICS AND ASTRONOMY, The American Institute of Physics, 335 E. 45th St., New York NY 10017. (212)661-9404. Contact: Manager, Public Information Division. For information contact Mary Toepfer, public information division secretary. Annual contest/award. Estab. 1987. Purpose of the contest/award: to stimulate and recognize writing that improves children's understanding and appreciation of physics and astronomy. Previously published submissions only; must be published between October 1 and September 30 (the following year). Deadline for entries: October 10. SASE for contest/award rules and entry forms. "Entries may be submitted by the publisher as well as the author." Entries not returned. No entry fee. Awards $3,000 and an engraved chair. Judging by a committee selected by the Governing Board of the AIP. Requirements for entrants: "entries must be articles or books, written in English or English translations, dealing primarily with physics, astronomy or related subjects directed at children, from preschool ages up to fifteen years old. Entries must have been available to and intended for young people."

SHOE TREE CONTESTS, National Association for Young Writer's Inc., 215 Valle del Sol Dr., Santa Fe NM 87501. (505)982-8596. Editor: Sheila Cowing. Contest/award offered 3 times a year/one each fiction, nonfiction, poetry. Estab. 1984. "The purpose of the awards is to stimulate young writers to do their best work. Fiction, poetry, nonfiction." Unpublished submissions only. Deadline for entries: January 1, fiction; April 1, poetry; June 1, nonfiction. SASE for contest/award rules and entry forms. SASE for return of entries. No entry fee. Awards first prize $25, second prize $10, honorable mention; all receive publication in *Shoe Tree.* "All writers may have work reprinted elsewhere after they write requesting permission, providing credit is given to *Shoe Tree.* All entries become property of NAYW." Works will be published in the issue of *Shoe Tree* following due date.
Tips: "Contests are open to all children between the ages of 6-14, first grade through eighth, at the time of entry. A statement of authenticity signed by the student and by a parent, teacher, or guardian must accompany the entry. Student's name, address, age, and the names of his or her school and teacher must accompany the entry."

GEORGE G. STONE CENTER FOR CHILDREN'S BOOKS RECOGNITION OF MERIT AWARD, George G. Stone Center for Children's Books, The Claremont Graduate School, 131 E. 10th St., Claremont CA 91711-6188. (714)621-8000 ext. 3670. Contest/Award Director: Doty Hale. Annual contest/award. Estab. 1965. Purpose of the contest/award: given to an author or illustrator of a children's book or for a body of work for the "power to please and expand the awareness of children and teachers as they have shared the book in their classrooms." Previously published submissions only. SASE for contest/award rules and entry forms. Entries not returned. No entry fee. Awards a scroll by artist Richard Beasley. Judging by a committee of teachers, professors of children's literature and librarians. Requirements for entrants: "nominations are made by students, teachers, professors, and librarians. Award made at annual Claremont Reading Conference in spring (March)."

SYDNEY TAYLOR AWARD FOR BEST OLDER CHILDREN'S BOOK OF JEWISH CONTENT, The Association of Jewish Libraries, % National Foundation for Jewish Culture, 330 7th Ave., New York NY 10001. Contest/Award Director: Aileen D. Grossberg. Annual contest/award. Estab. 1980. Purpose of the contest/award: to encourage more and superior Jewish children's books. Previously published submissions only; must be published year previous to date of award. Deadline for entries: December 31. Contest/award rules and entry forms available to publishers at the association address. Awards $1,000. Judging by committee of 6 librarians. Requirements for entrants: nominations by publishers. Works displayed at awards banquet and June convention.

SYDNEY TAYLOR AWARD FOR BEST YOUNGER CHILDREN'S BOOKS OF JEWISH CONTENT, Association of Jewish Libraries, % National Foundation for Jewish Culture, 330 7th Ave., New York NY 10001. Contest/Award Director: Aileen D. Grossberg. Annual contest/award. Estab. 1980. Purpose of the contest/award: to encourage the publishing and writing of excellent Jewish children's books. Previously published submissions only; must be published year prior to award. Deadline for entries: December 31. Publishers are requested to contact us at association address. Entries not returned. No entry fee. Awards $1,000. Judging by committee of 6 librarians. Requirements for entrants: nominations from publisher. Work displayed at awards banquet and convention in June.

SYDNEY TAYLOR MANUSCRIPT AWARD, Association of Jewish Libraries, % National Foundation for Jewish Culture, 330 7th Ave., New York NY 10001. Contest/Award Director: Lilian Schwartz. Annual contest/award. Estab. 1985. Purpose of the contest/award: to encourage authors to write for Jewish children stories of Jewish content. Unpublished submissions only. Deadline for entries: December 10. SASE for contest/award rules and entry forms. Entries not returned. No entry fee. Awards $1,000. Judging by 3 librarians. Works displayed at June banquet and convention. For more information contact L. Schwartz, Temple Emanu-EL Library, 99 Taft Ave., Providence RI 02906.

VFW VOICE OF DEMOCRACY, Veterans of Foreign Wars of the U.S., 34th & Broadway, Kansas City MO 64111. (816)756-3390. Director: Jeff Lawson. Annual contest/award. Estab. 1960. Purpose of the contest/award: to give high school students the opportunity to voice their opinions about their responsibility to our country and to convey them via the broadcast media to all of America. Deadline for entries: November 15. SASE for contest/award rules and entry forms. SASE for return of entries. No entry fee. Awards 1st-9th place; $16,000, $9,000, $6,000, $4,000, $3,000, $1,500, $1,000, $1,000, $1,000 respectively. Requirements for entrants: "10th, 11th and 12th grade students in public, parochial and private schools in the United States and overseas, are eligible to compete. Former national and/or 1st Place State winners are not eligible to compete again. U.S. Citizenship is required."

THE STELLA WADE CHILDREN'S STORY AWARD, AMELIA Magazine, 329 E St., Bakersfield CA 93304. (805)323-4064. Editor: Frederick A. Raborg, Jr. Annual contest/award. Estab. 1988. Purpose of the contest/award: with decrease in the number of religious and secular magazines for young people, the juvenile story and poetry must be preserved and enhanced. Unpublished submissions only. Deadline for entries: August 15. SASE for contest/award rules and entry forms. SASE for return of entries. Entry fee is $5 per adult entry; there is no fee for entries submitted by young people under the age of 17, but such entry must be signed by parent, guardian or teacher to verify originality. Awards $125 plus publication. Judging by editorial staff. "We use First North American serial rights only for the winning manuscript." Contest is open to all interested. If illustrator wishes to enter only an illustration without a story, the entry fee remains the same. Illustrations will also be considered for cover publication. Restrictions of mediums for illustrators: no restrictions, though submitted photos should be no smaller than 5×7. Illustrations (drawn) may be in any medium. "Winning entry will be published in the most appropriate issue of either AMELIA, CICADA or SPSM&H — subject matter would determine such. Submit clean, accurate copy."

WESTERN HERITAGE AWARDS, National Cowboy Hall of Fame, 1700 NE 63rd St., Oklahoma City OK 73111. (405)478-2250. Director of Public Relations and Publications: Marcia Preston. Annual contest/award. Estab. 1960. Purpose of the contest/award: the WHA is presented annually to encourage the accurate and artistic telling of great stories of the West. There are twelve categories of entries: art book, nonfiction book, juvenile book, western novel, western poetry, western short story, western magazine article, western feature film (movie), factual television, fictional television, music. Previously published submissions only; must be published the calendar year before the awards are presented. Deadline for entries: December 31. SASE for contest/award rules and entry forms. Entries not returned. No entry fee. Awards a Wrangler award, a reproduction of a C.M. Russell bronze. Judging by a panel of judges selected each year with distinction in various fields of western art and heritage. Requirements for entrants: the material must pertain to the development or preservation of the West. "There is an autograph party preceding the awards. Film clips are shown during the awards presentation."

LAURA INGALLS WILDER AWARD, Association for Library Service to Children—a division of the American Library Association, 50 E. Huron, Chicago IL 60611. (312)944-6780. Executive Director, ALSC: Susan Roman. Contest/award offered every 3 years. Purpose of the contest/award: to recognize an author or illustrator whose books, published in the U.S. have over a period of years made a substantial and lasting contribution to children's literature. Awards a medal. Judging by committee which chooses several authors—winner is chosen by vote of ALSC membership.

PAUL A WITTY OUTSTANDING LITERATURE AWARD, International Reading Association, Special Interest Group, Reading for Gifted and Creative Learning, School of Education, Box 32925, Fort Worth TX 76129. (817)921-7660. Contest/Award Director: Dr. Cathy Collins. Annual contest/award. Estab. 1979. Categories of entries: poetry/prose at elementary, junior high and senior high levels. Unpublished submissions only. Deadline for entries: February 1, 1989. SASE for contest/award rules and entry forms. SASE for return of entries. No entry fee. Awards $25 and plaque, also certificates of merit. Judging by 2 committees for screening and awarding. Works will be published in Reading Association publications.
Tips: "The elementary students' entries must be legible and may not exceed 1,000 words. Secondary students' prose entries should be typed and may exceed 1,000 words if necessary. At both elementary and secondary levels, if poetry is entered, a set of 5 poems must be submitted. All entries and requests for applications must include a self-addressed, stamped envelope."

YOUNG WRITER'S CONTEST, Young Writer's Contest Foundation, Box 6092, McLean VA 22106. (703)893-6097. Executive Director: Kathie Janger. Annual contest/award. Estab. 1984. Purpose of the contest/award: to challenge first through eighth graders and to give them recognition; in so doing, we aim to improve basic communication skills. Unpublished submissions only. Deadline for entries: November 30. SASE for contest/award rules and entry forms. Entries not returned. Entry fee is $10 per school (or, if school does not participate, the individual may pay the fee). "All participating students and schools receive certificates; winners' entries are published in our anthology: RAINBOW COLLECTION: Stories and Poetry by Young People." Judging by writers, editors, journalists, teachers, reading specialists. "All rights surrounding winners' entries are given to YWCF, via consent and release form. Participants must be currently enrolled in grades 1-8; no more than 12 entries per school may be submitted; we accept poems, stories, and essays. RAINBOW COLLECTION: Stories and Poetry by Young People is published in May of each year, and is distributed (16,500 cc. in 1988) to libraries, school systems, and charitable organizations. The YWCF complements classroom writing programs and creates a cycle of encouragement and performance; writing is critical to all fields of endeavor; we reward the students' efforts—not just the winners'."

Resources

Writer's and Illustrator's Agents

It's not always easy to determine when you, as a writer or illustrator, will need the services of an agent. Many established writers/illustrators are quite successful at selling their work because they have established a reputation in the field and have the right contacts. Some professionals, based on prior experience, also are skilled at negotiating their own contracts. It may be helpful, first of all, to explain what an agent can or can't do for you.

An agent can evaluate your manuscript or artwork for you to determine whether it's salable; he can sell to contacts in the marketplace you may not know yourself; he has the time to invest in selling your work that you may not have; he can negotiate a contract on your behalf (you do get final say though on issues of concern to you); and an agent can collect fees from the publisher for you as well as maintain your financial records. What an agent can't do for you is act as a writing or art teacher. Neither will an agent act as your social secretary, edit your manuscript (that's the editor's job), or defend you in court (unless he is also an attorney). Though many agents offer reading and critique services (for writers), no one will waste time on a writer who obviously has no writing ability. Agents are in business to make a profit.

And that's probably why there are fewer agents who handle juvenile writing and illustrating—there is less money to be made. There are no miniseries, fewer foreign rights, smaller print runs and fewer reprints. Also, the juvenile market is more open to first-time writers and illustrators, and unsolicited manuscripts or queries than any other area of publishing.

Agents generally charge 10 to 15 percent commission from the sale of your writing or art material. Such fees will be taken from your advance and royalty payments. If an agent also deals with foreign sales of rights, you can expect a 20 percent commission deducted from your earnings because he will probably be sharing this fee with an agent based in that country. Some agents now offer reading and critique services for manuscripts; this isn't an industry standard though. Reading services will probably be charged to unpublished writers; the fee should be less than $75. If the agent agrees to represent you, and your manuscript is sold, you may be reimbursed this amount. (It depends on the agent.) Criticism services shouldn't be confused with editing a manuscript, as mentioned before. Some agents who specialize in different genres of writing feel they know salable material well enough to offer "pointers" on tightening up manuscripts or revising style. Such services can range from $25 to $200 or more. One word of warning—be sure to find out exactly what results you can expect from a reading or critique fee. The listings in this section specify whether such editorial services are offered, how much is charged, and if the fee is refundable upon a manuscript sale.

While agents don't charge clients for general "overhead" office expenses, they will exact a fee for specific duties such as photocopying, phone expenses, postage for mail services, or messenger services. How do you know when you should get an agent? This will involve some honesty with yourself about how polished a writer or artist you are at this point in your career. You'll have to determine whether you can afford to pay an agent 10 or 15 percent of your royalties, and if you are so busy writing that you don't have time to market yourself, track your income, adequately analyze your own contracts to your best interests, or put someone else in charge of maintaining those contacts you've already established. Also, not every agent is interested in representing unpublished writers or artists. This means you will have to have some track record of publication prior to approaching an agent.

Finding the right agent is a two-way street. The agent will want to know about your credentials as a writer or artist. This means that your manuscript or artwork must be as polished and professional-looking as possible, as well as your cover or query letters and/or outlines. An agent will want to be sure you can represent yourself through writing or art—clearly organized information will tell him a lot about you.

Prior to signing with an agent you need to do some research as well. Does he know his market well enough to represent you to editors? Information in the following listings includes reporting time on queries and/or manuscripts or art samples, possible reading or critique fees, other "hidden" marketing expenses (such as photocopying mentioned earlier), what rights he markets, what his contract requirements are (i.e., how long the agreement runs, what expenses you are responsible for and how they will be paid), how an agreement can be terminated, as well as what special services are offered (i.e., lecture/promotional tours, tax/legal consultations). Some agents may balk at giving you a list of their clients to contact, but this information can be very helpful to you.

These listings also specify which agents are members of Independent Literary Agents Association, Inc. (ILAA) and Society of Author's Representatives, Inc. (SAR). These organizations require their members to adhere to a code of ethics in business practice. There are other organizations that will be specified too, especially for illustration agents who may be members of the Graphic Artists Guild (GAG) or the Society of Photographers and Artists Representatives (SPAR). All listings included in this section are open in varying degrees to reviewing the work of new potential clients. Read through each listing to get a feel for what each agent can do...and remember to ask as many questions about them as they will about you. For an agent/client relationship to function effectively, each must be comfortable with the other's abilities.

BARBARA BAUER LITERARY AGENCY, 179 Washington Ave., Matawan NJ 07747. (201)739-5210,16. Business Representative: Kay Morgan. Estab. 1884. Branch Office: 59 W. Front St., Keyport NJ 07735. (201)583-4988. Represents 10-12 clients. Specializes in new and unpublished authors. "New writers are welcome to attend our seminar in Las Vegas on August 10 and 11, 1989, at the Palace Station Hotel and Casino in Las Vegas, Nevada. This will be an educational experience for anyone who needs to know how to get inside the publishing houses. We are very excited about it. Keynote speaker: Dr. Herman Estrin. Topic: "You Are What You Speak'." Ms/illustration packages: send with SASE. Has sold *The Mystery of the Singing Mermaid*, Ann Young, (Weekly Reader Book Clubs).

BOOKSTOP LITERARY AGENCY, 67 Meadow View Rd., Orinda CA 94563. (415)254-2664. Agent: Kendra Bersamin. Estab. 1984. Member of SCBW. Clients specialize in picture books, young readers, middle readers, young adult books, illustration of own books, juvenile art. 50% of clients are new/unpublished writers; 30% new/unpublished illustrators. Qualifications for representation: must have high-quality work that will sell to the trade market. Prefers to review new material via the entire ms. Reports in 6 weeks on a ms or ms/illustration package. Has sold *Natalie Underneath*, Betsy James (picture book, Dutton); *Umbrella Day*, Melissa Mathis (picture book, Philomel); *Long Night Dance*, James (young adult fantasy, Dutton). Commission: 15% on domestic sales, 20% on foreign sales. Criticism service fee: $25 an hour. I charge for postage, copies and telephone. 75% of business derived from commission on ms sales; 25% from criticism services.

ANDREA BROWN, LITERARY AGENCY, 13B, 301 W. 53 St., New York NY 10019. (212)581-7068. President: Andrea Brown. Estab. 1981. Member of ILAA. 15-18 clients specialize in picture books, 10 in young readers, 10-15 in middle readers, 10-12 in young adult books, 5 writers illustrate own books, 10 clients specialize in juvenile art. 25% of clients are new/unpublished writers; 5% new/unpublished illustrators. Qualifications for representation: "Illustrators—who have published children's book material only. Writers—queries only by unpublished writers with a SASE. Other writers should send samples of work published. Taking on few brand new writers." Prefers to review new material via a query with outline/proposal; ms/illustration packages (queries with photos of art—SASE). Reports in approximately 2 weeks on a query, 8 weeks on a ms, 4 weeks on a ms/illustration package, 2 weeks on illustrations. Handles (approximately) 30% nonfiction, 40% fiction, 10% ms/illustration package, 20% illustrations only. Commission: 15% on domestic sales, 20% on foreign sales. "We call new, unpublished authors collect." 99% of business derived from commission on ms sales.
Tips: "We do exclusively children's books. Young adults is slow now, and we can't get enough good middle-group books. Not interested in unpublished picture book people."

MARIE BROWN ASSOCIATES, 412 W. 154th St., New York NY 10032. (212)690-7613. Contacts: Marie Brown/B.J. Ashanti. Estab. 1984. Represents 40 clients. Qualifications for representation: "Writer should be published (magazines, journals, etc.). We specialize in multi-cultural books and Afro-American writers and illustrators." Prefers to review new material via an outline plus sample chapters; ms/illustration packages (submit photocopy of ms). Reports in 4-6 weeks on a query, ms, ms/illustration package. Handles 50% fiction, picture books, 50% young readers. Charges reading fee, but not for manuscripts under 40 ms pages. Criticism service includes analysis of manuscript and overview of the market. Critique written by selected readers who specialize in children's literature.

MARIA CARVAINIS AGENCY, INC., 235 W. End Ave., New York NY 10023. (212)580-1559. President: Maria Carvainis. Estab. 1977. Member of Independent Literary Agents Association, Writers Guild of America, Authors Guild of America, and Romance Writers of America. Represents 60 clients. 15% of clients specialize in young adult books. 15% of clients are new/unpublished writers. Accepting new clients on a selective basis.

Qualifications for representation: "I look for three criteria to be met-1) a strong writing talent 2) a special story or book concept and 3) a strong execution of the story or book concept." Prefers to review new material via a query. Reports in 2-3 weeks on a query, 4-12 weeks on a ms. Handles 100% fiction (10% middle readers, 90% young adults). "I would like to see more nonfiction. Commission: 15% on domestic sales, 20% on foreign sales. Criticism service only offered to agency's clients. "I offer evaluation of the strength of the book's development and execution of its potential given my experience for more than a decade as an editor at Macmillan Publishing, Basic Books, Avon Books and Crown Publishers." 100% of business derived from commission on ms sales.

Tips: "The juvenile market is one of the most healthy and expanding sectors of the publishing industry. I expect it to remain so."

MARTHA CASSELMAN, LITERARY AGENT, 1263 Twelfth Ave., San Francisco CA 94122. (415)665-3235. Sole proprietor: Martha Casselman. Assistant: Cheryl Carroll. Estab. 1978. Member of ILAA. Represents 6 clients in juvenile and young adults. 2 clients specialize in picture books, 2 in young adults, 2 illustrators specialize in juvenile art. 80% of clients are new/unpublished writers. Qualifications for representation: "Authors should be familiar with the field." Commission: 15% domestic sales; 10% foreign sales. Charges for copying, overnight mailing services. "I have made a cautious entry into the juvenile and young adult market. Sales have been to reputable publishers. Juvenile and young adult will continue to be a small part of the agency's projects."

RUTH COHEN, INC., Box 7626, Menlo Park CA 94025. (415)854-2054. President: Ruth Cohen. Estab. 1982. Member of ILAA. Represents 60-70 clients. 5 clients specialize in picture books, 14 in young readers, 15 young adult books, 5 writers illustrate own books, 5 clients specialize in juvenile art. 50% of clients are new/unpublished writers. Qualifications for representation: "Submission of quality material in the form of a partial ms and illustrations (if illustrator has been published before) or a partial ms for older children if author has not been published before; plus list of credits and SASE. Prefers to review new material via an outline plus 3 sample chapters; ms/illustration packages (must include SASE). Reports in 14 days on a query, 21 days on a ms or ms/illustration package, 14 days on illustrations. Commission: 15% domestic sales; 20% foreign sales. Charges for foreign/telex or phone calls and overseas mailing charges.

CRAVEN DESIGN STUDIOS, INC., 461 Park Ave. S., New York NY 10016. (212)696-4680. President: Tema Siegel. Estab. 1981. Represents 20 illustrators. Qualifications for representation: "Illustrators should have a few years experience and have some published pieces. How many pieces published does not matter as much as how good they are and how well they represent a specific style." Ms/illustrations packages: submit samples—photocopies that do not have to be returned—or a self addressed mailer—I will call for portfolio if interested. Reports in 2 weeks on illustrations. Handles 100% illustrations (10% picture books, 10% young readers, 3% middle readers, 2% young adults); also 85% textbooks. Commission: 25% domestic sales; 25% foreign sales. 100% of business derived from commission on illustrations.

RICHARD CURTIS ASSOCIATES, Ste. 1, 164 E. 64th St., New York NY 10021. (212)371-9481. Estab. 1974. Represents 75 clients. Head of Children's Books: Ms. Rob Cohen. Member of ILAA. Handle 25% nonfiction, 75% fiction (25% picture books, 25% young readers, 25% young adults). So far, only one illustrator. Qualifications for representation: "We would prefer children's book authors who have already sold one or two books, but we will read queries from unpublished authors." Query format: outline plus sample chapters or, for short juvenile books, we will take complete ms with illustrations. For longer young adult books, 1 or 2 sample illustrations would be preferable. Query only for illustrators. Response in 2 weeks on a query, 4 weeks on ms and ms/illustration packages. Some better known clients: young adult mystery author John Bellairs and illustrator Barry Moser. Commission: 10% domestic sales; 20% foreign sales. 100% of business derived from commission on ms sales.

Tips: "This is a difficult market and we are just getting started, so we have very strict standards for acceptance. But we love to see good books."

PETER ELEK ASSOCIATES, Box 223, Canal St. Station, New York NY 10013. (212)431-9368. Executive Assistant: Liza Lagunoff. Estab. 1979. Represents 30 clients. 8 clients specialize in picture books, 8 in young readers, 2 in middle readers, 1 in young adult books, 5 clients specialize in juvenile art. 20% of clients are new/unpublished writers; 50% new/unpublished illustrators. Accepting new clients "very selectively." Qualifications for representation: "intent on making a career as a professional writer; experience writing for children (not simply a teacher, librarian or parent)." Prefers to review new material via a query; with outline proposal. Reports in 14 days on a query, 21 days on a ms or ms/illustration package. Handles 30% nonfiction (60% picture books, 40% middle readers); 50% fiction (60% picture books, 20% young readers, 20% middle readers); 20% ms/illustration package (80% picture books, 10% young readers, 10% middle readers). Has sold *Exploring the Titanic*, Dr. Robert Ballard (middle readers, Scholastic); *Earl's Too Cool for Me*, Leah Komaiko (picture book, Harper & Row); *Ollie Forgot*, Tedd Arnold (picture book, Dial). Commission: 15% domestic sales; 20% foreign sales. If required, charges for ms copying, courier charges. 100% of business derived from commission on ms sales.

Tips: "Sadly too many individuals are encouraged by 'schools' and writing courses to believe that they are innovative and have the ability to write for children. Few have studied publishers' catalogs and bookstore/library shelves to see what is already there."

ETHAN ELLENBERG/LITERARY AGENT, #5-C 548 Broadway, New York NY 10012. (212)431-4554. President: Ethan Ellenberg. Estab. 1984. Represents 35 clients. 3 clients specialize in picture books, 1 in young readers, 1 writer illustrates own books. 100% of clients (in children's books) are new/unpublished writers; 100% new/unpublished illustrators. (In adult books 50% of clientele published before.) Qualifications for representation: a professionally prepared manuscript and/or illustrations ready for submission to publishers. "Query , sample chapters or entire ms are all acceptable to submit as long as they include SASE. No preference." Reports in 2-3 weeks for all submissions, no matter what. Handles 50% fiction, 50% ms/illustration package. Has sold *The Devil Ate My Blintzes*, Ben Hillman (age 0-8, Waterfront Press). Commission: 15% domestic sales; 20% foreign sales. "The only expense I charge is a photocopying fee for duplication of ms for submission."

Tips: "I am actively seeking new clients and I look forward to hearing from anyone serious about children's books. Before opening my own agency I was in charge of the contracts for juvenile publishing at Bantam, so I know the field well. I enjoy children's books and I'm excited about the opportunities the field has."

ANN ELMO AGENCY INC., 60 E. 42 St., New York NY 10165. (212)661-2880, 2881, 2883. President: Ann Elmo; or Lettie Lee. Estab. 1945. Member of SAR, Authors League, Dramatist Guild. Represents 50 regular clients. 5 clients specialize in young readers, 3 in young adult books, 5 writers illustrate own books. Qualifications for representation: "Writers need not have credits in juvenile writing to be accepted as long as they have valid ideas in marketable form." Prefers to review new material via a query or entire ms; ms/illustration packages (typed double-spaced). Reports in 1 week on ms, 4-8 weeks on ms/illustration package. Commission: 15% domestic sales; 25% foreign sales.

J. KELLOCK & ASSOCIATES LTD., 11017-80 Ave., Edmonton Alberta T6G 0R2 Canada. (403)433-0274. President: Joanne Kellock. Estab. 1981. Represents approximately 70 clients. 5 clients specialize in picture books, 10 in young adult books, 10 writers illustrate own books, some clients specialize in juvenile art. 30% of clients are new/unpublished writers; 1% new/unpublished illustrators. Qualifications for representation: "It is always preferable to acquire a writer who has one or two books on the market, but new talent must be looked at providing any project is well thought out, professionally written, competition studied, and required age group carefully considered. Helpful if illustrators have a reputation as an artist, and are VERY serious about becoming an illustrator for children's material. They must love such children's books." Prefers to review new material via a query; outline/proposal; outline plus 3 complete sample chapters; or one finished piece of art work, 3 b&w sketches. Reports in 1 week on a query, 3-4 weeks on a ms, 2 weeks on a ms/illustration package, 1 week on illustrations. Handles 2% nonfiction picture books, and 5% middle readers; 3% fiction picture books, 15% young readers and 12% young adults; 4% ms/illustration package picture books, 2% young readers, 15% middle readers, 9% young adults; 3% illustration only picture books, 15% middle readers, 9% young adult books. Has sold *Ida Mae Evans Eats Ants*, Mary Blakeslee, (middle readers, McClelland & Stewart/HB Avon, N.Y. Paperback); *Sixteen is Spelled Ouch*, Joan Weir (young adults, Stoddart/Toronto); *Why the Reindeer Were Chosen*, Moe Price (picture book, Mathew Price Inc./U.K.). Commission: 15% English language sales; 20% foreign sales. Reading/criticism service fee fiction and nonfiction: under 2,000 words, $37.50; 2,000-10,000 words, $45; 10,000-20,000 words, $90; 20,000-100,000 words, $165; more than 100,000 words, $225. "We do not require an additional fee for a second and third reading of the same manuscript providing all editorial corrections have been made (line editing) and all editorial comments have been taken into consideration when rewriting (substantive editing). I basically concern myself with style working with subject/whether or not work fits into the right age group; character development, action, point of view/voice. My reader sometimes deals with ms from new writers. Require a SASE with all submissions. Charges for postage and long distance calls." 70% of business derived from commission on ms sales and 30% from reading fees/criticism service. "I do not charge for reading three chapters, and that is usually enough to tell me if a ms works. I do not request complete ms if ms not working."
Tips: "I do very well with sales of children's work, and consequently more and more writers of this material seek me out. I fight hard for my children's writers, particularly if sale is to Canadian publisher, as here children's writers are still somehow considered second class. I also sell TV/film."

BARBARA S. KOUTS, LITERARY AGENT, 788 Ninth Ave., New York NY 10019. (212)265-6003. Literary Agent: Barbara Kouts. Estab. 1980. Member of ILAA. Represents 22 clients. 4 clients specialize in picture books, 8 in young readers, 10 in young adult books, 2 writers illustrate own books. 60% of clients are new/unpublished writers. Qualifications for representation: "I am looking for writer's with some background in writing (i.e., published stories or articles). But I will look at new material, too." Prefers to review new material via a query. Reports in 1-2 weeks on query, 3-4 weeks on ms. Handles 40% nonfiction (10% picture books, 45% middle readers, 45% young adult books); 60% fiction (25% picture books, 25% young readers, 25% middle readers, 25% young adult books). Has sold *A Man Named Thoreau*, Robert Burleigh (middle readers, Atheneum); *The Makeover*, Jane Parks-McKay (young adult book, Morrow Junior Books); *The Enchanted Tapestry*, Robert San Souci (picture book, Dial). Commission: 10% domestic sales; 20% foreign sales. Charges photocopying fee. 100% of business derived from commission on ms sales.

CAROL JUDY LESLIE LITERARY AGENCY, Ste. 515, 156 Fifth Ave., New York NY 10010. (212)633-1220. President: Carol Judy Leslie. Estab. 1986. Represents 30-40 clients. 2 clients specialize in young readers, 1 in young adult books, 3 writers illustrate own books. 10% of clients are new/unpublished writers; 10-15% new/unpublished illustrators. Qualifications for representation: "I represent the books of both photographers and illustrators, but usually require projects to come in including the text. Often these books are in the 'children of all ages' category." Prefers to review new material via an outline/proposal; ms/illustration packages: text and illustration samples with SASE. Reports in 2 weeks on ms/illustration package. Handles 50% nonfiction (50% picture books, 50% young adult books); 50% fiction (75% picture books, 25% young adult books); 75% ms/illustration packages (100% picture books). Has sold *The Gift Angel*, Airdire Thomsen (all ages, Simon & Schuster); *Ophelia's English Adventure* Michele Clise (all ages, Clarkson N. Potter); *Omni's Odysseys*, (series, young adult science fiction, Scholastic US/Collins UK). Commission: 15% domestic sales; 15% foreign sales. 100% of business derived from commission on ms sales.

LIGHTHOUSE LITERARY AGENCY, 1112 Solana Ave., Box 2105, Winter Park FL 32790. (407)647-2385. Director: Sandra Kangas. Estab. 1988. Member of Authors Guild. Represents 20 clients. 3 clients specialize in picture books, 1 in young readers, 1 in young adult books. 35% of clients are new/unpublished writers. Qualifications for representation: "Some prior success is a plus, but not a requirement. More important is a professional work attitude. We enjoy working with authors who are receptive to criticism, those who realize that good writing is the art of rewriting." Prefers to review entire ms. "Do not send your only copy." Ms/illustration packages: send quality copies or samples of artwork. Do not send original artwork until requested to do so. Reports in 2 weeks on a query, ms, ms/illustration package or illustrations. Handles 30% nonfiction (50% picture books, 25% young readers, 25% middle readers); 70% fiction (50% picture books, 25% young readers, 25% middle readers). Commission: 10% domestic sales; 20% foreign sales. Offers criticism service. "The author/illustrator receives a written critique one or more pages long. Comments are on clarity, originality, visualization, story development, entertainment value, pace, organization of material, technical skills and marketability. Lighthouse hires experienced readers to help with this service." 90% of business derived from commission on ms sales; 10% (projected) criticism service. "Critiques are offered to help improve unmarketable work. We offer to handle marketable work, with or without the critique."
Tips: "Authors should realize that children's books are among the most difficult books to write. Facts must be correct, values must be considered, and the market is competitive. Study the market, know the children, read the best children's authors and study the award-winning books. There is a great need for good children's material."

LITERARY MARKETING CONSULTANTS, Ste. 701, One Hallidie Plaza, San Francisco CA 94102. (415)391-7508. Agent: Sydney Winter. Estab. 1984. Represents 15 clients. 1 client specializes in picture books, 1 in young readers, 5 in young adult books, 1 client specializes in juvenile art. 5% of clients are new/unpublished writers; 1% new/unpublished illustrators. "We welcome queries from new writers. However, these must be excellent quality to interest us enough to show further curiosity about the author's project. The query must be original, neatly typed, contain a SASE, and 1) a paragraph about the author, 2) a paragraph about the story, 3) any plans for illustrations/format, and 4) advise regarding target age group and approximate word count." Prefers to review new material via a query. "Do not submit ms/illustrations at all! Advise us of them in the query. We will not be responsible for any unsolicited material we receive." Reports in 1 month on a query, 2 months on a ms. Handles 98% fiction (1% young readers, 2% middle readers, 97% young adult books); 2% ms/illustration package (2% young readers). Commission: 15% domestic sales; 20% foreign sales. Offers a criticism

service "for our clients-no fee. A criticism can be a) via phone or b) letter (about 2-5 pages, usually) and is done by experienced writers in the particular genre, but only for our clients in any case." Charges a one-time marketing fee, so we don't have to charge for extras like criticism or "necessaries" like expenses. 95% of business derived from commission on ms sales. "We only critique work that we agree to market for the writer."
Tips: "Look at what is already out there before sending us a query; we want controversial, thrilling and very fresh ideas from our authors."

GINA MACCOBY LITERARY AGENCY, Ste. 3D, 124 W. 24th St., New York NY 10011. (212)627-9210. President: Gina Maccoby. Estab. 1986. Represents 45 clients. 8 clients specialize in picture books, 8 in young readers, 2 in young adult books, 2 writers illustrate own books, 2 clients specialize in juvenile art. 20% of clients are new/unpublished writers; 10% new/unpublished illustrators. Qualifications for representation: "I have to love the work and feel confident that I can place it." Prefers to review new material via a query. Ms/illustration packages: query first; all manuscripts and illustrations that are submitted must be accompanied by a self-addressed, stamped mailer for the material's return should that be necessary. Reports in 2 weeks on a query, 2-6 weeks on a ms, ms/illustration package or illustrations. Handles 30% nonfiction (20% young readers, 80% middle readers); 50% fiction (60% picture books, 10% middle readers, 30% young adult books); 10% ms/illustration package (50% picture books; 50% young readers); 10% illustrations only (100% picture books). Has sold *The Prince In The Golden Tower*, Flora Karpin (picture book, Viking); *Yoo Hoo Moon*, Mary Blocksma (begin-to-read, Bantam); *The Great Little Madison*, Jean Fritz (middle readers, Putnams). Commission: 10% domestic sales; 20% foreign sales. "Certain charges will be made against the author's account if and when they arise. These include the cost of photocopying manuscripts, cost of bound books or bound proofs purchased from the U.S. publisher for submission to foreign subagents, bank charges where applicable (conversion of foreign currency), airmail postage to Europe and Japan."

MEWS BOOKS LTD., 20 Bluewater Hill, Westport CT 06880. (203)227-1836. President: Sidney B. Kramer. Estab. 1975. Represents 50 "active at one time" clients. 10 picture books; 20 young readers; 30 writers illustrating own mss; 1 client specializes in juvenile art. 20% of clients are new/unpublished writers. Qualifications for representation: "We look for professional handling of material presented. If material calls for illustration, send very rough sketches so that the ultimate work can be visualized. Recommendation by published author or expert is useful. Work should have clear purpose and age delineation. Previously published authors (in any category) have greater credibility with publishers." Prefers to review new material via query; character and plot outline/proposal. No original illustrations are accepted by us. "We try to process material within 30 days." SASE. Have sold to Simon & Schuster, Western Publishing, Crown, Parents. Commission: 15% domestic sales (10% for authors previously published extensively); 20% foreign sales. "New authors who do not have professional credentials only: We will submit accepted material to 3 or 4 publishers and charge $150 for our handling." 100% of business derived from commission on ms sales.
Tips: "President offers individual, domestic, and international legal service to authors in need of negotiating assistance (as an attorney and former publisher). The agency offers extensive foreign representation."

PAMELA NEAIL ASSOCIATES, 27 Bleecker St., New York NY 10012. (212)673-1600. Contact: Lisa Worth. Estab. 1982. Member of SPAR, Society of Illustrators. Represents 15 clients. 5 clients specialize in picture books, 5 in young readers, 5 in young adult books, 5 clients specialize in juvenile art. Qualifications for representation: "We represent illustrators and are willing to review work. Artists should send promos and slides —

NO ORIGINALS and if they wish the materials returned, must include a SASE." Prefers to review printed promos, no originals.

THE NORMA-LEWIS AGENCY, 521 Fifth Ave., New York NY 10175. (212)751-4955. Partner: Norma Liebert. Estab. 1980. Qualifications for representation: "he/she must write a ms that we think is marketable." Prefers to review new material via a query; ms/ illustration packages: do not send any original artwork, send reproductions only. Reports in 2 weeks on a query, 4 weeks on a ms. Handles 50% nonfiction, 50% fiction. Commission: 15% domestic sales; 20% foreign sales. 100% of business derived from commission on ms sales.

JANE ROTROSEN AGENCY, 318 E. 51st St., New York NY 10022. (212)593-4330. Literary Agent: Jane Rotrosen. Estab. 1974. Member of ILAA. Represents 160 clients. Prefers to review new material via a query; outline proposal; outline plus sample chapters. Reports in 2 weeks on a query or illustrations, 6 weeks on a ms or ms/illustration package. Commission: 15% domestic sales; 20% foreign sales. Charges for long distance phone calls, foreign postage. 100% of business derived from commission on ms sales.

S.I. INTERNATIONAL, 43 E. 19th St., New York NY 10003. (212)254-4996. Children's Director: Mr. Don Bruckstein. Estab. 1958. Member of Graphic Artists Guild. Represents 18 clients. 5 clients specialize in picture books, 5 in young readers, 6 in young adult books, 2 writers illustrate own books, 10 clients specialize in juvenile art. Qualifications for representation: "previous illustration work-published." Prefers to review new material via a portfolio. Reports in 2 weeks on ms/illustration package, 1 week on illustrations. Commission: 25% domestic sales; 35% foreign sales.

SANDRA WATT & ASSOCIATES, Ste. 4053, 8033 Sunset Blvd., Los Angeles CA 90046. (213)653-2339. Agent: Robert Drake. Estab. 1976. Member of ILAA, WGAW, SAG, AFTRA. Represents 50 clients. 5 clients specialize in young adult books. 75% of clients are new/unpublished writers. Qualifications for representation: "be talented, competent and professional." Prefers to review new material via a query. Reports on a query in 1 week, 8 weeks on a ms. Handles 80% fiction (10% young adult books). Commission: 15% domestic sales; 25% foreign sales. Charges marketing fee: $50-100. 100% of business derived from commission on ms sales.

WRITERS HOUSE, 21 W. 26 St., New York NY 10010. (212)685-2400. Vice President/ Director: Susan Cohen. Contact: Sheila Callahan. Estab. 1973. Member of ILAA. Represents 300 clients. Clients specialize in picture books, young readers, young adult books, writers illustrating own book. Small percent of clients are new/unpublished writers. Accepting new clients "on a limited basis." Qualifications for representation: "material we think we can sell and a person we'd like to work with." Prefers to review new material via a query or outline plus 2 sample chapters. Reports on a query in 2-3 weeks, 6-8 weeks on a ms, 2-3 weeks on ms/illustration package. Handles mostly fiction books; smaller % of nonfiction as ms/illustration packages. Susan Cohen has sold: *Guys From Space*, Daniel Pinkwater (picture book, Macmillan); *Treehouse Times*, Page McBrier (4-book series, middle grades, Avon); *Rachel Chance*, Jean Thesman (young adult book, Houghton Mifflin). Amy Burkower has sold: *Starring Becky Suslow*, Doris Orgel (8-12 year olds, Viking); *Baby-Sitters Club*, Ann Martin (Scholastic); *Sweet Valley High*, Francine Pascal (Bantam); *Choose Your Own Adventure*, Edward Packard & Raymond Montgomery (Bantam); *Bunnicula*, James Howe (Atheneum). Commission: 15% domestic sales; 20% foreign sales. New commission for all new clients. Charges for extraordinary expenses (big photocopying jobs, telexes, messengers) deducted from disbursements to writers. Most of business % derived from commission on ms sales; some from foreign and performance rights sales and agency also represents submission rights for some small publishers.

TOM ZELASKY LITERARY AGENCY, 3138 Parkridge Crescent, Chamblee GA 30341. (404)458-0391. Agent: Tom Zelasky. Estab. 1986. Represents 7 clients. All clients are new/unpublished writers. Qualifications for representation: "A writer's work must be professional in quality, i.e., has the subject matter been researched from psychological background meaningful to the growth of the written age category. Is the material written in an applicable form for the reader; it should not be written because the writer emotionally and stubbornly wants to impose his own, narrow approach." Prefers to review new material via a query and outline proposal. Reports in 2 weeks on a query, 6-8 weeks on a ms. Handles 10-15% each on nonfiction, fiction, ms/illustration package and illustrations only. Commission: 10-15% domestic sales; 15-25% foreign sales. Reading fee is $75. "Reader and agent" write the critiques. "Additional costs, after reading fee is used up, is deducted from royalties earned." Payment of criticism fee ensures writer's representation by agency.

Tips: "If you send us a manuscript, please include a self-addressed envelope (SASE) large enough to contain the work in case it is returned to you. Also, provide postage, but do not affix the stamps to the envelope."

Organizations

Writing and art organizations serve a myriad of functions. Some organizations publish newsletters which keep their membership up-to-date on industry trends, member news, important business or legal considerations; as well as print educational pieces written by successful people in the field. Many organizations also offer workshops, some of which are open to nonmembers, as well as contests, which can also be open to nonmembers. Still other organizations offer legal counsel, if needed, or health-care insurance packages.

There are many different organizations listed in this section. Some are open to beginning or amateur writers/artists; some are for professionals only. Often industry organizations offer varied levels of affiliation such as full membership for published writers/illustrators and associate membership for those still working toward that goal. You can write to some groups for the information and membership forms; others may require a recommendation by a member of that club. Check the listings that arouse your interest; qualification information is included in most. Do write to the group for more information or get member names so you can determine beforehand if this is the right group for you. For many writers and artists, however, belonging to such professional organizations is a good educational function, as well as an outlet for support from fellow "struggling" peers. Also, membership in a group can show a publisher you are serious about your craft. While this doesn't guarantee your work will be published, it will add points to your credibility as a serious writer/artist.

THE AUTHORS GUILD, 234 W. 44th St., New York NY 10036. (212)398-0838. Assistant Director: Peggy Randall. Purpose of organization: membership organization of 6,700 members that offers services and information materials intended to help authors with the business and legal aspects of their work, including contract problems, copyright matters, freedom of expression and taxation. Qualifications for membership: book author published by an established American publisher within 7 years or any author who has had three works, fiction or nonfiction, published by a magazine or magazines of general circulation in the last 18 months. Associate membership also available. Annual dues-$75. Different levels of membership include: associate membership with all rights except voting available to an author who has work in progress but who has not yet met the qualifications for active membership. This normally involves a firm contract offer from a publisher. Workshops/conferences: "The Guild and Authors of America League conduct several symposia each year at which experts provide information, offer advice, and answer questions on subjects of interest and concern to authors. Typical subjects have been the rights of privacy and publicity, libel, wills and estates, taxation, copyright, editors and editing, the art of interviewing, standards of criticism and book reviewing. Transcripts of these symposia are published and circulated to members." Symposia open to members only. "The *Author's Guild Bulletin*, a periodical journal, contains articles on matters of interest to writers, reports of Guild activities, contract surveys, advice on problem clauses in contracts, transcripts of Guild and League symposia, and information on a variety of professional topics. Subscription included in the cost of the annual dues."

THE AUTHORS RESOURCE CENTER, Box 64785, Tucson AZ 85740-1785. (602)325-4733. Director: Martha R. Gove. Purpose of organization: to help writers understand the business and professional realities of the publishing world — also have literacy agency that markets member's books. Qualifications for membership: serious interest in writing books and articles. Membership cost: starts at $50 per year, maximum $150 1st year. Different levels of membership include: aspiring and professional. "Professional development workshops are open to members and the general public. TARC instructors are actively publishing and often have academic credentials. The bimonthly TARC newsletter includes reports about TARC activities, markets, resources, legal matters, writers' workshops, reference sources, announcement of members' books, reviews, and other news important to writers." Non-member subscription: $50/year.

CANADIAN AUTHORS ASSOCIATION, Ste. 104, 121 Avenue Rd., Toronto ON M5R 2G3 Canada. (416)926-8084. Contact: Executive Director. Purpose of organization: to help "emerging" writers and provide assistance to "professional" writers. "Membership is divided into three categories for individuals: Active (voting): Persons engaged in writing in any genre who have produced a sufficient body of work; Associate (non-voting): Persons interested in writing who have not yet produced sufficient material to qualify for Active membership, or those who, though not writers, have a sincere interest in Canadian literature; Apprentice (non-voting): Persons interested in learning to write who may join the Association as Apprentices for a period not exceeding two years, unless they are bona fide students." Membership cost: $90-professional members, $75-associates, $50-apprentice. Workshops/conferences: 68th Annual Conference June 22-26, 1989 in North York (Toronto) Ont. "The conference draws writers, editors and publishers together in a congenial atmosphere providing seminars, workshops, panel discussions, readings by award-winning authors, and many social events." Open to non-members. Publishes a newsletter of members and writing market. For members only. Also publishes a quarterly journal and a bienniel writer's guide available to non-members. "The Association created a major literary award program in 1975 'to honor writing that achieves literary excellence without sacrificing popular appeal'. The awards are in four categories—fiction, (for a full-length novel); nonfiction (excluding works of an instructional nature); poetry (for a volume of the works of one poet); and drama (for a single play published or staged). The awards consist of a handsome silver medal and $5,000 in cash; they are funded by Harlequin Enterprises, the Toronto-based international publisher." Contest open to nonmembers. Also contests for writing by students, and for young readers (see Vicky Metcalf and Canadian Author & Bookman Awards).

INTERNATIONAL BLACK WRITERS, Box 1030, Chicago IL 60690. (312)995-5195. Executive Director: Mable Terrell. Purpose of organization: to encourage, develop and display writing talent. Qualifications for membership: the desire to write and willingness to work to excel in the craft. Membership cost: $15/year. Different levels of membership include: senior citizens and youth. Workshops/conferences: June 9-11, 1989 conference, Charlotte, NC. Open to nonmembers. Publishes a newsletter detailing issues of importance to writers, competitions. Nonmembers subscription: $15/year. Sponsors an annual writing competition in poetry, fiction and nonfiction. Deadline: May 30th. Awards include plaque and certificates. Contest open to nonmembers.

LEAGUE OF CANADIAN POETS, 24 Ryerson Ave., Toronto, Ontario M5T 2P3 Canada. (416)363-5047. Executive Director: Angela Rebeiro. President: Douglas Burnet Smith. Executive Assistant: Dolores Ricketts. The L.C.P. is a national organization of published poets. Our constitutional objectives are to advance poetry in Canada and to promote the professional interests of the members. Qualifications for membership: full—publication of at least one book of poetry by a Canadian publisher; associate membership—an active interest in poetry, demonstrated by several magazine/periodical publication credits. Membership fees: full—$160/year, associate—$30/year. Hold an Annual General Meeting every spring; some events open to nonmembers. We also organize reading programs in schools and public venues. We pubilsh a newsletter which includes information on poetry/poetics in Canada and beyond. Also publish the books

Poetry Markets for Canadians; *Who's Who in the League of Canadian Poets*; *When is a Poem* (teaching guide) and its accompanying anthology of Canadian Poetry *Here is a Poem*; plus a series of cassettes. We sponsor a National Poetry Contest, open to Canadians living here and abroad. Rules: Unpublished poems of any style/subject, under 75-lines, typed, with name/address on separate sheet. $5 entry fee per poem. $1,000-1st prize, $750-2nd, $500-3rd; plus best 50 published in an anthology, Inquire with SASE. Contest open to nonmembers. Organize three annual awards: The Gerald Lampert Memorial Award for a first book of poetry published in Canada in the preceding year; The Pat Lowther Memorial Award for a book of poetry written by a woman in the preceding year; The F.R. Scott Translation Award for a translation of poetry by a Canadian in the previous year. Please write for more details.

NATIONAL WRITERS CLUB, Ste. 620, 1450 S. Havana, Aurora CO 80012. (303)751-7844. Executive Director: James Lee Young. Purpose of organization: association for freelance writers. Qualifications for membership: associate membership — must be serious about writing; professional membership — published and paid (cite credentials). Membership cost: $40-associate; $50-professional; $15 setup fee for first year only. Workshops/conferences: TV/Screenwriting Workshops, NWC Annual Summer Conference (usually July). Open to nonmembers. Publishes industry news of interest to freelance writers; how-to articles; market information; member news and networking opportunities. Nonmember subscription $25. Sponsors poetry contest; short story/article contest; book manuscript contest. Awards cash awards for top three winners; books and/or certificates for other winners; honorable mention certificate places 11-20. Contests open to nonmembers.

NATIONAL WRITERS UNION, 7th Floor, 13 Astor Place, New York NY 10003. (212)254-0279. Executive Director: Kim Fellner. Purpose of organization: labor union of nonstaff writers dedicated to collective action for fair and equitable treatment of writers. Qualifications for membership: eligible if writer has published a book, play, 3 articles, 5 poems, one short story, or an equivalent amount of newsletter, publicity, technical, commercial, government, or institutional copy. Also eligible if writer has written an equal amount of unpublished material and is actively writing and seeking publication. Membership cost: $50 if annual writing income is under $5,000; $85 for $5,000-25,000 range; $120 for income above $25,000. Workshops/conferences: national executive board meets six times a year; delegates assembly meets once a year; workshops — magazine writers, book authors, technical writers, and many other groups meet regularly through any of their respective 11 locals nationwide. "Interested potential members may attend." Publishes national union newspaper mailed to entire membership quarterly. Some locals sponsor contests — poetry for example. Awards very small cash prizes; publication in local newsletter.

NEBRASKA WRITERS GUILD, 1473 N. 96th Ave., Omaha NE 68114. (402)391-3182. President: Harry A. Dolphin. Purpose of organization: to assist regional writers in their professional development. Qualifications for membership: active members qualify by having marketed some of their production. Prose writers must have sold a minimum of 5,000 words published in media with minimum 2,500 circulation. Poets' requirements are established on a different basis. Associate members accepted. Membership cost: no initiation fees, current annual dues are $10. Different levels of membership include: very special writers (currently, 3) are honorary members; 30-year members are life members; active members (explained above). Associates submit material for evaluation. Workshops/conferences: 1989 conferences will be April 22 in Chadron, Nebraska (the storied Sandhills), and the October 21 conference will be in Omaha. Open to nonmembers. Publishes news pertaining to members and information of assistance to members.

POETRY SOCIETY OF AMERICA, 15 Gramercy Park, New York NY 10003. (212)254-9628. Director: Elise Paschen. "The PSA's mission is to secure a wider recognition for poetry as one of the important forces making for a higher cultural life; to kindle a more intelligent appreciation of poetry; and to assist poets, especially younger American poets. Membership in the Society is open to all persons in sympathy with the general purposes of the Society." Membership cost: member-$30; sustaining member-$100; patron member-$250; benefactor-$500; angel-$1,000 and above. "Workshops are held each fall and spring, and are taught by professional poets. Past workshop instructors have included Nicholas Christopher, Stephen Dobyns, and Mary Jo Salter. We also sponsor a Peer Group Workshop for PSA members. We publish the PSA Newsletter, which contains articles, book reviews, interviews, news of members, and news of contests and submissions (3 times/year). "The Poetry Society's extensive awards program, now exceeding $14,000 in annual prizes, is aimed at advancing excellence in poetry and encouraging skill in traditional forms as well as experiments in contemporary forms. It is also designed to call the attention of the public and the literary world to poets and poetry. The prizes are presented at the Awards Ceremony held at the National Arts Club in New York City each spring. Included in our awards is the prestigious Shelley Memorial Award given, since 1929, by nomination only. Prize varies between $2,000 and $4,000." Some contests open to nonmembers. For more contest information, send SASE to above address.

SAN DIEGO WRITERS/EDITORS GUILD, 3235 Homer Street, San Diego CA 92106. (619)223-5235. Treasurer: Elizabeth W. Smith. "The Guild was formed January, 1979 to meet the local writers' needs for assignments and editors who seek writers. The use of the Guild as a power to publicize poor editorial practices has evolved. We hope to meet writers' needs as we become aware of them and as members are willing to provide services." Activities include: monthly social meetings with a speaker, monthly newsletter, membership directory, workshops and conferences, annual writing contest, other social activities. Qualifications for membership: published book; three published, paid pieces (nonfiction, fiction, prose, poetry), paid editor, produced screenplay or play, paid and published translations, public relations, publicity or advertising. "All professional members must submit clear evidence of work and a brief resume. After acceptance, member need not requalify unless membership lapses." Membership cost: $25 annual fees, $40 member and spouse, $12.50 full-time student and out of state or country member. Different levels of membership include: associate and professional. Workshops/conferences: Fiesta/Siesta Conference, Murrieta Hot Springs and Spa, Murrieta, CA 92362, April 28-30, 1989. Open to nonmembers. Publish a newsletter giving notice of meetings, conferences, contests. Sponsors annual writers contest. Open competition, professional, nonprofessional, members, nonmembers. Awards cash and certificate of award. Contest open to nonmembers.

SCIENCE FICTION WRITERS OF AMERICA, INC., Box 4236, West Columbia SC 29171. (803)791-5942. Executive Secretary: Peter Dennis Pautz. Purpose of organization: to encourage public interest in science fiction literature, and provide organization format for writers/editors/artists within the genre. Qualifications for membership: at least one professional sale or other professional involvement within the field. Membership cost: annual active dues-$52.50; affiliate-$36.75; one-time installation fee of $10; dues year begins July 1st. Different levels of membership include: affiliate requires one professional sale or professional involvement; active requires three professional short stories or one novel published. Workshops/conferences: annual awards banquet, usually in April or May. Open to nonmembers. Publishes newsletter. Nonmember subscription: $12.50 in U.S. Sponsors SFWA Nebula Awards for best published SF in the categories of novel, novella, novelette, and short story. Awards trophy. Contest open to nonmembers.

SOCIETY OF CHILDREN'S BOOK WRITERS, Box 296, Mar Vista Station, Los Angeles CA 90066. (818)347-2849. Chairperson, Board of Directors: Sue Alexander. Purpose of organization: to assist writers and illustrators working or interested in the field. Qualifications for membership: an interest in children's literature and illustration. Membership cost: $35/year. Different levels of membership include: full membership—published authors/illustrators; associate membership—unpublished writers/illustrators. Workshops/conferences: 30-40 events around the country each year. Open to nonmembers. Publishes a newsletter focusing on writing and illustrating childrens books. Sponsors Don Freeman Award for illustrators, 2 grants in aid.

SOCIETY OF SOUTHWESTERN AUTHORS, % Susy Smith, Apt. 128, 8215 N. Oracle Rd., Tucson AZ 85704. (602)297-9642. Purpose of organization: to promote mutually supportive fellowship, recognition of achievement, stimulation and encouragement of professional writers. Qualifications for membership: professional authorship of books, articles, plays, movie and TV scripts. Membership cost: $10 year. Different levels of membership include: regular members, associate members. Workshops/conferences: we hold a writer's seminar the last week of each January at the University of Arizona to raise funds for scholarship awards for promising young writers. Open to nonmembers. "The Write Word" keeps members up-to-date on the activities and achievements of fellow members." Sponsors yearly scholarship awards for nonprofessional writers of short stories and articles. Awards $500 for winners in each category. Contest open to nonmembers.

WOMEN WRITERS WEST, Box 1637, Santa Monica CA 90406. (213)657-0108. President: Rita White. "Women Writer's West (WWW) is a nonprofit, non-political support group for women and men who write. Through this network, we exchange information on the many readings, workshops, classes and literary events that take place in Southern California. Membership is open to all who support and encourage creativity. Our members are published and to-be-published, fiction writers, poets, nonfiction writers, free-lancers, TV and screenwriters, and diary keepers, as well as practitioners of the teaching and healing arts." Cost of membership: $15/year. Workshops/conferences: monthly meeting includes speaker or workshop; annual 1-day conference—1989 date unknown, usually spring. Publishes newsletter about writing. Nonmember subscription: $7.50. Sponsors contest. Awards cash prizes (small), books. Contest open to nonmembers.

Workshops shouldn't be overlooked as vehicles to keep your writing and/or illustrating skills at their best. Even if you are an established professional, knowledge of new trends sweeping the publishing industry will always provide you with a competitive edge.

Not all of the workshops listed in this section are directly related to writing or illustrating for children. Included are courses for mystery, science fiction, and romance, as well as general art workshops designed to instruct in watercolors and oils. For writers, any of these categories can overlap into the juvenile publishing market, and probably will result in fresh new approaches. Illustrators always benefit by exploring new styles and techniques in their medium, as well as developing a teacher/student relationship to further refine their skills.

The listings in this section will tell you what courses are offered, where and when, and costs. Write for more information. Some of the larger writing and art organizations offer a variety of workshops in different regions of the U.S. throughout the year, so you may be able to save on travel costs.

THE ART & BUSINESS OF HUMOROUS ILLUSTRATION, Cartoon Art Museum, 665 3rd St., San Francisco CA 94107. (415)546-3922. Administrator: Barry Gantt. Writer and illustrator workshops geared toward professional levels. "Class focus is on cartooning, but we do cover some marketing topics about children's books." Workshops held fall and spring. Length of each session: 10 weeks. Maximum class size: 30. Cost of workshop: $130, includes art and writing instruction. Write for more information.

CLARION SCIENCE FICTION & FANTASY WRITING WORKSHOP, Lyman Briggs School, E-28 Holmes Hall, MSU, East Lansing MI 48824-1107. (517)353-6486. Administrative Assistant: Mary Sheridan. Writer and illustrator workshop geared toward intermediate levels. Emphasizes science fiction and fantasy. "An intensive workshop designed to stimulate and develop the talent and techniques of potential writers of speculative fiction. Previous experience in writing fiction is assumed. Approximately 25 participants will work very closely together over a six week period, guided by a series of professional writers of national reputation." Workshop held summer—June 25-August 5, 1989. Length of session: six weeks. Maximum class size: 17-25. Cost of workshop: $1,100-1,900, includes tuition for 7 credits of upper level course work; lodging (single room) and some subsidy toward meals. Requirements prior to registration: submission of two manuscripts (up to 2,500 words each) for review. Write for more information.

DIXIE COUNCIL OF AUTHORS AND JOURNALISTS, INC., % Ann Ritter, 1214 Laurel Hill Dr., Decatur GA 30033. (404)320-1076. Executive Secretary: Ann Ritter. Writer workshops geared toward beginner, intermediate, advanced, professional levels. Emphasizes general fiction, nonfiction, marketing, agents, editors. Classes/courses offered: 6-8 class periods each of 5 days. Guest speaker each evening. Workshops held: each June, usually beginning on Father's Day; one week, daily classes. Length of each session: 5 days. Maximum class size: averages 20. Writing facilities: comfortable motel rooms, acres of moss-draped oaks, beach. Cost of workshop: estimated at $89-$100. Cost includes classes, individual conference/evaluation with instructor, contests (more than $1,000 in awards). Write for more information. "1989 is the 29th annual writing conference sponsored by DCAJ."

DRURY COLLEGE/SCBW WRITING FOR CHILDREN WORKSHOP, Drury College, Springfield MO 65802. (417)865-8731. Assistant Director, Continuing Education: Lynn Doke. Writer and illustrator workshop geared toward beginner, intermediate, advanced, professional levels. Emphasizes all aspects of writing for children and teenagers. Classes/courses offered include: "A Picture Book from Idea to Publication," "What Makes Children Laugh," "Nuts and Bolts for Beginners," "Writing from Personal Experience." Workshop held in November. Length of each session: 1 hour. Maximum class size: 25-30. Cost of workshop: varies, includes sessions, refreshments. Write for more information.
Tips: "Our workshop is held in conjunction with the Children's Literature Festival of the Ozarks, a meeting of 2,000 school children and 12-15 nationally known authors."

FIFTH ANNUAL CHILDREN'S LITERATURE CONFERENCE, Hofstra University, 232 Memorial Hall, Hempstead NY 11550. (516)560-5997. Writers/Illustrators Contact: Lewis Shena, director, Liberal Arts Studies. Writer and illustrator workshops geared toward beginner, intermediate, advanced, professional levels. Emphasizes: fiction, nonfiction, poetry, submission procedures, picture books. Workshops held April 29, Saturday, 9:30 a.m. - 4:00 p.m. Length of each session: 4 hours. Maximum class size: 20. Cost of workshop includes: workshop, reception, lunch, panel discussions with guest speakers, e.g. "What An Editor Looks For." Write for more information. Co-sponsored by Society of Children's Book Writers.

HIGHLIGHTS FOUNDATION WRITERS WORKSHOP AT CHAUTAUQUA, 711 Court St., Honesdale PA 18431. (717)253-1192. Conference Director: Jan Keen. Writer workshops geared toward beginner, intermediate, advanced levels. Classes/courses offered include: "Children's Interests," "Writing Dialogue," "Beginnings and Endings," "Science Writing," "My Stories for Young Readers." Workshops held July 16-23, 1989, Chautauqua Institution, Chautauqua, NY. Length of each session: 1 1/2 hrs. Maximum class size: 100. Cost of workshop: $985; includes registration fee, gate ticket fee, workshop supplies and all meals. Write for more information.

MYSTERY WRITERS OF AMERICA, Midwest Chapter, Box 8, Techny IL 60082. (312)441-3942. Director: Betty Nicholas. "We have a broad spectrum of sessions and the level of the registrants varies from beginners to regularly selling professionals." Deals with techniques for writing mystery fiction. Faculty includes professional mystery writers as well as representatives of law enforcement and related fields whose expertise can be helpful to mystery writers. One-day workshop held in June, Northwestern University, Evanston IL. Maximum registration: 100. Cost of workshop: $50 for members, $60 for nonmembers; includes lunch. Write for specific information on the current year's program.

SELF PUBLISHING CHILDREN'S BOOKS, % Writers Connection, Ste. 180, 1601 Saratoga-Sunnyvale Rd., Cupertino CA 95014. (408)973-0227. Program Director: Meera Lester. Writer and illustrator workshops geared toward beginner, intermediate levels. Emphasizes all aspects of self-publishing children's literature, from writing through production and marketing. Length of each session: six-hour session usually offered on a Saturday. Maximum class size: 35-40. Writing/art facilities available: at the Cupertino location, our desktop publishing system is set up. Writing tables, overhead projector, and white board is provided as well as access to our bookstore of 200 titles of writing, reference, and how-to books. Write for more information.

SOUTHERN CALIFORNIA SOCIETY OF CHILDREN'S BOOK WRITERS ILLUSTRATORS DAY, 1669 12th St., Santa Monica CA 90404. (213)450-9054, 457-3501. Illustrator Regional Advisor: Judith Enderle. Illustrator workshops geared toward beginner, intermediate, advanced, professional levels. Emphasizes illustration and illustration markets. Classes/courses offered include: presentations by Art Director, children's book editor, and panel of artists/author-illustrators. Workshops held annually—this year's (89) Illustrator's day is Nov. 11. Length of each session: full day. Maximum class size: 100. "Editors and art directors will view portfolios. We want to know if each conferee is bringing a portfolio or not." Cost of workshop: $80 members, $90 nonmembers, includes lunch, handouts.

Tips: "This is a chance for illustrators to meet editors/art directors and each other."

SUMMER WRITERS CONFERENCE, Hofstra U - U.C.C.E. - Memorial 232, Hempstead NY 11550. (516)560-5997. Writers/Illustrators Contact: Lewis Shena, director, Liberal Arts Studies. Writer and illustrator workshops geared toward beginner, intermediate, advanced, professional levels. Emphasizes fiction, nonfiction, poetry, children's literature, stage/screen. Classes/courses offered: "Besides workshops, we arrange a series of readings and discussions." Workshops held Monday-Friday—2 weeks—July 10-21, 1989. Length of each session: approximately 2 1/2 hours of workshop and 1-2 hours of informal meetings. Maximum class size: 25. Writing/art facilities available: lecture room, tables, any media required will be gotten. Cost of workshop: noncredit $486; includes 1 workshop per day—special readings—special speakers. (Dorm rooms available at additional cost). Write for more information.

VASSAR INSTITUTE OF PUBLISHING AND WRITING: CHILDREN'S BOOKS IN THE MARKETPLACE, Box 300, Vassar College, Poughkeepsie NY 12601. (914)437-5900. Program Coordinator: Claudia Duffy. Writer and illustrator workshops geared toward beginner, intermediate, advanced, professional levels. Emphasizes "the editorial, production, marketing and reviewing processes, on writing fiction and nonfiction for all ages, creating the picture book, understanding the markets and selling your work." Classes/courses offered include: "Writing Fiction," "The Editorial Process," "How to Write a Children's Book and Get It Published." Workshop held in 1989—June 18-25 (normally the 2nd or 3rd week in June). Length of each session: 3½ hour morning critique sessions, afternoon and evening lectures. Maximum class size: 55 (with three instructors). Cost of workshop: approximately $580, includes room, board, and tuition for all critique sessions, lectures and social activities. "Manuscripts are pre-prepared and discussed at morning critique sessions. Portfolio review done on pre-prepared works." Write for more information.

Tips: "This conference gives a comprehensive look at the publishing industry as well as offering critiques of creative writing and portfolio review."

WILLAMETTE WRITERS 21ST ANNUAL WRITERS CONFERENCE, #120, 811 E. Burnside, Portland OR 97214. (503)233-1877. Conference Chair: Jo Anne Colbath. Writer workshops geared toward beginner, intermediate, advanced, professional levels. Emphasizes all areas of writing from nonfiction to horror/fiction. Classes/courses offered include: romance writing; A-B-C's of writing, basic techniques; desk top publishing; How to Research—Step by Step Process; science fiction panel. Workshops held August 11-13, 1989. Length of each session: 1 1/2 hours. Cost of workshop: $125/member, $150/nonmember; includes full conference registration, all workshops and Saturday lunch, Saturday evening banquet, Sunday brunch. Write for more information.

WRITERS AT WORK CONFERENCE IN PARK CITY, Box 8897, Salt Lake City UT 84108. (801)322-5136. Director: Steve Wunderli. Writer workshops geared toward intermediate, advanced, professional levels. Emphasizes craft of the story. Classes/courses offered include: writing for children and teenagers. Workshop held June 11-14. Length of each session: 3 days. Maximum class size: 25. Cost of workshop: $200, includes tuition. Write for more information.

Glossary

Advance. A sum of money that a publisher pays a writer prior to the publication of a book. It is usually paid in installments, such as one-half on signing the contract; one half on delivery of a complete and satisfactory manuscript. The advance is paid against the royalty money that will be earned by the book.

All rights. The rights contracted to a publisher permitting a manuscript's use anywhere and in any form, including movie and book-club sales, without additional payment to the writer.

ASAP. Abbreviation for as soon as possible.

B&W. Abbreviation for black and white artwork or photographs.

Backlist. A publisher's list of books not published during the current season but still in print.

Biennially. Once every two years.

Bimonthly. Once every two months.

Biweekly. Once every two weeks.

Bleed. Area of a plate or print that extends beyond the actual trimmed sheet to be printed.

Book packager. Draws all elements of a book together, from the initial concept to writing and marketing strategies, then sells the book package to a book publisher and/or movie producer. Also known as book producer or book developer.

Business-size envelope. Also known as a #10 envelope, it is the standard size used in sending business correspondence.

Camera-ready. Art that is completely prepared for copy camera platemaking.

Caption. A description of the subject matter of an illustration or photograph; photo captions include names of people where appropriate. Also called cutline.

Clean-copy. A manuscript free of errors and needing no editing; it is ready for typesetting.

Contract. A written agreement stating the rights to be purchased by an editor or art director and the amount of payment the writer or illustrator will receive for that sale.

Contributor's copies. Copies of the issues of magazines sent to the author or illustrator in which his/her work appears.

Copy. Refers to the actual written material of a manuscript.

Copyediting. Editing a manuscript for grammar usage, spelling, punctuation, and general style.

Copyright. A means to legally protect an author's/illustrator's work. This can be shown by writing ©, your name, and year of work's creation.

Cover letter. A brief letter, accompanying a complete manuscript, especially useful if responding to an editor's request for a manuscript. A cover letter may also accompany a book proposal. A cover letter is not a query letter.

Cutline. See caption.

Disk. A round, flat magnetic plate on which computer data is stored.

Division. An unincorporated branch of a company.

Dot-matrix. Printed type in which individual characters are composed of a matrix or pattern of tiny dots.

Final draft. The last version of a "polished" manuscript ready for submission to the editor.

First North American serial rights. The right to publish material in a periodical before it appears in book form, for the first time, in the United States or Canada.

Flat fee. A one-time payment.

Galleys. The first typeset version of a manuscript that has not yet been divided into pages.

Genre. A formulaic type of fiction, such as adventure, mystery, romance, science fiction or western.

Glossy. A black and white photograph with a shiny surface as opposed to one with a non-shiny matte finish.

Gouache. Opaque watercolor with an appreciable film thickness and an actual paint layer.

Halftone. Reproduction of a continuous tone illustration with the image formed by dots produced by a camera lens screen.

Hard copy. The printed copy of a computer's output.

Illustrations. May be artwork, photographs, old engravings. Usually paid for separately from the manuscript.

Imprint. Name applied to a publisher's specific line or lines of books.

IRC. International Reply Coupon; purchased at the post office to enclose with text or artwork sent to a foreign buyer to cover his postage cost when replying or returning work.

Keyline. Identification, through signs and symbols, of the positions of illustrations and copy for the printer.

Kill fee. Portion of the agreed-upon price the author or artist receives for a job that was assigned, worked on, but then canceled.

Layout. Arrangement of illustrations, photographs, text and headlines for printed material.

Letter-quality submission. Computer printout that looks like a typewritten manuscript.

Line drawing. Illustration done with pencil or ink using no wash or other shading.

Mechanicals. Paste-up or preparation of work for printing.

Middle reader. The general classification of books written for readers 9-11 years of age.

Modem. A small electrical box that plugs into the serial card of a computer, used to transmit data from one computer to another, usually via telephone lines.

Ms, mss. Abbreviation for manuscript(s).

One-time rights. Permission to publish a story in periodical or book form one time only.

Outline. A summary of a book's contents in 5-15 double spaced pages; often in the form of chapter headings with a descriptive sentence or two under each one to show the scope of the book.

Package sale. The editor buys manuscript and illustrations/photos as a "package" and pays for them with one check.

Payment on acceptance. The writer or artist is paid for his work at the time the editor or art director decides to buy it.

Payment on publication. The writer or artist is paid for his work when it is published.

Photocopied submissions. Submitting photocopies of an original manuscript instead of sending the original. Do not assume that an editor who accepts photocopies will also accept multiple or simultaneous submissions.

Photostat. Black-and-white copies produced by an inexpensive photographic process using paper negatives; only line values are held with accuracy. Also called stat.

Picture book. A type of book aimed at the preschool to 8-year-old that tells the story primarily or entirely with artwork.

PMT. Photostat produced without a negative, somewhat like the Polaroid process.

Print. An impression pulled from an original plate, stone, block, screen or negative; also a positive made from a photographic negative.

Proofreading. Reading a manuscript to correct typographical errors.

Query. A letter to an editor designed to capture his/her interest in an article you purpose to write.

Reading fee. An arbitrary amount of money charged by some agents and publishers to read a submitted manuscript.

Reporting time. The time it takes for an editor to report to the author on his/her query or manuscript.

Reprint rights. Permission to print an already published work whose rights have been sold to another magazine or book publisher.

Response time. The average length of time it takes an editor or art director to accept or reject a manuscript or artwork and inform you of the decision.

Rights. What you offer to an editor or art director in exchange for printing your manuscripts or artwork.

Rough draft. A manuscript which has been written but not checked for errors in grammar, punctuation, spelling or content. It usually needs revision and rewriting.

Roughs. Preliminary sketches or drawings.

Royalty. An agreed percentage paid by the publisher to the writer or illustrator for each copy of his work sold.

SASE. Abbreviation for self-addressed, stamped envelope.

Second serial rights. Permission for the reprinting of a work in another periodical after its first publication in book or magazine form.

Semiannual. Once every six months.

Semimonthly. Twice a month.

Semiweekly. Twice a week.

Serial rights. The rights given by an author to a publisher to print a piece in one or more periodicals.

Simultaneous submissions. Sending the same article, story, poem or illustration to several publishers at the same time. Some publishers refuse to consider such submissions. No simultaneous submissions should be made without stating the fact in your letter.

Slant. The approach to a story or piece of artwork that will appeal to readers of a particular publication.

Slush pile. What editors call the collection of submitted manuscripts which have not been specifically asked for.

Software. Programs and related documentation for use with a particular computer system.

Solicited manuscript. Material which an editor has asked for or agreed to consider before being sent by the writer.

Speculation (Spec). Writing or drawing a piece with no assurance from the editor or art director that it will be purchased or any reimbursements for material or labor paid.

Subsidiary rights. All rights other than book publishing rights included in a book contract, such as paperback, book club and movie rights.

Subsidy publisher. A book publisher who charges the author for the cost of typesetting, printing and promoting a book. Also vanity publisher.

Synopsis. A brief summary of a story or novel. If part of a book proposal, it should be a page to a page and a half, single-spaced.

Tabloid. Publication printed on an ordinary newspaper page turned sideways.

Tear sheet. Page from a magazine or newspaper containing your printed story, article, poem or ad.

Thumbnail. A rough layout in miniature.

Transparencies. Positive color slides; not color prints.

Unsolicited manuscript. A story, article, poem, book or artwork sent without the editor's or art director's knowledge or consent.

Vanity publisher. See subsidy publisher.

Word length. The maximum number of words a manuscript should contain as determined by the editor or guidelines sheet.

Word processor. A computer that produces typewritten copy via automated typing, text-editing, and storage and transmission capabilities.

Young adult. The general classification of books written for readers ages 12-18.

Young reader. The general classification of books written for readers 5-8 years old. Here artwork supports the text as opposed to picture books.

___ *Newbery Medal Winners*

Throughout this book you have read advice from publishers that emphasizes the importance of studying best-selling publications. The best way to understand the types of manuscripts most respected by book experts is to research them prior to submitting your own material. Included here are names of Newbery Medal winners, including the name of each publication and publisher. Take time to study these books. Each award-winning manuscript represents the best of all literary endeavors during that particular calendar year.

The first Newbery Medal was offered in 1921 by Frederic G. Melcher (an author of children's books) to the author of the most distinguished children's book published the previous year. The Newbery Medal is named after John Newbery, an 18th century children's book publisher and seller, and is presented annually by the Children's Services Division of the American Library Association (ALA). The award is restricted to citizens or residents of the U.S. In addition to a winning manuscript, varying numbers of honor books are also selected; the winner receives a gold medal and the honored author(s) a certificate. The Newbery winner is selected each January at the ALA midwinter convention. Both the Newbery and Caldecott Medals are officially presented to the winners at the ALA's annual convention in June. For more information about the Newbery Medal, see that listing on page 133 in the Contests and Awards section.

Here is a compilation of Newbery winners from present to past:

1989—*Joyful Noise: Poems for Two Voices*, by Paul Fleischman (Harper & Row, ages 9 and up)

1988—*Lincoln, A Photobiography*, by Russell Freedman (Ticknor & Fields, nonfiction)

1987— *The Whipping Boy*, written by Sid Fleischman/illustrated by Peter Sis (Greenwillow, fiction)

1986—*Sarah, Plain and Tall*, by Patricia MacLachlan (fiction)

1985— *The Hero and the Crown*, by Robin McKinley (Greenwillow, fiction)

1984—*Dear Mr. Henshaw*, written by Beverly Cleary/illustrated by Paul O. Zelinsky. (Morrow, fiction)

1983—*Dicey's Song*, by Cynthia Voigt (Macmillan, fiction)

1982—*A Visit to William Blake's Inn: Poems for Innocent and Experienced Travelers*, written by Nancy Willard/illustrated by Alice and Martin Provensen (Harcourt, literature)

1981—*Jacob Have I Loved*, by Katherine Paterson (Crowell, fiction)

1980—*A Gathering of Days*, by Joan W. Blos (Scribner, fiction)

1979—*The Westing Game*, by Ellen Raskin (Dutton, fiction)

1978—*Bridge to Terabithia*, written by Katherine Paterson/illustrated by Donna Diamond (Crowell, fiction)

1977—*Roll of Thunder, Hear My Cry*, written by Mildred Taylor/illustrated by Jerry Pinkney (Dial, fiction)

1976—*The Grey King*, written by Susan Cooper/illustrated by Michael Heslop (Atheneum, fiction)

1975—*M.C. Higgins, the Great*, by Virginia Hamilton (Macmillan, fiction)

1974—*The Slave Dancer*, written by Paula Fox/illustrated by Eros Keith (Bradbury, fiction)

1973—*Julie of the Wolves*, written by Jean George/illustrated by John Schoenherr (Harper, fiction)

1972—*Mrs. Frisby and the Rats of Nimh*, written by Robert C. O'Brien/illustrated by Zena Bernstein (Atheneum, fiction)

1971—*Summer of the Swans*, written by Betsy Byars/illustrated by Ted CoConis (Viking, fiction)

1970—*Sounder*, written by William H. Armstrong/illustrated by James Barkley (Harper, fiction)

1969—*The High King*, by Lloyd Alexander (Holt, fiction)

1968—*From the Mixed-Up Files of Mrs. Basil E. Frankweiler*, by E.L. Konigsburg (Atheneum, fiction)

1967—*Up a Road Slowly*, by Irene Hunt (Follett, fiction)

1966—*I, Juan de Pareja*, by Elizabeth Borton de Trevino (Farrar, fiction)

1965—*Shadow of a Bull*, written by Mala Wojciechowska Rodman/illustrated by Alvin Smith (Atheneum, fiction)

1964—*It's Like This Cat*, written by Emily Neville/illustrated by Emil Weiss (Harper, fiction)

1963—*A Wrinkle in Time*, by Madeleine L'Engle (Farrar, fiction)

1962—*The Bronze Bow*, by Elizabeth Speare (Houghton, fiction)

1961—*Island of the Blue Dolphins*, by Scott O'Dell (Houghton, fiction)

1960—*Onion John*, written by Joseph Krumgold/illustrated by Symeon Shimin (Crowell, fiction)

1959—*The Witch of Blackbird Pond*, by Elizabeth Speare (Houghton, fiction)

1958—*Rifles for Watie*, written by Harold Keith/illustrated by Peter Burchard (Crowell, fiction)

1957—*Miracles on Maple Hill*, written by Virginia Sorensen/illustrated by Beth and Joe Krush (Harcourt, fiction)

1956—*Carry On, Mr. Bowditch*, written by Jean Lee Latham/illustrated by J.O. Cosgrove (Houghton, nonfiction)

1955—*The Wheel on the School*, written by Meindert De Jong/illustrated by Maurice Sendak (Harper, fiction)

1954—*And Now Miguel*, written by Joseph Krumgold/illustrated by Jean Charlot (Crowell, fiction)

1953—*Secret of the Andes*, written by Ann Nolan Clark/illustrated by Jean Charlot (Viking, fiction)

1952—*Ginger Pye*, by Eleanor Estes (Harcourt, fiction)

1951—*Amos Fortune, Free Man*, written by Elizabeth Yates/illustrated by Nora S. Unwin (Dutton, nonfiction)

1950—*The Door in the Wall*, by Marguerite de Angeli (Doubleday, fiction)

1949—*King of the Wind*, written by Marguerite Henry/illustrated by Wesley Dennis (Rand McNally, fiction)

1948—*The Twenty-One Balloons*, by William Pene du Bois (Viking, fiction)

1947—*Miss Hickory*, written by Carolyn Sherwin Bailey/illustrated by Ruth Chrisman Gannett (Viking, fiction)

1946—*Strawberry Girl*, by Lois Lenski (Lippincott, fiction)

1945—*Rabbit Hill*, by Robert Lawson (Viking, fiction)

1944—*Johnny Tremain*, written by Esther Forbes/illustrated by Lynd Ward (Houghton, fiction)

1943—*Adam of the Road*, written by Elizabeth Gray Vining/illustrated by Robert Lawson (Viking, fiction)

1942—*The Matchlock Gun*, written by Walter Edmonds/illustrated by Paul Lantz (Dodd, fiction)

1941 — *Call It Courage*, by Armstrong Sperry (Macmillan, fiction)

1940 — *Daniel Boone*, by James Daugherty (Viking, nonfiction)

1939 — *Thimble Summer*, by Elizabeth Enright (Holt, fiction)

1938 — *The White Stag*, by Kate Seredy (Viking, nonfiction)

1937 — *Roller Skates*, written by Ruth Sawyer/illustrated by Valenti Angelo (Viking, fiction)

1936 — *Caddie Woodlawn*, written by Carol Ryrie Brink/illustrated by Kate Seredy (Macmillan, fiction)

1935 — *Dobry*, written by Monica Shannon/illustrated by Atanas Katchamakoff (Viking, fiction)

1934 — *Invincible Louisa*, by Cornelia Meigs (Little, nonfiction)

1933 — *Young Fu of the Upper Yangtze*, written by Elizabeth Foreman Lewis/illustrated by Kurt Wiese (Holt, fiction)

1932 — *Waterless Mountain*, written by Laura Adams Armer/illustrated by Sidney and Laura Armer (McKay, fiction)

1931 — *The Cat Who Went to Heaven*, written by Elizabeth Coatsworth/illustrated by Lynd Ward (Macmillan, fiction)

1930 — *Hitty, Her First Hundred Years*, written by Rachel Field/illustrated by Dorothy P. Lathrop (Macmillan, fiction)

1929 — *Trumpeter of Krakow*, written by Eric P. Kelly/illustrated by Angela Pruszynska (Macmillan, fiction)

1928 — *Gay Neck*, written by Dhan Gopal Mukerji/illustrated by Boris Artzybasheff (Dutton, nonfiction)

1927 — *Smoky, the Cowhorse*, by Will James (Scribner, fiction)

1926 — *Shen of the Sea*, written by Arthur B. Chrisman/illustrated by Else Hasselriis (Dutton, fiction)

1925 — *Tales from Silver Lands*, written by Charles J. Finger/illustrated by Paul Honore (Doubleday, literature)

1924 — *The Dark Frigate*, written by Charles Boardman Hawes/illustrated by A.L. Ripley (Little, fiction)

1923 — *Voyages of Dr. Dolittle*, by Hugh Lofting (Lippincott, fiction)

1922 — *The Story of Mankind*, by Hendrik Willem Van Loon (Liverwright, nonfiction)

Caldecott Medal Winners

Throughout this book you have read advice from publishers that emphasizes the importance of studying best-selling publications. The best way to understand the types of illustrations most respected by book experts is to research them prior to submitting your own material. Included here are names of Caldecott Medal winners, including the name of each publication and publisher. Take time to study these books. Each award-winning set of illustrations represents the best of all artistic endeavors during that particular calendar year.

The first Caldecott Medal was created and donated by Frederic G. Melcher (an author of children's books) in 1938 to the artist of the most distinguished picture book published in the U.S. the previous year. This medal was named for Randolph Caldecott, a well known English illustrator of children's books. The Caldecott award is now presented annually to the artist of the best illustrated book by the Children's Services Division of the American Library Association (ALA). The artist, as with Newbery recipients, must be a citizen or resident of the U.S. A winning book, as well as varying numbers of honor books, are selected each January at the ALA's mid-winter convention. The winner receives the gold Caldecott Medal, and honor-book winners are presented with a certificate. Similar to the Newbery, awards are presented at the ALA's annual June convention. For more information about the Caldecott Medal refer to that listing on pages 129-130 in the Contests and Awards section.

Here is a compilation of Caldecott winners from present to past:

1989 — *Song and Dance Man*, illustrated by Stephen Gammell/written by Karen Ackerman (Knopf, ages 4-8)

1988 — *Owl Moon*, illustrated by John Schoenherr/written by Jane Yolen (Putnam, easy reader)

1987 — *Hey, Al*, illustrated by Richard Egielski/written by Arthur Yorinks (Farrar)

1986 — *Polar Express*, by Chris Van Allsburg (Houghton, easy reader)

1985 — *St. George and the Dragon*, illustrated by Trina Schart Hyman/written by Margaret Hodges (Little Brown, literature)

1984 — *The Glorious Flight*, by Alice and Martin Provensen (Viking, nonfiction)

1983 — *Shadow*, illustrated by Marcia Brown/written by Blaise Cendrars (Macmillan, nonfiction)

1982 — *Jumanji*, by Chris Van Allsburg (Houghton, easy reader)

1981 — *Fables*, by Arnold Lobel (Harper, literature)

1980 — *The Ox-Cart Man*, illustrated by Barbara Cooney/written by Donald

Hall (Viking, easy reader)

1979—*The Girl Who Loved Horses*, by Paul Goble (Dutton, easy reader)

1978—*Noah's Ark*, by Peter Spier (Doubleday, easy reader)

1977—*Ashanti to Zulu: African Traditions*, illustrated by Leo and Diane Dillon/ written by Margaret W. Musgrove (Dial, nonfiction)

1976—*Why Mosquitos Buzz in People's Ears*, illustrated by Leo and Diane Dillon/written by Verna Aardema (Dial, nonfiction)

1975—*Arrow to the Sun*, by Gerald McDermott (Viking, easy reader)

1974—*Duffy and the Devil*, illustrated by Margot Zemach/written by Harve Zemach (Farrar, easy reader)

1973—*The Funny Little Woman*, illustrated by Blair Lent/written by Arlene Mosel (Dutton, easy reader)

1972—*One Fine Day*, by Nonny Hogrogian (Macmillan, easy reader)

1971—*A Story—A Story*, by Gail Haley (Atheneum, nonfiction)

1970—*Sylvester and the Magic Pebble*, by William Steig (Simon and Schuster, easy reader)

1969—*The Fool of the World and the Flying Ship*, illustrated by Uri Shulevitz/ written by Arthur Ransome (Farrar, nonfiction)

1968—*Drummer Hoff*, illustrated by Ed Emberley/written by Barbara Emberley (Prentice-Hall, easy reader)

1967—*Sam, Bangs, and Moonshine*, by Evaline Ness (Holt, easy reader)

1966—*Always Room for One More*, illustrated by Nonny Hogrogian/written by Leclaire Alger (Holt, easy reader)

1965—*May I Bring a Friend?*, illustrated by Beni Montresor/written by Beatrice Schenk de Regniers (Atheneum, easy reader)

1964—*Where the Wild Things Are*, by Maurice Sendak (Harper, easy reader)

1963—*The Snowy Day*, by Ezra Jack Keats (Viking, easy reader)

1962—*Once a Mouse*, by Marcia Brown (Scribner, easy reader)

1961—*Baboushka and the Three Kings*, illustrated by Nicolas Sidjakov/written by Ruth Robbins (Parnassus, easy reader)

1960—*Nine Days to Christmas*, by Marie Hall Ets (Viking, easy reader)

1959—*Chanticleer and the Fox*, illustrated by Barbara Cooney/written by Geoffrey Chaucer (Crowell, easy reader)

1958—*Time of Wonder*, by Robert McCloskey (Viking, easy reader)

1957—*A Tree is Nice*, illustrated by Marc Simont/written by Janice Udry (Harper, easy reader)

1956—*Frog Went A-Courtin'*, illustrated by Feodor Rojankovsky/written by John Langstaff (Harcourt, easy reader)

1955—*Cinderella*, illustrated by Marcia Brown/written by Charles Perrault (Scribner, literature)

1954—*Madeline's Rescue*, by Ludwig Bemelmans (Viking, easy reader)

1953—*The Biggest Bear*, by Lynd Ward (Houghton, easy reader)

1952—*Finders Keepers*, illustrated by Nicholas Mordvinoff/written by William Lipkind (Harcourt, easy reader)

1951—*The Egg Tree*, by Katherine Milhous (Scribner, easy reader)

1950—*Song of the Swallows*, by Leo Politi (Scribner, easy reader)

1949—*The Big Snow*, by Berta and Elmer Hader (Macmillan, easy reader)

1948—*White Snow, Bright Snow*, illustrated by Roger Duvoisin/written by Alvin Tresselt (Lothrop, easy reader)

1947—*The Little Island*, illustrated by Leonard Weisgard/written by Golden MacDonald (Doubleday, easy reader)

1946—*The Rooster Crows*, by Maude and Miska Petersham (Macmillan, easy reader)

1945—*Prayer for a Child*, illustrated by Elizabeth Orton Jones/written by Rachel Field (Macmillan, nonfiction)

1944—*Many Moons*, illustrated by Louis Slobodkin/written by James Thurber (Harcourt, easy reader)

1943—*The Little House*, by Virginia L. Burton (Houghton, easy reader)

1942—*Make Way for Ducklings*, by Robert McCloskey (Viking, easy reader)

1941—*They Were Strong and Good*, by Robert Lawson (Viking, fiction)

1940—*Abraham Lincoln*, by Ingri and Edgar d'Aulaire (Doubleday, nonfiction)

1939—*Mei Li*, by Thomas Handforth (Doubleday, easy reader)

1938—*Animals of the Bible*, by Dorothy P. Lathrop (Lippincott, nonfiction)

Age-Level Index/ Book Publishers

The age-level index is set up to help you more quickly locate book markets geared to the age group(s) for which you write or illustrate. Read each listing carefully and follow the publisher's specific information about the type(s) of manuscript(s) each prefers to read and the style(s) of artwork each wishes to review.

Picture books (preschool-8-year-olds)

Abingdon Press
Advocacy Press
Aegina Press/University Editions
African American Images
Aladdin Books/Collier Books for
    Young Adults
Atheneum Publishers
Barrons Educational Series
Bookmaker's Guild, Inc.
Bradbury Press
Branden Publishing Co.
Calico Books
Carnival Enterprises
Carolina Wren Press
Carolrhoda Books, Inc.
Childrens Press
Child's World, Inc., The
Chronicle Books
Clarion Books
Coteau Books Ltd.
Council for Indian Education
Davenport, Publishers, May
Dial Books for Young Readers
Doubleday
Dutton Children's Books
Eakin Publications
Exposition Phoenix Press
Farrar, Straus & Giroux
Four Winds Press
Godine, David R.
Green Publications, Kendall
Greenwillow Books
Harbinger House
Harcourt Brace Jovanovich
Harvest House Publishers
Holt & Co., Inc., Henry
Homestead Publishing
Houghton Mifflin Co.
Humanics Children's House
Ideals Publishing Corporation

Kar-Ben Copies, Inc.
Kruza Kaleidoscopix, Inc.
Little, Brown and Company
Lothrop, Lee & Shepard Books
Maryland Historical Press
McElderry Books
Metamorphous Press
Morehouse-Barlow
National Press Inc.
New Seed Press
Oddo Publishing, Inc.
Orchard Books
Paulist Press
Perspectives Press
Philomel Books
Pippin Press
Price Stern Sloan
St. Paul Books and Media
Scojtia, Publishing Co., Inc.
Standard Publishing
Sterling Publishing Co., Inc.
Tom Thumb Music
Trillium Press
Walker and Co.
Waterfront Books

Young readers (5-8-year-olds)

Abingdon Press
Advocacy Press
Aegina Press/University Editions
African American Images
Aladdin Books/Collier Books for
    Young Adults
Atheneum Publishers
Barrons Educational Series
Bookmaker's Guild, Inc.
Bradbury Press
Calico Books
Carnival Enterprises
Carolina Wren Press

Carolrhoda Books, Inc.
Childrens Press
China Books
Chronicle Books
Clarion Books
Coach House Press, Inc.
Council for Indian Education
Dial Books for Young Readers
Dillon Press, Inc.
Double M Press
Doubleday
Dutton Children's Books
Eakin Publications
Exposition Phoenix Press
Farrar, Straus & Giroux
Godine, David R.
Green Publications, Kendall
Greenwillow Books
Harbinger House
Harvest House Publishers
Holt & Co., Inc., Henry
Homestead Publishing
Houghton Mifflin Co.
Humanics Children's House
Ideals Publishing Corporation
Kruza Kaleidoscopix, Inc.
Lerner Publications Co.
Little, Brown and Company
Lothrop, Lee & Shepard Books
Maryland Historical Press
McElderry Books
Messner, Julian
Metamorphous Press
Morehouse-Barlow
National Press Inc.
New Seed Press
Oddo Publishing, Inc.
Orchard Books
Paulist Press
Perspectives Press
Philomel Books
Pippin Press
Players Press, Inc.
Price Stern Sloan
Proforma Books
St. Paul Books and Media
Scojtia, Publishing Co., Inc.
Shoe Tree Press
Simon & Pierre Publishing Co. Ltd.
Standard Publishing
Trillium Press
Twenty-First Century Books
Walker and Co.
Waterfront Books

Middle readers (9-11-year-olds)

Abingdon Press
Aegina Press/University Editions
African American Images
Aladdin Books/Collier Books for Young Adults
Archway/Minstrel Books
Atheneum Publishers
Avon Books
Barrons Educational Series
Bookmaker's Guild, Inc.
Bradbury Press
Breakwater Books
Carnival Enterprises
Carolrhoda Books, Inc.
Childrens Press
China Books
Chronicle Books
Clarion Books
Coach House Press, Inc.
Council for Indian Education
Crossway Books
Dial Books for Young Readers
Dillon Press, Inc.
Double M Press
Doubleday
Dutton Children's Books
Eakin Publications
Enslow Publishers Inc.
Exposition Phoenix Press
Facts on File
Farrar, Straus & Giroux
Fawcett Juniper
Fleet Press Corporation
Four Winds Press
Free Spirit Publishing
Godine, David R.
Green Publications, Kendall
Greenhaven Press
Greenwillow Books
Harbinger House
Harcourt Brace Jovanovich
Holt & Co., Inc., Henry
Homestead Publishing
Houghton Mifflin Co.
Kruza Kaleidoscopix, Inc.
Lerner Publications Co.
Liguori Publications
Little, Brown and Company
Lothrop, Lee & Shepard Books
Maryland Historical Press
McElderry Books

Messner, Julian
Metamorphous Press
Misty Hill Press
Morehouse-Barlow
Mosaic Press
National Press Inc.
New Day Books
New Day Press
New Seed Press
Oddo Publishing, Inc.
Orchard Books
Pando Publications
Paulist Press
Perspectives Press
Philomel Books
Pippin Press
Press of Macdonald & Reinecke, The
Price Stern Sloan
Rosen Publishing Group, The
St. Paul Books and Media
Sandlapper Publishing Co., Inc.
Scojtia, Publishing Co., Inc.
Shaw Publishers, Harold
Shoe Tree Press
Simon & Pierre Publishing Co. Ltd.
Skylark/Books for Young Readers
Standard Publishing
Star Books, Inc.
Sterling Publishing Co., Inc.
Trillium Press
Twenty-First Century Books
Walker and Co.
Waterfront Books
Western Producer Prairie Books

Young adults
(12 and up)

Abingdon Press
Aegina Press/University Editions
African American Images
Aladdin Books/Collier Books for
    Young Adults
Archway/Minstrel Books
Atheneum Publishers
Avon Books
Barrons Educational Series
Bookmaker's Guild, Inc.
Bradbury Press
Branden Publishing Co.
Breakwater Books
Childrens Press
Chronicle Books

Clarion Books
Coach House Press, Inc.
Consumer Report Books
Council for Indian Education
Crossway Books
Davenport, Publishers, May
Dial Books for Young Readers
Double M Press
Dutton Children's Books
Eakin Publications
Enslow Publishers Inc.
Facts on File
Farrar, Straus & Giroux
Fawcett Juniper
Fleet Press Corporation
Four Winds Press
Free Spirit Publishing
Green Publications, Kendall
Greenhaven Press
Greenwillow Books
Harbinger House
Harcourt Brace Jovanovich
Harvest House Publishers
Holt & Co., Inc., Henry
Homestead Publishing
Houghton Mifflin Co.
Hunter House Publishers
Lerner Publications Co.
Liguori Publications
Little, Brown and Company
Lothrop, Lee & Shepard Books
Maryland Historical Press
McElderry Books
Meriwether Publishing Ltd.
Messner, Julian
Metamorphous Press
Misty Hill Press
Morehouse-Barlow
National Press Inc.
New Day Press
New Readers Press
New Seed Press
Orchard Books
Pando Publications
Paulist Press
Perspectives Press
Philomel Books
Proforma Books
Rosen Publishing Group, The
St. Paul Books and Media
Sandlapper Publishing Co., Inc.
Scojtia, Publishing Co., Inc.
Shaw Publishers, Harold
Shoe Tree Press

Simon & Pierre Publishing Co. Ltd.
Standard Publishing
Starfire
Trillium Press
Walker and Co.
Waterfront Books
Western Producer Prairie Books

Age-Level Index/ Magazine Publishers

The age-level index is set up to help you more quickly locate magazine markets geared to the age group(s) for which you write or illustrate. Read each listing carefully and follow the publisher's specific information about the type(s) of manuscript(s) each prefers to read and the style(s) of artwork each wishes to review.

Picture materials (preschool-8-year-olds)

Apple Blossom Connection, The
Brilliant Star
Chickadee
Day Care and Early Education
Dolphin Log
Highlights for Children
Humpty Dumpty's Magazine
Lighthouse
My Friend
National Geographic World
Pennywhistle Press
Skylark
Stone Soup
Together Time
Turtle Magazine
Tyro Magazine
Wee Wisdom Magazine

Young readers (5-8-year-olds)

Animal World
Apple Blossom Connection, The
Brilliant Star
Calli's Tales
Chickadee
Children's Playmate
Day Care and Early Education
Equilibrium
Friend Magazine, The
Highlights for Children
Hob-Nob
Home Altar, The
Humpty Dumpty's Magazine
In-Between
Kid City
Lighthouse
My Friend
Noah's Ark
Pennywhistle Press
Pockets
Primary Friend

School Magazine (*Blast Off!, Countdown, Orbit, Touchdown*
Single Parent, The
Skylark
Stone Soup
Tyro Magazine
Wee Wisdom Magazine
Young American

Middle readers (9-11-year-olds)

Apple Blossom Connection, The
Brilliant Star
Children's Digest
Clubhouse
Cobblestone
Crusader
Discoveries
Dolphin Log
Equilibrium
Faces
Friend Magazine, The
Highlights for Children
Hob-Nob
Home Altar, The
In-Between
Junior Trails
Lighthouse
My Friend
National Geographic World
Noah's Ark
Odyssey
On the Line
Owl Magazine
Pennywhistle Press
Pockets
R-A-D-A-R
Ranger Rick
School Magazine (*Blast Off!, Countdown, Orbit, Touchdown*)
Shofar
Single Parent, The
Skylark
Stone Soup

3-2-1 Contact
Touch
Tyro Magazine
Venture
Wee Wisdom Magazine
Young American
Young Crusader, The

**Young adults
(12 and up)**

Aim Magazine
Animal World
Apple Blossom Connection, The
Careers
Clubhouse
Cobblestone
Equilibrium
Exploring
Faces
Hob-Nob
In-Between
Insights
Jackie
Keynoter
Lighthouse
Listen
My Friend
Odyssey
Owl Magazine
Pennywhistle Press
Pioneer
Single Parent, The
Skylark
Stone Soup
Straight
3-2-1 Contact
TQ
Tyro Magazine
Venture
Wee Wisdom Magazine
With
Young American
Youth Update

General Index

A

Abingdon Press 20
Addams Children's Book Award, Jane 127
Advocacy Press 21
Aegina Press/University Editions, Inc. 21
African American Images 22
Agora: The Magazine for Gifted Students 116
Aim Magazine 81
Aladdin Books/Collier Books for Young Adults 22
Alberta Writing for Youth Competition 127
America & Me Essay Contest 127
American Association of University Women Award in Juvenile Literature, The 128
AMHA Morgan Art Contest 128
Animal World 81
Annual Contest 128
Apple Blossom Connection, The 82
Archway/Minstrel Books 23
Art & Business of Humorous Illustration, The 153
Atheneum Publishers 23
Authors Guild, The 148
Authors Resource Center, The 148
Avon Books 24
Avon Flare Young Adult Novel Competition 128

B

Ballantine 25
Bantam Books Inc. 25
Bantam Doubleday 25
Barrons Educational Series 25
Bartle Annual Playwriting Award, Margaret 129
Bauer Literary Agency, Barbara 139
Big Apple Awards, The 129
Bitterroot 116
Book of the Year for Children 129
Bookmaker's Guild, Inc. 26
Bookstop Literary Agency 140

Boston Globe-Horn Book Awards, The 129
Bradbury Press 27
Branden Publishing Co. 28
Breakwater Books 28
Brilliant Star 82
Brown Associates, Marie 140
Brown Literary Agency, Andrea 140

C

Caldecott Award 129
Calico Books 28
Calli's Tales 83
Canadian Author & Bookman Creative Writing Contest 130
Canadian Authors Association 149
Careers 83
Carnival Enterprises 29
Carolina Wren Press/Lollipop Power Books 29
Carolrhoda Books, Inc. 30
Carvainis Agency, Inc., Maria 140
Casselman, Literary Agent, Martha 141
Chickadee 84
Children's Book Award 130
Children's Digest 85, 117
Children's Ministries 85
Children's Playmate 85, 117
Childrens Press 31
Children's Reading Round Table Award 130
Children's Television Workshop 85
Child's World, Inc., The 32
China Books 32
Christopher Award, The 130
Chronicle Books 33
Clarion Books 33
Clarion Science Fiction & Fantasy Writing Workshop 153
Clubhouse 85, 117
Coach House Press, Inc. 34
Cobblestone 86
Cohen, Inc., Ruth 141
Consumer Report Books 34
Coteau Books Ltd. 35
Council for Indian Education 35
Craven Design Studios, Inc. 141
Creative Kids 117

Creative With Words Publications 118
Crossway Books 36
Crusader 87
Curtis Associates, Richard 141

D

Davenport, Publishers, May 37
Day Care and Early Education 87
Delacorte Juvenile 130
Dial Books for Young Readers 37
Dillon Press, Inc. 38
Discoveries 87
Dixie Council of Authors and Journalists, Inc. 153
Dolphin Log 88
Double M Press 38
Doubleday 39
Dragonfly: East/West Haiku Quarterly 118
Drury College/SCBW Workshop 154
Dutton Children's Books 39

E

Eakin Publications, Inc. 40
Elek Associates, Peter 142
Ellenberg/Literary Agent, Ethan 142
Elmo Agency Inc., Ann 142
Enslow Publishers Inc. 41
Equilibrium 89
Exploring 89
Exposition Phoenix Press 41

F

Faces 90
Facts on File 41
Farrar, Straus & Giroux 42
Fawcett Juniper 42
Fiction Contest 130
Fifth Annual Children's Literature Conference 154
Fisher Children's Book Award, Dorothy Canfield 131
Fleet Press Corporation 42
Flying Pencil Press, The 118

Foster City Annual Writers Contest 131
Four Winds Press 43
Free Spirit Publishing 44
Freeman Memorial Awards, Don 131
Friend Magazine, The 90
Futurific 119

G

Gallaudet University Press 44
Gifted Children Monthly 119
Girls Club of Santa Barbara, The 44
Godine, Publisher, David R. 44
Good News Publishers 46
Green Publications, Kendall 45
Greenhaven Press 46
Greenwillow Books 46
Gulliver Books 47

H

Harbinger House, Inc. 47
Harcourt Brace Jovanovich 48
Harvest House Publishers 48
HBJ Children's Books 49
Hearst Corporation, The 49
High Adventure 91
Highlights for Children 91, 119
Highlights Foundation Writers Workshop at Chautauqua 154
Hob-Nob 92
Holt & Co., Inc., Henry 49
Home Altar, The 93
Homestead Publishing 49
Houghton Mifflin Co. 50
Howard-Gibbon Medal, Amelia Frances 131
Humanics Children's House 50
Humpty Dumpty's Magazine 93
Hunter House Publishers 51

I

Ideals Publishing Corporation 51
In-Between 94
Insights 95
International Black Writers 149

J

Jackie 95
Jefferson Cup Award 131
Junior Trails 96

K

Kar-Ben Copies, Inc. 52
Kellock & Associates Ltd., J. 143
Keynoter 97
Kid City 97
Kouts, Literary Agent, Barbara S. 143
Kruza Kaleidoscopix, Inc. 53

L

Laubach Literacy International 54
League of Canadian Poets 149
Lerner Publications Co. 54
Leslie Literary Agency, Carol Judy 144
Lieberman Student Poetry Award,
    Elias 132
Lifeprints 119
Lighthouse 98
Lighthouse Literary Agency 144
Liguori Publications 54
Listen 98
Literary Marketing Consultants 144
Little, Brown and Company 55
Lothrop, Lee & Shepard Books 55

M

Maccoby Literary Agency, Gina 145
Macmillan Publishing Co. 56
Maryland Historical Press 56
McElderry Books, Margaret K. 56
Meriwether Publishing Ltd. 57
Merlyn's Pen, The National Magazine
    of Student Writing 120
Messner, Julian 57
Metamorphous Press 58
Metcalf Awards, Vicky 132
Metcalf Short Story Award, Vicky 132
Mews Books Ltd. 145
Misty Hill Press 58

Morehouse-Barlow 59
Morrow & Co. Inc., William 59
Mosaic Press 59
My Friend 99, 121
Mystery Writers of America 154
Mythic Circle, The 121

N

National Geographic World 100
National Jewish Book Award for Chil-
    dren's Literature 132
National Jewish Book Award—Picture
    Books 133
National Press Inc. 60
National Writers Club 150
National Writers Union 150
Neail Associates, Pamela 145
Nebraska Writers Guild 150
New Day Books 60
New Day Press 61
New Jersey Poetry Contest 133
New Readers Press 61
New Seed Press 62
Newbery Medal Award 133
1989 Manningham Poetry Trust Stu-
    dent Contests 133
1989 National Written & Illustrated by
    .. Awards Contest for Students,
    The 133
Noah's Ark 100
Noah's Ark, a Newspaper for Jewish
    Children 121
Norma-Lewis Agency, The 146

O

Oddo Publishing, Inc. 62
Odyssey 100
Ogs Essay Contest 134
On The Line 101
Orchard Books 63
Owl Magazine 101

P

Padre Productions 64
Pando Publications 64

Paulist Press 65
Penguin/USA 66
Pennywhistle Press 102
Perspectives Press 66
Philomel Books 66
Pioneer 102
Pippin Press 67
Players Press, Inc. 68
Pocket Books 68
Pockets 103
Poetry Society of America 151
Press of Macdonald & Reinecke, The 68
Price Stern Sloan 69
Primary Friend 103
Prism Magazine 122
Proforma Books 69
Publish-a-Book Contest 134
Putnam & Grosset Group, The 70

R

R-A-D-A-R 104
Ranger Rick 104
Reflections 122
Rhyme Time Creative Writing Contest 134
Rhyme Time Poetry Newsletter 123
Rosen Publishing Group, The 70
Rotrosen Agency, Jane 146

S

St. Paul Books and Media 70
San Diego Writers/Editors Guild 151
Sandburg Literary Arts Awards, Carl 134
Sandlapper Publishing Co., Inc. 71
School Magazine (*Blast Off!, Countdown, Orbit, Touchdown*) 106
Science Fiction Writers of America, Inc. 151
Science Writing Award in Physics and Astronomy 135
Scojtia, Publishing Co., Inc. 72
Self Publishing Children's Books 154
Shaw Publishers, Harold 72
Shoe Tree 123
Shoe Tree Contests 135

Shoe Tree Press 73
Shofar 106
S.I. International 146
Simon & Pierre Publishing Co. Ltd. 74
Simon & Schuster 74
Single Parent, The 106
Skylark 107
Skylark/Books for Young Readers 74
Society of Children's Book Writers 152
Society of Southwestern Authors 152
Southern California Society of Children's Book Writers Illustrators Day 154
Standard Publishing 74, 108
Star Books, Inc. 75
Starfire 75
Sterling Publishing Co., Inc. 75
Stone Center for Children's Books Recognition of Merit Award, George G. 135
Stone Soup 108, 124
Straight 108
Straight Magazine 124
Summer Writers Conference 155

T

Taylor Award for Best Older Children's Book of Jewish Content, Sydney 135
Taylor Award for Best Younger Children's Books of Jewish Content, Sydney 136
Taylor Manuscript Award, Sydney 136
3-2-1 Contact 109
Thumbprints 124
Thunder Creek Publishing Co-op Ltd. 76
Ticknor & Fields 76
Together Time 109
Tom Thumb Music 76
Touch 110
TQ 110
Trillium Press 76
Turtle 125
Turtle Magazine 111
Twenty-First Century Books 77
Tyro Magazine 111

U

United Methodist Publishing House 77

V

Vassar Institute of Publishing and Writing: Children's Books in the Marketplace 155
Venture 112
VFW Voice of Democracy 136
Voyager Paperbacks 77

W

Wade Children's Story Award, The Stella 136
Walker and Co. 77
Walker Publishing Co. Inc. 78
Waterfront Books 78
Watt & Associates, Sandra 146
Watts, Inc., Franklin 79
Wee Wisdom Magazine 112
Western Heritage Awards 136
Western Producer Prairie Books 79
Wilder Award, Laura Ingalls 137

Willamette Writers 21st Annual Writers Conference 155
With 114
Witty Outstanding Literature Award, Paul A. 137
Wombat: A Journal of Young People's Writing and Art 125
Women Writers West 152
Writers at Work Conference in Park City 155
Writers House 146
Writers Newsletter 125
Writing! 126

Y

Yolen Books, Jane 79
Young American 114
Young Crusader, The 115
Young Naturalist Foundation 115
Young Writer's Contest 137
Youth Update 115

Z

Zelasky Literary Agency, Tom 147

Record of Submissions

Date Sent	Title/Illustrations	Market	Editor/ Art Director

Date Returned	Date Accepted	Date Published	Copy Received	Expenses	Payment

Record of Submissions

Date Sent	Title/Illustrations	Market	Editor/ Art Director

Date Returned	Date Accepted	Date Published	Copy Received	Expenses	Payment

Other Books of Interest
for Children's Writers and Illustrators

Annual Directories
Artist's Market, edited by Susan Conner $18.95
Novel & Short Story Writer's Market, edited by Laurie Henry (paper) $17.95
Photographer's Market, edited by Connie Eidenier $19.95
Poet's Market, by Judson Jerome $17.95
Songwriter's Market, edited by Julie Whaley $17.95
Writer's Market, edited by Glenda Tennant Neff $22.95

Writing for Children
The Children's Picture Book: How to Write It, How to Sell It, by Ellen E. M. Roberts (paper) $15.95
Families Writing, by Peter R. Stillman (paper) $15.95
How to Write & Illustrate Children's Books, by Treld Pelkey Bicknell & Felicity Trotman $22.50
Nonfiction for Children: How to Write It, How to Sell It, by Ellen E. M. Roberts $16.95
Writing for Children & Teenagers, 3rd Edition, by Lee Wyndham/Revised by Arnold Madison (paper) $12.95
Writing Short Stories for Young People, by George Edward Stanley $15.95
Writing Young Adult Novels, by Hadley Irwin & Jeannette Eyerly $14.95

Illustration
Drawing & Painting with Ink, by Fritz Henning $24.95
Fantasy Art, by Bruce Robertson $24.95
Illustration & Drawing: Styles & Techniques, by Terry R. Presnell $22.95
Painting Watercolor Portraits that Glow, by Jan Kunz $27.95
People Painting Scrapbook, by J. Everett Draper $26.95
Putting People in Your Paintings, by J. Everett Draper $22.50

Reference Books
Beginning Writer's Answer Book, edited by Kirk Polking (paper) $12.95
The Complete Guide to Self-Publishing, by Tom & Marilyn Ross (paper) $12.95
How to Write a Book Proposal, by Michael Larsen $9.95
How to Write with a Collaborator, by Hal Bennett with Michael Larsen $11.95
Knowing Where to Look: The Ultimate Guide to Research, by Lois Horowitz (paper) $15.95
Literary Agents: How to Get & Work with the Right One for You, by Michael Larsen $9.95
Time Management for Writers, by Ted Schwarz $10.95
12 Keys to Writing Books that Sell, by Kathleen Krull (paper) $12.95
The 29 Most Common Writing Mistakes & How to Avoid Them, by Judy Delton $9.95
Word Processing Secrets for Writers, by Michael A. Banks & Ansen Dibell (paper) $14.95
The Writer's Digest Guide to Manuscript Formats, by Dian Dincin Buchman & Seli Groves $16.95

Graphics/Business of Art
Airbrushing the Human Form, by Andy Charlesworth $27.95 (cloth)
Artist's Friendly Legal Guide, by Conner, Karlen, Perwin & Spatt $15.95 (paper)
Basic Graphic Design & Paste-Up, by Jack Warren $12.95 (paper)
Color Harmony: A Guide to Creative Color Combinations, by Hideaki Chijiiwa $15.95 (paper)
Complete Airbrush & Photoretouching Manual, by Peter Owen & John Sutcliffe $23.95 (cloth)
The Complete Guide to Greeting Card Design & Illustration, by Eva Szela $27.95 (cloth)
Creative Ad Design & Illustration, by Dick Ward $32.95 (cloth)
Design Rendering Techniques, by Dick Powell $29.95 (cloth)
Dynamic Airbrush, by David Miller & James Effler $29.95 (cloth)
Getting It Printed, by Beach, Shepro & Russon $29.50 (paper)
The Graphic Artist's Guide to Marketing & Self Promotion, by Sally Prince Davis $15.95 (paper)
How to Design Trademarks & Logos, by Murphy & Rowe $24.95 (cloth)
How to Draw Charts & Diagrams, by Bruce Robertson $24.95 (cloth)
How to Draw & Sell Cartoons, by Ross Thomson & Bill Hewison $17.95 (cloth)
How to Draw & Sell Comic Strips, by Alan McKenzie $18.95 (cloth)
How to Understand & Use Design & Layout, by Alan Swann $24.95 (cloth)
Illustration & Drawing: Styles & Techniques, by Terry Presnall $22.95 (cloth)

Marker Rendering Techniques, by Dick Powell & Patricia Monahan $32.95 (cloth)
Presentation Techniques for the Graphic Artist, by Jenny Mulherin $24.95 (cloth)
Studio Secrets for the Graphic Artist, by Jack Buchan $29.95 (cloth)
Type: Design, Color, Character & Use, by Michael Beaumont $24.95 (cloth)

Watercolor

Getting Started in Watercolor, by John Blockley $19.95 (paper)
Make Your Watercolors Sing, by LaVere Hutchings $22.95 (cloth)
Painting Nature's Details in Watercolor, by Cathy Johnson $24.95 (cloth)
Watercolor Interpretations, by John Blockley $19.95 (paper)
Watercolor Painter's Solution Book, by Angela Gair $24.95 (cloth)
Watercolor Fast & Loose, by Ron Ranson $21.95 (cloth)
Watercolor—The Creative Experience, by Barbara Nechis $16.95 (paper)
Watercolor Tricks & Techniques, by Cathy Johnson $24.95 (cloth)
Watercolor Workbook, by Bud Biggs & Lois Marshall $19.95 (paper)
Watercolor: You Can Do It!, by Tony Couch $25.95 (cloth)

Mixed Media

Catching Light in Your Paintings, by Charles Sovek $18.95 (paper)
Colored Pencil Drawing Techniques, by Iain Hutton-Jamieson $23.95 (cloth)
Exploring Color, by Nita Leland $26.95 (cloth)
Keys to Drawing, by Bert Dodson $21.95 (cloth)
The North Light·Illustrated Book of Painting Techniques, by Elizabeth Tate $27.95 (cloth)
Oil Painting: A Direct Approach, by Joyce Pike $26.95 (cloth)
Painting Seascapes in Sharp Focus, by Lin Seslar $24.95 (cloth)
Pastel Painting Techniques, by Guy Roddon $24.95 (cloth)
The Pencil, by Paul Calle $16.95 (paper)
People Painting Scrapbook, by J. Everett Draper $26.95 (cloth)
Putting People in Your Paintings, by J. Everett Draper $22.50 (cloth)
Tonal Values: How to See Them, How to Paint Them, by Angela Gair $24.95 (cloth)

A complete catalog of Writer's Digest Books and North Light Books is available FREE by writing to the address shown below. To order books directly from the publisher, include $2.50 postage and handling for one book, 50¢ for each additional book. Allow 30 days for delivery.

Writer's Digest Books/North Light Books
1507 Dana Avenue
Cincinnati, Ohio 45207

Credit card orders call TOLL-FREE 1-800-543-4644 (outside Ohio), 1-800-551-0884 (Ohio only).

Write to this same address for information on *Writer's Digest* magazine, Writer's Digest Book Club, Writer's Digest School, Writer's Digest Criticism Service, North Light Book Club, Graphic Artist's Book Club, *The Artist's Magazine*, and *HOW* Magazine.

Prices subject to change without notice.